REPORT OF THE REVIEW

OF THE LONDON RENAL SERVICES

MAY 1993

London: HMSO

COMMITTEE MEMBERS

Professor N P Mallick - Professor of Renal Medicine Manchester
Chairman

Mr P C Coe - Chief Executive, East London and the City Health Authority

Dr N J B Evans - Chairman, United Kingdom, Transplant Support Services Authority

Professor D P Gray - Dean of Postgraduate Studies, Exeter.

Professor D N S Kerr - Lately Dean, Royal Postgraduate Medical School

Dr G Maidment - Consultant Physician Windsor

Professor M G McGeown - Professorial Fellow, Queens University, Belfast

Dr P Roderick - Consultant in Public Health Medicine, North West Thames Regional Health Authority

Professor J R Salaman - Professor of Transplant Surgery, University of Wales

Mr J R Stopes-Roe - Locality Director (Newham), East London and the City Health Authority

Mr J Wellbeloved - Lately Director, National Kidney Research Fund.

Mrs L J Whitworth - Nurse Manager, Renal Services, Manchester.

Dr A J Williams - Consultant Renal Physician, Swansea.

The following gave professional assistance:

Dr A M Davison ; Dr J D Briggs; Professor P Druet; Dr E Jones; Dr N Mayes; Professor P J Morris; Professor Sir Keith Peters; Dr V Raleigh; Professor E Ritz; Dr N Sellwood; Mr G Shipp; Dr I T Wood.

Mr I R Jones and Mr V Crumbleholme gave research and administrative assistance.

In addition to the bodies involved through the implementation group we have been in communication with the following:

Royal College of Physicians
Royal College of Surgeons
British Transplantation Society
Renal Association
British Association of Paediatric Nephrologists
Wellcome Foundation
Medical Research Council
National Kidney Research Fund
British Kidney Patients Association
National Federation of Kidney Patients Association

We received communications from many other sources not otherwise acknowledged here and we record our gratitude to all who helped in this task.

CONTENTS   **Page**

APPENDICES

REPORT OF THE REVIEW OF LONDON RENAL SERVICES

INTRODUCTION

1.   Following the publication of *Making London Better* six specialty review groups were established by the London Implementation Group to undertake a systematic review of key tertiary clinical services provided in Greater London. Three main aims were pursued by each of the review teams: to assess current and projected needs for each speciality; to develop criteria for the development of major tertiary centres; and to advise on the future pattern of service provision, including the location of major centres in order to achieve the most effective services for the local resident population.

2.   The purpose of this review has been to determine if the service to patients with kidney disease in London is appropriate. We have considered not only inner and outer London, but the four Thames regions as a whole, since there is substantial overlap in the provision for patients throughout this area.

3.   We have used the document produced after wide consultation, by the Renal Association and the Royal College of Physicians[1] as the basis of our recommendations. The forthcoming, complementary document on standards and audit will supplement the information available to all concerned.

4.   The definition of "autonomous" or "tertiary", and of "sub-regional" or "district general hospital" centres, and of "satellite dialysis units" are broadly in line with that document. We have proposed a particular form of tertiary centre in London at five University centres, each carrying transplantation responsibilities. Other autonomous and less complex nephrology services are detailed. We provide a costed structure for each level of service we recommend.

5.   Renal medicine is a complex specialty and a concentration of activities is necessary to provide sufficient consultant staff for continuous cover, and for the support and training of both junior doctors and other professional staff. Increasing sub-specialisation also points to the need for a tertiary centre to be staffed by a number of consultants. A corollary of such a concentration of staff is the requirement that they provide outreach services (support for satellite dialysis units, and outpatient clinics) so as to permit the ready access of patients to the facilities they require.

6.   The steady development of dialysis techniques and organ transplantation has given the speciality a high public profile. The survival rates for patients after renal transplantation are impressive, and this is generally the treatment of choice, both for the patient's quality of life, and for cost-effectiveness to the NHS. However the limited availability of cadaver organs constrains the scope for transplantation.

---

[1]*Provision of Services for Adult Patients with Renal Disease in the United Kingdom*, November 1991, The Renal Association.

7.   In this review we have looked closely at the present provision of services in each of the renal units in London, to which many patients across the four Thames regions travel for treatment and advice. We have consulted the users of these services, as represented by the various kidney patient associations. Their responses are summarised in Appendix G. We have also looked at services elsewhere in the Thames regions, to see how roles and responsibilities might develop in the future. Our recommendations are radical, but we are convinced that they will significantly increase the quality, accessibility and cost-effectiveness of the renal services available to the population of the south-east of England. We have considered the potential at each university tertiary site for future academic development, and taken both national and international advice on this matter.

8.   We wish to record our appreciation of the assistance accorded to us by all those working in each centre. We respect their achievements and believe that they have served London well. We hope that our recommendations will assist them in continuing to do so and will be to the benefit of the patients they seek to serve.

INCIDENCE AND PREVALENCE OF RENAL DISEASE

9.   Prospective studies carried out in various parts of the United Kingdom during the last five years have shown that, under the age of 80, some 80 patients per million population (pmp) per year will develop endstage renal failure and be suitable for renal replacement therapy (RRT). This and other evidence allows us to predict the future workload of the renal units. There is a sharp age-specific rise in the incidence of endstage renal failure (Table 1 of Appendix A). For reversible or acute renal failure, the incidence is likely to be below 70 pmp per year, and again there is a sharp age-specific rise in incidence. It should also be recognised that with increasing age, both additional diseases are commoner and life expectation shorter.

10.   The Thames population derived from the Indian sub-continent (Asian), and the Black population have a threefold higher prevalence and acceptance rate for RRT (see Appendix A). This may reflect partly the closer proximity of these populations to renal services, but it is also likely to reflect greater population need for RRT particularly secondary to diabetic and hypertensive nephropathy. As these ethnic groups are younger than whites one can predict a rising need with time. We have taken account of all these factors in our analysis so as to provide a picture of the likely patterns of need in the different Thames regions.

11.   We have developed a previously established modelling technique to estimate the future need for RRT in the four Thames regions using data supplied by EDTA and by Thames renal units. Appendix B sets out the details of the modelling we have undertaken. Our estimates of the final "steady state" position vary according to the availability of kidneys for transplantation and to the risk profile of patients accepted. We estimate that, at an acceptance rate of 80 pmp per year, there would be 11,000 to 12,000 patients on RRT of whom 6,000 to 7,000 would be on dialysis. This represents a doubling of the total stock on RRT, within which there would be an even greater proportional increase in those on maintenance haemo-dialysis. The overall population need is likely to be higher than 80 pmp if ethnicity and the population over age 80 is accounted for and this will increase further the estimated total stock at steady state.

12.   In addition to the provision of RRT, as outlined above, there is a substantial workload in adult renal medicine. Many patients admitted to intensive care units develop acute reversible renal impairment. We have estimated the incidence of acute renal failure and the corresponding workload in managing these conditions on the nephrologists at present in post. Also, since glomerular disease continues to account for the highest proportion of renal failure, we have estimated the resulting workload by analysing the number of native renal biopsies performed.

PRESENT PROVISION OF RENAL SERVICES IN LONDON

13.   At present there are eleven units within inner London (as defined in the Tomlinson Report) and one in outer London. The eleven are all in main teaching hospitals, and the twelfth is in a district general hospital associated with a teaching hospital. There are four units in district general hospitals in the shires. We visited all 12 London units and received evidence from the paediatric renal service at Great Ormond Street. The units at Southend, Stevenage, Canterbury and Brighton all returned data to us, which we have used together with data from units in neighbouring Regions (Cambridge, Oxford, RAF Halton, Portsmouth Ipswich) to ensure that we captured information on all patients on RRT in the four Thames Regions. All 16 units, so requested, responded promptly and fully to a detailed questionnaire covering workload, staffing, facilities, costs and academic output. These have been analysed fully and much of the data have been incorporated in the appendices, with summary material included in this report. This section outlines the workload of these units arising from the prevalence of renal disease, and other demands on nephrologists, described above. Table 1 summarises the activity of all 16 units.

Renal replacement therapy

14.   A detailed analysis of RRT workload arising from endstage renal failure is given in Appendix A. The combined stock of adult patients on RRT in the London units is 5061 (dialysis 2190, transplants 2971. The stock in the four "shire" units is 720 (dialysis 470, transplants 250). The population-based stock rates for adults resident in the four Thames regions is 506 pmp for all treatment modalities (dialysis 236 pmp, transplants 270 pmp). These rates are higher in the north Thames regions, and vary by DHA type (inner London 713 pmp, outer London 583 pmp, shires 384 pmp). This can be partly explained by the higher ethnic minority populations in inner London. Overall stock rates are higher in those from the Indian sub-continent (1258 pmp) and Blacks (1201 pmp) compared to Whites (417 pmp).   At present patients incur substantial costs met from exchequer funds in travelling to dialysis units for treatment (see appendices D and I).

15.   The number of adults accepted for RRT in 1992 by the London units was 884, and by the shire units 205. For residents in the four Thames regions, the total population rate was 73 pmp, which can be compared to the Renal Association's estimate of British average population need of 80 pmp. The Thames average rate of 73 pmp breaks down approximately into 111 pmp in inner London DHAs, 79 pmp in outer London DHAs and 51 pmp in shire DHAs. Acceptance rates are significantly low in some of the shire DHAs and well below 80 pmp suggesting that population need is not being met in these areas. Rates are significantly high in some Greater London DHAs with a high proportion of ethnic minorities.

3

TABLE 1   Summary of present provision in London

| HOSPITAL | New Pts 1992 | Transplant 1992 | Dialysis stations (main unit) | STOCK | | | | | | | CONSULTANT SESSIONS | | | WORK RATIO |
				Unit HD	Home HD	Sat HD	CAPD	CCPD	Tot dial	Tot TxP	Physn	Acad	Txp	
St Bart's	72	19	13	79	30	14	123	0	233	277	25	3	11	30
London	103	49	16	83	33	0	156	0	266	318	23	8	11	32
Royal Free	65	47	18	49	38	0	89	0	183	294	16	5	11	39
Guy's	86	50	15	41	34	0	117	0	195	442	22	22	11	29
King's	74	74	13	62	9	0	74	2	147	356	28	5	11	27
St Thomas's	43	19	19	59	19	0	84	8	162	174	18		0	26
Helier	112	57	14	36	28	3	140	8	169	268	11		11	112
St George's	37		3	7	0	0	45	0	53	13	5	4	0	58
Charing Cross	64	16	15	98	40	0	84	8	230	168	22	10	0	26
Hammersmith	54	21	9	35	0	0	93	0	119	225	20	15	11	22
St Mary's	103	46	14	87	6	25	132	4	226	242	24		11	47
UCH/Middx	73	29	20	89	0	0	120	0	207	199	20	22	11	26
Southend	41		12	54	0	0	4	0	58	0	6		0	75
Brighton	62	38	13	53	25	0	40	21	139	139	16		0	43
Canterbury	50	10	8	34	6	14	90	0	130	90	17		0	32
Stevenage	52	2	20	55	0	20	68	0	143	21	22		0	26

Notes: 1. The total of dialysis stock is not consistent with the sum of dialysis modes. The stock data has been used for epidemiological analysis.

2. Transplant sessions include other renal failure surgery.

3. "Work ratio" represents the number of new dialysis patients per year per wte consultant physician (counting "academic" sessions as half of an "NHS" session).

4

Acute renal failure

16.   Acute renal failure describes an episode of renal failure occurring abruptly, severe enough to influence patient morbidity and survival, which may need specialist advice and management and may have workload and planning implications.   There are many causes of acute renal failure .   It may occur de novo due to other morbid conditions such as severe trauma, post-operative complications, severe burns, severe prolonged hypertension due to haemorrhage, sepsis, or to a wide variety of renal insults including urinary tract obstruction.   Acute renal failure was once a relatively common sequel of severe childbirth complications but this has now become rare.

17.   Patients with acute renal failure are often severely ill and there may be failure of more than one organ system.   They require high quality medical and nursing care in specialised units, where there are facilities for dialysis (haemodialysis, peritoneal dialysis) haemofiltration, and respiratory support if needed.   A small number may need plasma exchange.   Severe cases may not require dialysis but nevertheless provide a significant workload for the renal unit staff.   We have found that 2117 patients received dialysis for acute renal failure during 1991 and 1992.   The population requirement for treatment of acute renal failure is difficult to estimate because of the many ways in which acute renal failure may arise.   A conservative estimate, on the basis of present information, would be 70 pmp per annum.   (See Appendix A)

General nephrology

18.   The annual rates for acute renal failure and parenchymal renal disease for residents of the Thames region are approximately 75 pmp and 80 pmp as defined by the workload (acute renal replacement therapy; native renal biopsies) of the 16 renal units in the Thames RHA's.   Furthermore approximately 125 patients are treated annually with plasma exchange by the renal units.

Renal Transplantation

19.   There are currently 13 NHS units in the Thames regions at which kidneys are transplanted into adults.   Details of their workload, staffing and results are given in Appendix C.   The total amount of renal transplant activity in the Thames regions is relatively high, averaging 35 compared with the national figure of 29 transplants pmp per year.   It is unlikely that the level can exceed about 40 pmp per year in the foreseeable future, whatever the prevailing legal position (personal communication from J D Briggs, past-President British Transplantation Society).

20.   This activity, totalling at present some 485 transplants per year, is split between the 13 centres, which vary widely in their size and patient-mix, as for example

- Activity ranges from 6 to 73 transplants/year.
- Elderly patients range from 1% to 11% aged over 65 years.
- Ethnicity ranges from 1% to 31% non-white.

Presumably these variations in patient mix represent both the characteristics of the populations from which the patients are drawn and the selectivity of the units.

21. Not surprisingly, the outcomes of transplantation also varied, as for example

- Patient survival ranged from 79% to 96%
- Graft survival ranged from 73% to 94%.

Both figures are for first grafts, and 1-year survivals. Though the figures are too small for multivariate analysis, we considered that - allowing for case-mix - none of the present units is obviously below-standard as judged by survival outcomes. Indeed, some units have exceptionally good crude figures.

22. We were struck by the total resource devoted to this level of transplant activity, particularly as regards nurse staffing. Though it is difficult to quantify comparisons accurately, we considered that some of the nursing teams were dealing with only a third of the number of transplants we would have expected.

23. Transplant services south of the Thames are well coordinated at present. The three surgeons each at a different hospital have developed a rotation for organ retrieval and transplantation and increasingly they have a common policy for recipient selection and management. There is no such discernable arrangement north of the Thames. Evidence to us suggests that, despite significant effort, it is only recently that progress has been made in defining the considerations on which a common waiting list of patients can be created.

Medical staffing

24. This is detailed in Appendix H. The physicians and surgeons are young. The siting of the units and the age of the physicians reflect the fact that these services have only developed over the last thirty years virtually exclusively in teaching hospitals and have gradually increased their consultant base. Junior staff levels have been analysed and the consequences of change documented in Appendix H.

Nurse staffing

25. Most centres have senior nurse leadership providing a co-ordinated, quality service. Where this is not the case, the nursing service is un-coordinated and not developing. There are many highly skilled, high graded nurses, but few, trained health care assistants - a poor skill mix. The use of health care assistants frees skilled staff to care for the acutely ill. In most areas there is considerable shift overlap, a reduction would make for greater efficiency.

26. There is some rotation of staff in all units but no one unit rotates staff to all areas. Rotation of staff ensures quality of care for patients as the individual nurse gains experience in all areas of RRT. At present there are few nurse practitioners whose skills in counselling, education, diagnosis and prescribing are invaluable for provision of quality care of patients in the community and clinics.

27. All tertiary centres should provide ENB 136 Renal Course (dip). Not all do at present - missing a valuable source of recruitment and training. Within the M25 there is a paucity of nursing research. The academic resource of the speciality, in the capital, is not being tapped. The potential of the nurse is not being exploited.

28.   All centres, but one, provide a training/counselling programme for their nursing staff with regard to viral infections. The routine testing of all patients is recommended. Teamwork between clinicians, both medical and nursing is essential for the provision of good care. This is not happening in all centres. However, the renal nursing service throughout the capital, on the whole, is good and delivers a quality service to its patients.

Estate and equipment

29.   We have evaluated the estate in terms of bed-holding, dialysis stations and equipment available. This is documented in the appendices. There is under-utilisation of resources, in that, collectively, maintenance dialysis units are not fully utilised on the basis of a three-shift working day. In our analysis of the financial plans and future requirements we have made some estimates as to capital charging, but this is difficult to achieve precisely.

Costings

30.   The questionnaire which was sent to each of the renal centres in London asked for units' business plans for 1992/93 and 1993/94, and for details of service costings. It was anticipated that the responses received would assist in building a picture of the full cost profile of renal services in London, provide an indication of the relative cost efficiency of each centre, and provide financial information to help estimate of the cost of the service configurations we propose.

31.   In the event the response to this request has been extremely varied with only two centres providing detailed financial information, some providing none and most providing only summary information and treatment tariffs by modality. It has therefore not proved possible at this stage to prepare baseline costs against which the cost and relative efficiency of the proposed services can be measured. We consider that such information is likely to be available for most of the London renal centres and should be collected on the basis of an agreed cost template to ensure like for like costing of services in the different centres.

32.   An analysis of the response received from each centre is included in Appendix D, together with a table of those service costs and treatment tariffs which have been provided to us. This information is obviously incomplete and has not been used in any part of the further cost analysis work which we have undertaken.

33.   In the absence of robust baseline information for the London centres it was decided that the most pragmatic solution to constructing the cost of the services proposed for London would be "built cost" profiles from other renal centres where information was readily available to the Review Group.

PLANNING FOR FUTURE PROVISION

34.   In considering future provision we have brought together the academic, transplantation and tertiary referral functions and amalgamated services. Consideration of site potential for multi disciplinary work in the years ahead and future academic excellence have been important to us. There is extensive consultation with cardiovascular, diabetic, intensive care and other departments and a range of support services is needed. These are

set out in the Renal Association/Royal College of Physicians document. Present costs are difficult to evaluate on the evidence provided. We have preferred to provide a detailed cost profile which should be used as a template in constructing budgets (see Appendix D). Clinical standards are high and the amalgamations we propose will create new services with considerable strengths. We seek to create opportunities for steady and rewarding developments in clinical service and research.

35. There is also a vigorous academic presence, with five chairs of renal medicine in London, and some centres are actively seeking to create new ones. The emerging changes within the University of London, with the consolidation into five medical schools, imposes constraints on the siting of academic developments. It is generally accepted that an academic focus thrives best in conjunction with an active tertiary referral centre. While each school might support a chair in renal medicine it is unlikely that any would find it appropriate to support more than one, and on different sites. Most renal clinicians in London, undertake research and in this respect there is no absolute distinction between NHS and University appointments. University clinicians are concerned that their clinical load is so great that reserved time for basic scientific research is reduced. We make staffing proposals to provide properly protected research time.

Transplantation

36. Transplantation has become a relatively straightforward procedure provided it is carried out by a skilled and experienced team. Hence it is desirable to concentrate renal transplantation into relatively few specialised "tertiary" centres. However the operation itself is only an episode in the long-term management of the patient. Therefore it is also important that the transplant centres should consider outreach services for patients in the community and should coordinate their activities with the other renal units whose patients are transplanted and which will provide the bulk of continuing care.

37. There are constraints on the configuration of transplant services. As noted above, it is unlikely that cadaver organ availability will exceed 40 pmp per year in the foreseeable future. It follows, therefore, that the total population of the Thames regions of around 14 million would yield up to 600 transplants per year. Table 1 shows that the current total is around 480 per year.

38. The Royal Colleges of Surgeons and Physicians, the British Transplantation Society and transplantation teams within London have all told us that transplant centres should each conduct at least 100 grafts annually. This "critical mass" would ensure high quality of outcome, would justify a strong team of 3 or 4 transplant surgeons and of physicians and would allow the economical use of nursing staff and support staff, and would provide the clinical experience necessary for surgical and medical trainees and form a vigorous focus for research. On this basis, there are clearly too many centres for transplantation; four or five would be more appropriate.

Dialysis

39. The ideal configuration of dialysis services is different. The aim of planning should be that no patient should spend more than about half an hour travelling from home to the dialysis unit. This would require the development of a network of "satellite" dialysis units, each under the aegis of the specialist nephrological service at its parent hospital. The

parent hospital could be one of the tertiary centres, or it could be a sub-regional DGH centre. In either case, the parent hospital would be responsible for providing the full range of renal services, either on its site, or at its satellites. Patients referred to a tertiary centre for transplantation would normally be returned for continuing care to their parent centre.

40.   On the basis of the modelling of need that we have conducted (see Appendix B) it seems probable that some 200 pmp will require maintenance haemodialysis as steady-state is approached. On a three-shift per day working basis, this equates to some 35 dialysis stations pmp. University and other tertiary referral centres (see paragraph 48) might each provide 15 stations, so that the bulk of dialysis must be provided at other sites. If centres in sub-regional DGHs (see paragraph 48) each house 10 stations, then at least two further satellite centres will be needed pmp. We emphasise that we do not expect steady-state to be reached for perhaps fifteen years, but planning should be undertaken to provide for the gradual increase in numbers. The model we have provided should assist here.

41.   The Business Plan submissions have provided the Review Group with a considerable amount of information about the estate and renal facilities currently available. The future provision of renal services requires the provision of new facilities (see paragraphs 47-50).

42.   Whilst at this stage it is not possible to be specific about the siting of all of these facilities, it is probable that new facilities will need to be created in one of the University Centres, in 3 of the main DGH sites, 2 of the subregional DGH sites and for most of the Satellite Units. In these latter, the facilities which currently exist on six sites will need to be expanded and for the balance the option exists to consider:-

-    Provision of purpose built facilities
-    adaptation of existing premises
-    provision by the private sector

43.   Details of the type and size of facilities required in both the main units and the Satellite Units are contained in Appendix D.

44.   Colleagues have voiced concern that the amalgamation of units would lead to there being very large numbers of patients under treatment. We do not advocate such an outcome. We believe that tertiary facilities should be used for what they alone can provide. After transplantation, outpatient care should be predominantly with the parent unit, of course in a fully coordinated manner with the transplantation centre. The new patient rate we advocate for a tertiary centre should not result in an unmanageable workload. Inspection of Figure 5 in Appendix H shows that the inpatient workload of a combined unit will be contained within the bed number (50-60) we propose for a tertiary centre. We recognise that there must be an orderly rundown of the present number of patients treated in central London dialysis units as more geographically accessible units develop, and that outpatient care too should be dispersed to outreach clinics with greater involvement of nurse practitioners. These developments, again, will reduce the central workload.

Academic appraisal

45.   We obtained details of funding for the different units from national funding bodies, and each unit returned to us the details of its grant income, research activities and publications. These were analysed. We took advice from the funding bodies and from both international and national authorities. We took account of the overall rating of each university clinical medical department by the HEFCE, since nephrology is not usually rated separately. A substantial body of clinically related research is in progress, and basic science research is practised increasingly at selected centres. A firm consensus emerged that the RPMS and University College had the strongest academic base. It was agreed too that the siting of one university tertiary centre at Guy's/St Thomas's was appropriate in terms of academic reputation and strength, and that the developments in the north-east sector would best be achieved by the amalgamation of the RLH and St Bartholomew's at the most appropriate site for service purposes. There was firm support on academic grounds for the relocation of the service at St Helier to St George's.

RECOMMENDATIONS

46.   In order to obtain a critical mass for highly specialised tertiary centres, and at the same time to provide equitable access for patients who live at a distance from such centres, significant re-organisation of the service is required. We have not been constrained by the present RHA boundaries, but we have regarded the London area as falling into five "sectors": south-east, north-east, north-central, west and south-west. Our decisions as to the preferred sites for the University tertiary centres rest on the availability of the infra-structure such a centre requires, and on the development of an environment which will further inter-disciplinary research at both service and basic science level.

47.   We recommend that there be a central core of five tertiary referral centres in London, one in association with each of the teaching hospital groupings recommended in the Tomlinson Report, and now being developed. Each centre should include a transplantation service providing for approximately 3 million people, expert nephrology for approx 1.5 million people, and should support a minimum of 80 new patients annually for RRT. Each centre should have a university component with, at a minimum, a professor and senior lecturer. We list the proposed tertiary units in paragraphs 57 to 89 below.

48.   We recommend secondly that there should be established approximately five autonomous tertiary centres providing the same services as those above, but without transplantation or university provision. These should be situated strategically and predominantly in the shire counties so as to balance services provided by the central university units. It would be appropriate for these centres to have close links with one of the university units for service and staffing, and for academic developments. Of these, successful units already exist at Brighton, Canterbury and Stevenage. We propose that, over time, further units should be designated at DGH sites.

49.   In order to provide RRT to all the people whose requirements are otherwise covered by the tertiary centres approximately one unit per 3 million population in a DGH staffed by two general physicians with an interest in nephrology should provide RRT for 60-80 new patients annually. These intermediate, or sub-regional units will be geographically sited to allow for patient access and will lie between the university and DGH tertiary centres.

50.   Finally, we recommend that a network of satellite dialysis units should be developed, each one attached to one of the tertiary centres, or to one of the sub-regional district nephrology departments. On the basis of the estimates of dialysis workload set out in Appendix B, we would expect an eventual need for at least two satellite centres pmp (as set out in paragraph 49 above).

51.   We have looked at travel isochrones for a number of DGHs in the London area, and some of these, together with the population within a 30 minute road transport isochrone are listed in Appendix E. The choice of the most appropriate sites for the one or two tertiary centres, sub-regional DGH centres, and satellite units should be made on the basis of detailed local knowledge of purchaser and providers. We note that facilities are already available at Southend (Westcliffe on Sea) and that arrangements are contemplated or under development at Chelmsford and Goodmayes.

52.   Appendix F sets out the main functions of district and satellite renal units, and considers further the options for location and models of management.

53.   The timing and cost of the changes we recommend is clearly of importance. There are at present 921 patients on maintenance haemodialysis, and at three-shift working these would require 154 dialysis stations. However, at steady state this number would rise to 2800 patients, with a proportionate increase in station requirements. We note that this will take up to fifteen years and that planning should proceed as soon as possible to provide not only for the eventual number, but also for centres sited geographically to permit the standards of access we recommend.

54.   We recommend that the surgical teams both south and north of the Thames are aggregated to the centres we designate, and that, since there are at present insufficient surgeons for the teams we propose, over time new appointments should be made which have a predominant responsibility for transplantation and also for the access and other surgery which patients with renal failure require. We recognise, of course, that surgeons will need to remain practised in general surgery or another surgical specialty. The management of renal transplantation is best conducted jointly by an experienced team in which neither physician nor surgeon predominates. We hope that such an arrangement will prove possible in each of the centres we propose.

55.   We recommend that:

   a.   only the five designated centres be available for the delivery of renal transplantation;

   b.   that the staffing structure and bed complement for these centres be in place by 1/9/94 at Guy's Hammersmith and UCL, and by 1/4/95 at St George's, and by 1/4/96 at the Royal London;

   c.   that maintenance haemodialysis be continued at the dialysis units of King's St Helier, St Mary's, Bart's, the Royal Free, and Charing Cross. Consultant staffing should be provided either from the new university centres, or if service needs dictates that one or more of these hospitals becomes a sub-regional centre, then by locally appointed staff.

d.   that consideration be given urgently to developing the following DGH sites: Goodmayes, Northwick Park, Maidstone and perhaps Chertsey and Guildford, or at alternatives in these regions, more acceptable to purchasers and providers.

Recommendations for tertiary units

56.   The criteria we employed in choosing the best site for a University Tertiary Centre in each sector are set out in paragraphs 34 and 47. The detailed description of each unit can be found in the appendices. Full notes were taken of our observations on the visits to units. We summarise below some salient points which led to our conclusions.

South-east (Guy's/ St Thomas's, King's)

57.   Now that Guy's and St Thomas's have become one Trust we have considered them together. The choice therefore lies between this Trust and King's. The Trust has internationally recognised academic nephrology with a large research output. Paediatric nephrology and transplantation are well developed at Guy's/St Thomas's where the buildings are new and the dialysis facilities are well integrated and capable of expansion to provide for the needs of a tertiary unit. There are excellent laboratory facilities well suited for their purpose. The dialysis facilities at St Thomas's are not modern and the laboratories are physically remote from the dialysis unit but in more modern surroundings.

58.   In discussion we have ascertained that there are sound plans for integration. If the current site appraisal determines that St Thomas's rather than Guy's should be the clinical focus for the combined St Thomas's/Guy's Trust, then modern and enlarged facilities must be provided to replace those available at Guy's.

59.   King's has a big workload and a long history of renal transplantation, with an entrepreneurial tradition. Organ-harvesting is systematic and effective. It was also argued that the proximity of liver transplantation at Kings is important for synergy. Renal transplantation is currently at Dulwich but is planned to move the short distance to the King's site. While we recognise the importance of these two forms of transplantation, we believe it would be possible for a renal unit at Guy's to ensure adequate support for liver transplantation at King's, should King's not become a sub-regional centre.

60.   There have been considerable changes in the staffing of this unit in the last two years and while there is now a professor in post and he has young colleagues it is not clear how this service would develop either in regard to the management of its workload or to its research potential. We recognise that the Department of Medicine is supportive and that there is the potential for cooperation with the Department of Immunology but there are uncertainties which relate to the rapidity of recent change and the forthcoming possibilities of a move of the service from its present site.

61.   The academic review we conducted reinforces our view that the Guy's St Thomas's Trust is the preferred site for a university teaching centre in the South East and we recommend accordingly.

North-east (Royal London, St Bartholomew's)

62.   The Royal London Unit is sited in a hospital with nearly all relevant departments, including a major trauma centre in its A&E Department, recently upgraded to cope with the patients brought in by helicopter. It is surrounded by a growing local population.

63.   The present hospital and medical school buildings have little spare capacity but there is room on the site for a substantial increase in beds and university facilities, with plans awaiting finance. However the large renal service at St Bartholomew's could not be accommodated at RLH without expansion of current facilities.

64.   St Bartholomew's is a major hospital which at present includes nearly all relevant departments but it seems unlikely that all these will continue on site. The present facilities for renal medicine are adequate but not refurbished. There is a new theatre block, available for renal and other surgery. At the adjacent postgraduate campus at Charterhouse Square there is accommodation for the Professor and University colleagues and other research staff.

65.   The strengths of St Bartholomew's to become a tertiary centre is claimed to rest on its position on a central London site with easy lines of communication in all directions, with a high density of population close by.   The buildings are old, but are solid and it would be possible to provide the 50 beds needed for a tertiary unit.

66.   It is important that the tertiary centre for the north-east sector be sited together with a wide spectrum of other clinical disciplines.   A closely associated basic science establishment is desirable. The thrust of developments in this sector of London is clearly to increase the clinical presence of the RLH and to associate it closely with Queen Mary and Westfield College.

67.   We believe that the tertiary renal service should be sited at RLH and we so recommend. We recognise that a new joint Trust must develop its own plan, but believe that our University tertiary centre in this sector should be at the site with all the other major clinical specialities and support services. However it is clear that the RLH site will need substantial development if it is to house this and other specialist services likely to be recommended by other specialty reviews, and we recommend that the relocation of the staff and facilities from St Bartholomew's should not be completed until an adequate facility has been developed, which includes a proper component for the academic base now present at St Bartholomew's.   The Deans of both present schools have told us that they hope to integrate their academic departments, of which this is one, and we welcome their assurances.

North-central (Royal Free, University College/Middlesex,)

68.   The Institute of Urology joined with UCH in 1992 and is already well integrated. Plans for development at UCH include the transfer of clinical services from the cruciform building of UCH to vacant space in the Middlesex site. About 200 beds will remain on the UCH site, including the accident and emergency service. The well developed academic and clinical research already on site is to move into the vacated cruciform building at UCH.   UCH/Middlesex will be well placed for a major role in the whole concept of linkage/merger of medical schools.

69.   The clinical departments are supported by a strong college of nursing, with what is probably the best senior nursing lead for nephrology in London.   The present physical facilities for nephrology are good, as a floor was converted and opened about a year ago, to accommodate both nephrology and urology.   There are plans for development of a unit for treatment of adolescents, and this fits well with the strong interest in urological abnormalities on site.   Even if there were to be no eventual reprovision of facilities at the Odeon site of UCH the present development at the Middlesex could house the beds required to meet our profile for a university tertiary centre. There may have to be a review of the 67 urology beds in this complex, so as to make possible the delivery of a further 20 beds to the nephrology and transplantation service.   Such a reconfiguration would in any case provide a better balance between urology, nephrology and transplantation.   There is a very large amount of research on-going at the combined site, both basic science and clinically orientated.   Our academic review strongly supported the present achievements and potential of this site.

70.   The Royal Free Hospital serves a large local population which to some extent overlaps with that of UCH/Middlesex.   It has the clinical and laboratory support services for a tertiary centre, and has both liver and bone marrow transplantation.   There is a widely recognised research output.   A major consideration in deciding on a university tertiary centre and service, apart from the presence of renal transplantation is the presence of strong links with basic science departments.   In this respect UCH/Middlesex is much stronger than the Royal Free.   The latter lacks the powerful academic base available at UCH/Middlesex.

71.   The location of the tertiary centre for this sector here rather than at the Royal Free Hospital poses two problems.   First, transplantation for older children is now carried out at the Royal Free Hospital in liaison with the Great Ormond Street paediatric services. However, we have discussed this matter with our colleagues in the paediatric review group and it seems to all of us a suitable solution that transplantation for these children should move to the UCH/Middlesex complex, where it is hoped facilities for older children and adolescents will be expanded.   We note too that urological surgery for older children and adolescents is already provided at UCH/Middlesex for patients from Great Ormond Street. Our proposal therefore is in line with other suggestions for the closer integration of Great Ormond Street and the services at UCH/Middlesex.

72.   The second problem is that at present there are close links at clinical level between the liver and renal transplantation services at the Royal Free Hospital.   While we recognise the value of such an association, we do not feel that it overrides the requirements for future tertiary renal services being sited where their academic development is most likely to flourish, and this must be as we have suggested.   We anticipate that the expanded clinical presence at UCH/Middlesex will provide a continuing service to the liver transplantation programme at the Royal Free at both surgical and medical level.

73.   The potential of UCH/Middlesex for a well provided clinical service to be linked with the scientific work already being undertaken is considerable.   In this respect we note the strong support of funding bodies for this site.   For all these reasons the preferred site for the tertiary centre for the north-central sector is at UCH/Middlesex.

West (Charing Cross, Hammersmith, St Mary's)

74.   Charing Cross has a large regular dialysis programme but a smaller population of patients with renal transplants. During the past few years the transplant service has been to a large extent provided from the Hammersmith Hospital.

75.   The Charing Cross facilities are more spacious than average and there is the potential for considerable expansion. The unit runs a minimal care facility nearby with 6 stations and is shortly to open a satellite unit with 8 stations at West Middlesex Hospital. All the nephrologists carry responsibility for "general medicine". It has a varied clinically oriented research programme.

76.   Hammersmith has a dedicated transplant ward which is under-used and could take the whole current workload of North West Thames. The dialysis unit has been refurbished and could be expanded. The main strength of the RPMS is the high quality of the academic environment. The Nephrology/Immunology Departments in particular are of a very high standard, attracting large grants for research. The building to house the transferred Clinical Research Centre is nearing completion and this will undoubtedly serve to enhance further the academic standing of the hospital. Its high academic profile was confirmed by our independent academic review.

77.   St Mary's has a large workload, a modern 28 bed renal ward and an older dialysis unit. There is a satellite unit at Watford.   There is an active transplantation programme.There are two consultant nephrologists and there are plans to appoint a third in August 1993. Transplantation is performed by two surgeons whose other commitments include urology, although the medical school has considered appointing a professor of surgery with interest in transplantation later in the year.

78.   Recent research work has been in xenotransplantation, prevention of allograft rejection and the treatment of "highly sensitised" patients prior to transplantation. Both this work and the clinical service benefits from the presence of a strong academic department of renal histopathology.

79.   Despite the vigorous nephrology being practised at the other two centres, if all else were equal, we would recommend that renal services for this sector would best be provided by the expansion at Hammersmith Hospital. Academically this is an acknowledged centre with substantial support from outside funding bodies and a continuing record of training scientifically orientated academic physicians. Its expansion in the service field would require the appointment of additional experienced clinicians. We believe that this is readily possible, whereas the wholesale transfer of the research and academic facilities to another site would separate them from other departments with which there are shared research interests, and is less likely to succeed.

80.   An expanded renal service could not occur in isolation from other specialties at Hammersmith. It will take some time before it is clear how the translation of this special health authority into the market place will affect its services and its eventual configuration. Nevertheless we think that transplantation should be developed here and believe that this can be achieved satisfactorily from the present base. We have received written assurances from the Dean, the Professor of Renal Medicine and the Professor of Medicine that the development of Renal Services at Hammersmith will be supported to the level we require

for a tertiary centre.

81.   However we consider that in the present circumstances it would be prudent if the unit at Hammersmith developed a closer link with the service at Charing Cross Hospital with which it already has shared arrangements for transplantation. The large renal failure service at Charing Cross would complement the expertise in other fields (nephrology and transplantation) at Hammersmith and either site could be expanded as circumstances dictate to form a single preferred nephrology specialty centre for the western sector. It would be important to ensure an integrated staffing and managerial structure for these two sites. We emphasise that we do not believe that a two-site option can be other than temporary, but we consider that it is justified in the present circumstances.

82.   It has been put to us that St Mary's Hospital should be the renal centre for the western sector on the basis that the development of transplantation is central to the academic aspirations of this hospital. It has also been put to us that a fully-fledged renal service at St Mary's is important to a plan for the development of the medical faculty at Imperial College. We understand, however, that this plan is not universally accepted.

83.   We believe that Hammersmith Hospital with, for the present, a link to the Charing Cross nephrology service is the more appropriate option for linking tertiary renal services in west London into the academic focus of Imperial College. However we feel that there is a case for maintaining some renal services at St Mary's in view of the considerable commitment to other departments.

South-west (St George's, St Helier)

84.   St George's is a small unit with a brief but active history. The chronic renal failure service is about two years old but has recruited 64 new patients in its first two years and now has a stock of 50 on dialysis (nearly all CAPD) and 63 transplant follow-ups. A few live donor transplants are performed at St George's (tissue typing done at Guy's) but all cadaver transplants are carried out at St Helier which also provides some support services to the dialysis unit.

85.   We were shown an empty ward in a modern ward block which had been earmarked for conversion to a renal ward and supporting services if St George's is chosen as the tertiary centre for the south west sector. The hospital has a large population base around it though the Lambeth area is currently served largely by St Thomas's for renal services. Almost all relevant departments are currently at St George's.

86.   Because St George's is the academic focus of SW Thames we have explored with the Dean the attitude of the Medical School to developing St George's as the tertiary centre. He would support the creation of a chair in renal medicine, though St George's could not at present provide the funding. He would also supply adequate modern laboratory facilities for the academic department.

87.   St Helier Renal Unit is sited in the DGH at Carshalton which is also an associated university hospital taking medical students from St George's. It is the regional renal centre for SWTRHA. The hospital contains a wide range of other specialties though none has the same status as regional unit. The staff act as nephrologists to the Sutton branch of the Royal Marsden Hospital, and to the Atkinson Morley Hospital. They run peripheral clinics

at Epsom, East Surrey, Guildford, Kingston and Chertsey where they manage groups of patients on CAPD; haemodialysis was about to start at St Peter's Hospital Chertsey at the time of our visit. The Unit is the busiest in London, in terms of patients per consultant. The single handed transplant surgeon works closely with colleagues at Guy's and King's sharing the work of retrieval and the on-call duties.

88.   Our one serious reservation about St Helier is its academic isolation. It is supported by two enthusiastic patients' associations raising money for service and for academic developments. In our view it would be unwise to place a Professor of Nephrology in isolation from other academic departments. The academic review supported strongly the concept of the siting of a university tertiary centre at St George's and we so recommend. We strongly recommend that many of the attractive features of St Helier - its efficient organisation, patient-friendliness, collaboration with SET units, good records on kidney retrieval (involving mutual support with the Atkinson Morley) - should be retained and enhanced. The need to utilise some of the skills at St Helier by transfer of staff should be addressed.

89.   The creation of a new academic department at St George's would provide an excellent opportunity for the relocation of academic staff displaced from other centres by the reduction in the number of university units.

General recommendations

Medical and nursing staffing implications

90.   Overall, the workload carried by these central units is heavy. By the standards set out in the Renal Association document they have sufficient consultant medical but not surgical staff to cover the foreseen requirements for the eventual (rather than the present) stock of renal patients, as is demonstrated in Table 1. Medical staffing is covered in more detail in Appendix H. In order to provide, in the tertiary centres, for the workload we suggest, four physicians would be needed, with a fifth to cover the outreach services. We suggest that one post be provided from the combined sessions of the professor and senior lecturer whose time is otherwise reserved for academic work.

91.   For an autonomous centre without transplantation or university responsibilities, we recommend three physicians, and for a sub-regional centre in a DGH, two physicians with an interest in renal medicine. The junior staffing we suggest are consistent in number with the likely national provision for higher medical training in the specialty, but may not be sufficient to cover all the foreseeable workload. There may be a place for an associate specialist, staff grade or clinical assistant posts in some units, and we note that some such staff are already employed.

92.   The present nursing and non clinical staff provision is considered in appendix I. The staffing structures we recommend are incorporated in appendices D and I. Substantial relocation of nurses will be required, over time, nursing provision will be altered considerably and such change requires sympathetic management. We advocate, too, the increased use of non-nursing staff and also of nurse practitioners. We advise, and have costed for, the uniform implementation of economic shift patterns.

Teaching

93.   We note that undergraduates are allocated to units which practice general as well as renal medicine, for elective attachments to exclusively renal services, or on modular attachments which may include transplantation.   The teaching of renal disorders and of renal replacement therapy is quite complex, but each of the new combined schools should ensure that it is available to its undergraduates.   Post graduate teaching should be available at each University centre.   The Royal Postgraduate Medical School runs a course in renal disease; other centres should consider the opportunities for formal teaching of doctors in, or entering, the speciality.

Prevention

94.   With the exception of the skilled management of diabetes, and its complications for the kidney, which are addressed in detail in some of our centres, prevention of renal disease is difficult.   However the rate of its progression, and the complications which arise as renal failure worsens, with damage to bone, blood vessels and the heart, can all be modified by expert management at an early stage of renal impairment.   It is a concern to us that up to 50% of patients presenting to London units do so at the end stage of renal failure, when it is too late to apply such measures.   The development of outreach services should encourage early referral, and we recognise here a role for discussion with, and advice to, GPs who can be of vital assistance both in detecting renal disease and in assisting with its management.

Quality of Care

95.   Many of the quality issues described in The Patients Charter are not directly applicable to renal services but renal units do use criteria which have been identified as being of importance to the purchasers of health care.   Assessment of quality of care provided by renal units centres on provision of services for patients needing renal replacement therapy to sustain life.   Access to treatment is of paramount importance. Lack of defined areas of geographical responsibility make it difficult to compare London units in terms of success in providing access to treatment for all patients who require it, though some units have made greater efforts than others to provide locally accessible facilities, a course we recommend.   It would be invidious to rank quality of care delivered by the different London units from available data because the casemix varies from unit to unit.

96.   Prospective audit of quality of treatment using survival analysis and more detailed methods of analysing the efficiency of the dialysis techniques used may well be required by purchasers in future so that the quality of care that each unit provides can be monitored. We recommend strongly that units address this issue and point to the forthcoming Renal Association Document on Standards and Audit as a guide.

Central registry and organ exchange

97.   Outcome data are difficult to collect for renal medicine but we believe that they are important and have welcomed the initiatives of the Renal Association and the Royal College of Physicians in this area.   We recommend strongly that all renal units should provide data to the EDTA/ERA regularly, and eventually to a national registry from which

data can be drawn into the EDTA. The patchy nature of returns from British units to this Registry have impeded our analysis. While we understand the reasons for this in terms of the very heavy workload British units carry, we nevertheless consider that the collection of accurate data, and their availability for regional, national and international comparisons, are vital to the future assessment of quality. We believe British nephrologists will have little to fear from this. We recommend that the data set should include post code and ethnic origin so as to facilitate population-based analyses. In addition, the centres responsible for renal transplantation should play a full part in organ retrieval and in the national organ sharing schemes. A computer base and administrative assistance is needed. Units should incorporate these items in their costs.

Commissioning renal services

98. Compared to other services which DHA purchasers are responsible for commissioning, renal services are of relatively low volume, but high cost. These services are frequently excluded from mainstream block contracts, and handled on a cost and volume, or ECR basis. We recommend that, in order to give a more stable base for service commissioning, consideration should be given to creating larger, multi-district, consortia for purchasing renal services. Such an approach to commissioning would, we believe, create a well-balanced market comprising a smaller number of tertiary providers, and a larger number of district nephrology centres, and of satellite dialysis units.

99. In order to maintain an workable chain of clinical and management responsibility in this market, we recommend that purchasers should contract with a tertiary or district nephrology centre, as appropriate, leaving it to the centre to make agreed arrangements with satellite units for day-to-day dialysis and periodic outpatient reviews.

100. Purchasers should find helpful the data included in the full report in planning with providers, the provision of appropriate services and in establishing the cost of these services.

MAIN SPECIALTY CENTRES

Renal

Current service configuration

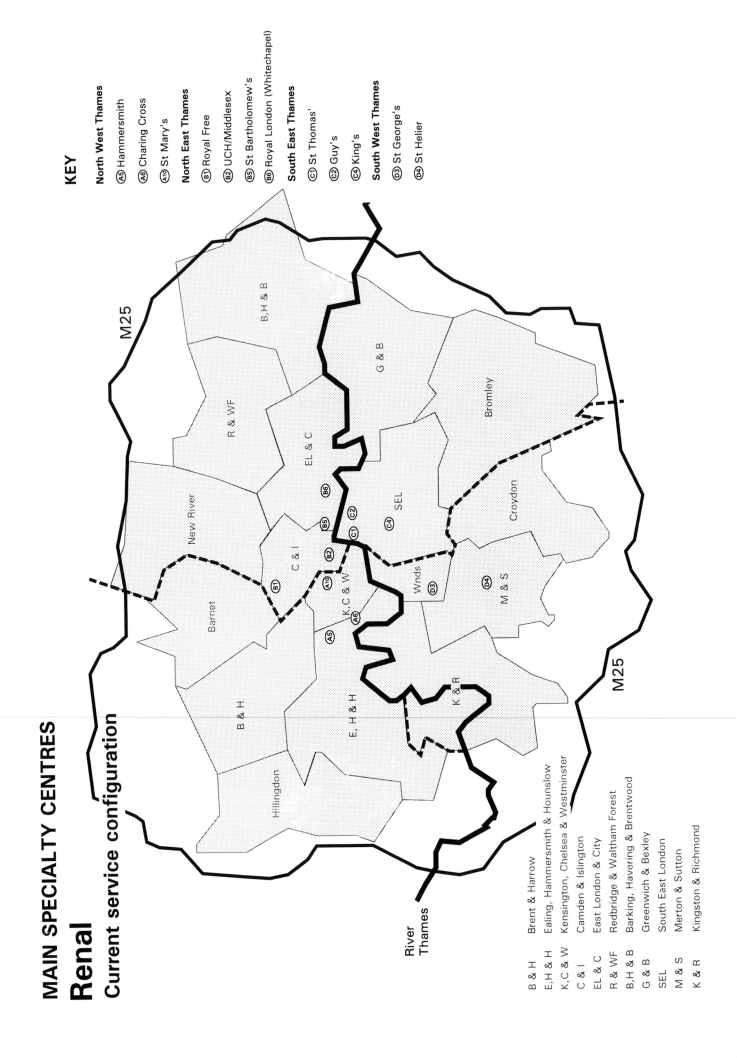

KEY

North West Thames
A5 Hammersmith
A6 Charing Cross
A10 St Mary's

North East Thames
B1 Royal Free
B2 UCH/Middlesex
B5 St Bartholomew's
B6 Royal London (Whitechapel)

South East Thames
C1 St Thomas'
C2 Guy's
C4 King's

South West Thames
D3 St George's
D4 St Helier

B & H   Brent & Harrow
E,H & H   Ealing, Hammersmith & Hounslow
K,C & W   Kensington, Chelsea & Westminster
C & I   Camden & Islington
EL & C   East London & City
R & WF   Redbridge & Waltham Forest
B,H & B   Barking, Havering & Brentwood
G & B   Greenwich & Bexley
SEL   South East London
M & S   Merton & Sutton
K & R   Kingston & Richmond

MAIN SPECIALTY CENTRES
Renal
Future service configuration

KEY

North West Thames
- (A5) Hammersmith
- (A6) Charing Cross

North East Thames
- (B2) UCH/Middlesex
- (B6) Royal London (Whitechapel)

South East Thames
- (C1) St Thomas'
- (C2) Guy's

South West Thames
- (D3) St George's

B & H — Brent & Harrow
E,H & H — Ealing, Hammersmith & Hounslow
K,C & W — Kensington, Chelsea & Westminster
C & I — Camden & Islington
EL & C — East London & City
R & WF — Redbridge & Waltham Forest
B,H & B — Barking, Havering & Brentwood
G & B — Greenwich & Bexley
SEL — South East London
M & S — Merton & Sutton
K & R — Kingston & Richmond

POPULATION NEED FOR CHRONIC (IRREVERSIBLE) AND

ACUTE (REVERSIBLE) RENAL FAILURE

CHRONIC RENAL FAILURE: POPULATION NEED FOR RENAL REPLACEMENT THERAPY

SUMMARY

The Renal Association estimate that the population need for renal replacement therapy (RRT) is 80 new cases per million per year under age 80, this figure is derived from studies in Devon, Lancashire and Northern Ireland. The impact of the substantial ethnic population in the Thames Regions on population needs to be considered. Some ethnic minorities (Asians and Blacks) have a higher prevalence of conditions which are known to cause to ESRF (especially non-insulin dependent diabetes and hypertension), they are likely therefore to have a greater need for RRT.

Overall 5.5% of the Thames population is Asian and 4.2% Black in the 1991 Census. There are sizeable populations in parts of Greater London, in some boroughs 40-50% of the population is from these groups. Asians and Blacks are younger than Whites, but this difference will diminish over the next few decades.

Studies in the UK and elsewhere have shown that Asians have a 3-4 fold increased prevalence of non-insulin dependent diabetes (NIDDM), about 30% of this is undiagnosed. They also have higher prevalence of hypertension. Blacks have a higher prevalence of hypertension and a much greater mortality from its complications (eg stroke), they too have a higher prevalence of diabetes.

There have been no UK population estimates of end-stage renal failure rates by ethnic group. Asians have been shown in Leicester to have a ten fold increased rate of acceptance onto RRT due to diabetic nephropathy. Studies in the US show that Blacks have a three to fourfold increased acceptance rate onto RRT, this occurs for most causes but is particularly high for hypertension.

Our analysis of the current RRT prevalence in the Thames Regions show adult rates per million (pm) of 417 for Whites, 1258 for Asians and 1201 for Blacks. Average acceptance rates in 1991-2 were 74pm, 238pm, and 237 pm respectively in these groups. These threefold increases are found in the under 55s and are therefore not likely to be due to access factors alone. Relative rates increase with age implying that as these ethnic groups age need for RRT will increase disproportionately.

The other major demographic determinant of need is the age structure of a population as the incidence of end-stage renal failure increases rises with age. The Thames population is projected to increase by only 1% by 1996 but there may be a shift in the distribution with numbers in inner London falling. The over 65 year old age group is not predicted to change but there is significant variation between district health authorities (DHAs) in the current proportion and projected change.

The stock and acceptance rates for RRT vary considerably between DHAs. There is evidence of under provision in the shires reflecting reduced access and under referral. The higher acceptance rates in parts of Greater London probably reflect greater need as well as closer proximity to renal units. Many Greater London DHAs have acceptance rates well above the national estimate.

In conclusion overall population need in the Thames Regions is likely to be greater than the national estimate of 80 per million because of the ethnic composition, 90-100 million is more realistic. Using the modelling techniques described in Appendix B, a 100 pm acceptance rate would increase the steady state estimate derived from an 80 pm acceptance by 14% and the dialysis stock by 23% (assuming that there is a limit on transplant supply). At a 100pm acceptance rate total stock would more than double and dialysis stock would more than treble. Some DHAs have a population need that may be almost double the national estimate, with a consequent impact on the steady state stock figure.

INTRODUCTION

This section reviews both the major determinants of population need for renal replacement therapy (RRT) and the demographic profile of patients currently receiving RRT in the Thames Regions. It is essential to consider the variation between districts in population need and their access to current treatment (as reflected by stock and acceptance rates) when deciding where renal services should be located. There are two sociodemographic factors, age and ethnicity, which are important determinants of population need for RRT and for which routine data from the 1991 census is now available at a district level. These are reviewed in detail, the effect of socioeconomic factors is unknown and is not considered.

To address these issues each renal unit in the Thames Regions supplied a demographic profile of their new patients in 1991-2 and their patient stock at the end of 1992/early 1993. The data items were district health authority (DHA) of residence, age, ethnicity and diabetic status. Units in neighbouring Regions (Cambridge, Oxford, Ipswich, Portsmouth and RAF Halton) were asked for a similar profile of their patients who were resident in the Thames Regions. The 1991 DHA boundaries have been used.

1.1. AGE

1.1.1 Population Based Studies

The Renal Association has undertaken two population based studies of advanced chronic renal failure (CRF). A study carried out in three English districts (North Devon, Exeter and Blackburn) during 1986-7 based case ascertainment on laboratory reports of a serum creatinine over 500 mmol/l (Feest, Mistry, Grimes and Mallick, 1990). In Northern Ireland, cases were ascertained by doctors' notification of patients with renal disease using similar criteria (McGeown 1990).

Both studies showed a marked age related increase in the incidence of CRF:

Table 1.   Age Related Incidence of Chronic Renal Failure

Age	Feest Rate/million (95% CI)	McGeown Rate/million (95% CI)	Pooled data Rate/million
0 -19	6 (-2 to 14)	24 (11 to 38)	20
20-39		37 (19 to 55)	37
40-49		90 (45 to 135)	90
20-49	58 (38 to 78)		
50-59	160 (96 to 224)	197 (124 to 271)	185
60-69	282 (197 to 367)	220 (138 to 302)	243
70-79	503 (370 to 636)	167 (81 to 253)	296
>80	588 (422 to 754)	78 (0 to 167)	345

The data are very similar except for the rates for the age groups below 20 and over 70, which may reflect ascertainment differences. The population of Northern Ireland was 1.5 million and had clearly defined boundaries without over-lap with adjoining areas.

Both studies then derived estimates of the population need for renal replacement therapy based on consideration of the suitability of patients, whether or not they had received it (some received therapy, some did not) (Table 2).

Table 2.   Population Need for Renal Replacement Therapy
Annual Rate Per Million (95% CI)

Age	Feest	McGeown
0-59		59 (44 to 90)
0-79	78 (63 to 93)	
All ages		77 (63 to 91)

These figures are likely to underestimate the true population rates because of incomplete case ascertainment. **The Renal Association have recommended a target of 80 patients per million under age 80 based on these studies.**

1.1.2   Age Distribution of the Population in the Thames Regions

Table 3 shows, for each DHA, the absolute numbers in each age and sex group and the proportions in older age categories. A map of the distribution of the population aged over 65 is shown in Figure 1. DHAs with large numbers in the older age groups will anticipate a higher population need for RRT, this is particularly true for DHAs on the South Coast.

Table 4 shows the 1991 population estimates and the 1996 projections for both the total population and for the over 65s. For the total population there is a 1% projected increase, most inner London DHAs show reductions. There is no projected increase in the over 65s but there is some variation between DHAs. Projections for the period after 1996 are unreliable.

1.1.3 Age Profile of Patients on Renal Replacement Therapy

This analysis is based on the returns by the renal units. Figures 2-4 show the age profile of all patients on RRT treated in the renal units in the four Thames Regions. Overall 21% of the stock is over 65 and 4.5% over 75, these proportions are lower for transplants. However a third of new patients accepted onto RRT are over 65, and 10% over 75 (Figure 5) partly reflecting a trend to take on older patients. The age profile of the stock differs between units (Figure 6).

1.2. ETHNICITY

There are significant ethnic minority populations in the Thames Regions especially in inner London. The primary diseases which cause end-stage renal failure (ESRF) are shown in Table 5. Some of these conditions (eg diabetes, hypertension) occur more commonly in Asians and Blacks and may therefore lead to an increased incidence of ESRF and need for RRT in the Thames Regions. The following are reviewed:

1.2.1 The ethnic breakdown of the population in the Thames Regions.

1.2.2 Diabetes mellitus in Asians and in Blacks. Diabetes prevalence of patients on RRT.

1.2.3 Hypertension in Asians and Blacks.

1.2.4 End-stage Renal Failure: Literature review.

1.2.5 The current acceptance and stock rates of patients in the Thames Regions by ethnic group.

1.2.6 The expected age adjusted rates of advanced chronic renal failure for each ethnic group.

1.2.7 Estimates of total population need for each DHA relative to the population estimate of 80 per million using varying ethnic relative risks.

In the following 'Asian' is taken as Indian, Pakistani, Bangladeshi or other Asian. 'Black' is Black Caribbean, Black African and Black Other. It is recognised that there was some underenumeration in the 1991 census particularly in inner-city areas, this may differentially affect ethnic groups and inflate their rates.

1.2.1 Ethnic Distribution of the Thames Population

The numbers in each ethnic group for the four Thames RHAs in the 1991 census, by age group, is shown in Table 6. 88.6% are White, 5.5% Asian, 4.2% Black, and 1.7% other.

The number of persons that are Asian or Black and their age distribution is shown in Figure 7 for Greater London and Inner London, and the proportions in Table 7. Greater London has a large population of both Asians and Blacks, and proportionally more of the Black population lives in Inner London. Figure 8 shows that North West and North East Thames have the largest Asian and Black populations, South East Thames has a sizeable Black population.

The age distribution of the main ethnic groups in Greater London is shown in figure 9. The Asian and Black populations currently have a significantly younger distribution than Whites with a marked deficit of people aged over 60. This difference will decrease over the next decade, with a consequent rise in the need for RRT.

The proportion of the population in Greater London that is of Asian and Black origin in ages 0-14, 15-54, 55-64 and 65+ is shown as maps in Figures 10-13. The highest proportions are found in the younger age bands. In several boroughs (and DHAs) in the north Thames Regions over 30% of the adult population aged 15-54 is Asian or Black. The age distribution is also shown as pie charts for Greater London, Inner London and the four Thames Regions in Figures 14,15,16.

1.2.2 Diabetes Mellitus

1.2.2.1 Diabetes in the Population

Drury, Watkins, Viberti and Walker (1989) reported that about 25% of patients developing diabetes below the age of 30 (all insulin dependent (IDDM)) develop diabetic nephropathy, but many die before they need replacement therapy. The total number of patients with diabetes mellitus in the UK is not known.

A joint working party of the British Diabetic Association, the Renal Association and the Research Unit of the Royal College of Physicians carried out a survey to identify the number of diabetic patients with untreated severe renal failure (serum creatinine over 500 mmol/l) in 1985 (Report of the British Diabetic Association et al,1988). Six Regions, with a total population of over 17 million were surveyed, five adjoining each other in central and northern England, thus minimizing the bias from inter-regional referral that would have occurred in south-east England. The sixth region was Northern Ireland. One hundred and eighty one patients with renal failure due to diabetes were identified, 166 of whom were of European origin, 12 were Asian and 1 was AfroCaribbean. In this mainly Caucasian population the overall mean number of diabetics with ESRF was 10.3 per million (95 % CI 8.8 to 11.8) in the single year. 64 % were insulin treated.

1.2.2.2 Diabetes Mellitus in Asians

Prevalence

Studies in Leicester (Feehally et al, 1993) and in Bolton (Bodansky et al, 1992) show that the prevalence of diabetes mellitus in Asian children does not differ from that in Whites.

Studies in different parts of the world all have shown a high prevalence of non-insulin dependent diabetes (NIDDM) amongst migrants of Indian subcontinent origin (Lancet editorial, 1986; Mather and Keen, 1985; Mather, Verma, Mehta and Keen, 1987; McKeigue, Marmot, Syndercombe et al, 1988; Beckles, Miller, Kirkwood et al, 1986). The risk is greater in males than in females. Furthermore the excess is apparent in Asian sub-groups, despite their dietary, economic and cultural heterogeneity. There is increasing concern in epidemiological literature on the role of diabetes in the high rates of ischaemic heart disease in Asians, and also about morbidity from other conditions associated with diabetes.

Mather and Keen (1985), using a patient questionnaire, reported an age-adjusted prevalence of known diabetes amongst Asians in Southall (a predominantly Punjabi-Sikh population) that was 3.8 times the rate in Europeans. In Asian patients aged 40-64 years the increase was five-fold, with a peak prevalence ratio of 7.6 at ages 50-54 years. Mather estimated that 8% of Asians aged 50-59 and 12% of those aged 60-69 were diabetic. An excess was not apparent below the age of 30. Mather's collaborative study of the prevalence of known diabetes in a suburb of Delhi, using similar ascertainment methods in both areas, showed similar results (Mather, Verma et al, 1987); no one under the age of 30 was identified as diabetic, and the age-specific prevalence at ages 40-64 corresponded closely.

McKeigue et al (1988) reported that 20% of Bangladeshis aged 35-69 in Tower Hamlets had diabetes, only two-thirds of whom had been diagnosed, and found a prevalence rate three times that in non-Asians. A similar prevalence has been reported in Asian populations in other parts of the world (Beckles et al, 1986; Zimmet, Taylor, Ram, et al, 1983; Omar, Seedat, Dyer, Rajput, Motala, Joubert, 1985). In another study in West London, McKeigue, Shah and Marmot (1991) again found a prevalence of diabetes of about 20% for ages 40-64, about 4.3 times that of Europeans. This applied to all sub-groups - Punjabis, Gujaratis, Hindus and Moslems.

Simmons, Williams and Powell (1989), in a study employing random blood glucose screening, estimated the prevalence of both diagnosed and non-diagnosed diabetes in Coventry. The population was predominantly Asian (Punjabi). For the age groups 20-79 the prevalence rate for Asian men was 11.2 % and for Asian women 8.9%, four times and double the rates in white men and women respectively. The diagnosis of diabetes had not been made previously in 30 % of the Asians (similar to the one-third found by McKeigue in Tower Hamlets). A prevalence study of known diabetics in the north east part of Leicester city showed a high incidence of NIDDM, increasing with age (Samanta, Burden, Fent, 1987). This study has recently been confirmed and expanded to show that the risk in females does not begin to increase until after the age of 50 (Feehally et al, 1993).

Studies from India have shown much lower prevalence rates that those quoted but they were based on varying criteria for diagnosis (Gupta, Joshi, and Dave, 1978; Ramachandran, et al,1988). However it has been shown fairly consistently that the prevalence is higher in urban than in rural populations in India, that it rises markedly after the age of 40, and that the excess is greater in men than in women. When the results of Ramachandran's study of an urban population in south India were adjusted to the age distribution of Mather's Southall population, overall prevalence was 10%.

There is known to be an excess of hospital admissions for diabetes amongst Asians in Britain (Cruickshank, Beevers, Osbourne, Haynes, Corlett and Selby, 1980; Donaldson and Taylor, 1983).

It can be concluded that the prevalence of NIDDM amongst middle-aged Asians in this country could be as high as 20%, four to five times that of the non-Caucasian population.

Mortality from Diabetes Mellitus Amongst Asians

Information on immigrant mortality is based on the country of birth of the deceased rather than on ethnic origin, since the latter was not recorded at death registration and in censuses up to 1981. Information is therefore limited to first-generation migrants and omits UK-born ethnic populations, who are now a rising proportion of the total ethnic minority population.

There have been two comprehensive cause-based analyses of immigrant mortality, for 1970-72, based on the 1971 Census (Marmot, Adelstein and Bulusu, 1984) and on the 1981 Census (Balarajan and Bulusu, 1990). The increased standardised mortality ratios (SMR) for 1979-83 (the most recent mortality data available) for diabetes mellitus amongst persons born in the Indian sub-continent and the AfroCaribbean Commonwealths are shown in Table 8.

Table 8. Standardised Mortality Ratios for Diabetes Mellitus in England and Wales 1979-83

Country of birth	SMR* (ages 20 -69)	
	Males	Females
Indian sub-continent	297 (148)	303 (93)
Caribbean Commonwealth	292 (82)	424 (71)
African Commonwealth	219 (20)	161 (8)

* England and Wales = 100, observed deaths in parentheses.
Source : OPCS data (Balarajan and Bulusu, 1990)

Balarajan, Bulusu, Adelstein and Shukla (1984) in a more detailed study of national data for 1975-77 found that the excess mortality is present in all the Indian sub-groups.

1.2.2.3 Diabetes Mellitus Amongst Blacks

Much less is known about the prevalence of diabetes in the Black population in the UK. Odugbesan, Rowe, Fletcher, Walford and Barnett (1989) estimated the prevalence of diabetes to be about twice that of the white population. McKeigue, Shah and Marmot (1991) found a three-fold excess in their West London study.

There is an excess mortality associated with diabetes of between two to fourfold (Table 8).

1.2.2.4 Diabetes in Patients on RRT in the Thames Regions

Diabetes is an important determinant of survival on RRT and in the past diabetic patients were less likely to receive RRT.

Currently 14% of dialysis patients treated in the Thames units are diabetic, the proportion by unit varying from 8-20%. The figures for transplant stock and new patients are 10% (units range 3-21%) and 17% (units range 5%-32%) respectively. This variation partly reflects the differing prevalence of diabetes (and ethnic populations) in their local catchment areas.

The differences between renal units in the age and diabetic profile of patients illustrates how crude outcome comparisons without adjustment for case mix are unreliable, and why such outcome data has not been used in this review.

Analysis of new acceptances in seven renal units showed that the distribution of risk categories is:

-     Low risk (under 55 non-diabetic) 42%,
-     Medium risk (55-64 non diabetic or diabetic under 55) 23%
-     High risk (65 and over or diabetic 55 and over) 35%.

This accords well with the estimates used in the modelling detailed in Appendix B.

1.2.3 Hypertension

Asians

Mortality due to hypertension is increased in Asians (Marmot, Adelstein,and Bulusu, 1984; Balarajan, and Bulusu, 1990). A significantly higher prevalence of hypertension was found amongst Asians in Southall (Keil, Weinrich, Keil, Britt and Hollis, 1980).

Blacks

Hypertension is a well recognised cause of mortality and morbidity in Black populations. The standardised mortality rates (SMR) for hypertension and stroke in the UK are substantially increased (Adelstein, Marmot 1989; Balarajan 1991).

In the United States it is well documented that the prevalence and severity of hypertension is greater in Blacks than in Whites (Roberta, Maurer 1977; McClellan, Turtle, Issa, 1988). There has been less work in the UK. Cruickshank et al. (1985) found that the mean blood pressure in AfroCaribbeans in Birmingham did not differ from that of whites, although both tails of the distribution were wider so that the proportion hypertensive was increased. In West London McKeigue, Shah, Marmot (1991) found higher mean diastolic and systolic blood pressure in AfroCaribbeans. In a smaller study in North West London Cruickshank et al. (1991) found a non-significant increase in the prevalence of raised diastolic and systolic pressure in AfroCaribbeans.

1.2.4. End-stage Renal Failure in Ethnic Minorities

1.2.4.1 Literature Review

To determine the incidence of end-stage renal failure in different ethnic groups population based studies are needed. However such studies have not previously been carried out in the UK. The proposed UK National Registry for Renal Patients should in the future give population based information on ethnic categorisation.

Most information comes from analysis of acceptance rates onto RRT, derived from studies in the United States. These rates reflect patterns of patient identification, referral and acceptance onto RRT and access to preventive services.

Findings in the United States

Over the last 20 years many studies in the United States (US) have demonstrated an increased risk of ESRF in US Blacks compared to Whites (Table 9). This is found for most underlying causes, the overall risk is between 2 and 4.5 times that of Whites in most studies. The risk increases with age and is not marked below age 35. The risk is greatest for hypertensive nephropathy and two thirds of all cases now accepted onto RRT in the US with this cause are Black. It is important to note that the White groups studied sometimes included other ethnic groups (eg Mexicans/Hispanics) who have a higher prevalence of ESRF, so the relative risks may be even greater. RRT has been funded by the Medicare programme since 1973 and access to RRT is not thought to be a differential factor between ethnic groups. The role of hypertension as the underlying cause may be overstated in Blacks but the consistency of the finding over different times and places is striking.

The prevalence rate of hypertension in US Blacks compared to Whites is increased, but this is not so marked as the relative rate of acceptance onto RRT with hypertensive ESRF (McClellan, Turtle, Issa, 1988; Whittle et al., 1991). Other explanations for the increased rates of hypertensive ESRF include variations in the severity of hypertension and poor access to preventive medical care. Attempts have been made to correct for such factors (prevalence of hypertension, diabetes, and severe hypertension, income and education status), but the risks remained increased (Weller, Wu, Ferguson, 1985; McClellan et al, 1988). However there is some evidence that Blacks present with chronic renal failure at a later stage suggesting that medical care is poorer (HDP,1977). A recent study has estimated national projections for hypertension related ESRF among middle aged groups. It is estimated that US blacks have an increased risk of hypertension of 1.6, and of 8.0 for hypertension related ESRF, compared to whites (Perneger et al 1993). The estimated population attributable proportion due to Black race is 44% for hypertension related ESRF.To explain these findings it has therefore been postulated that the kidneys of Blacks are more susceptible to damage.

The risk of ESRF from diabetic nephropathy, secondary to NIDDM is also increased in Blacks (MMWR, 1992). This risk persists after adjustment for hypertension control, diabetes prevalence, lack of regular health care and lack of college education (Brancati et al., 1992; Cowie et al., 1990).

The findings in US Blacks cannot be directly extrapolated to the UK because of differences in genetic, socioeconomic and cultural factors, and in access to health care. Nevertheless the US findings suggest that rates of ESRF may be increased in UK Blacks also.

UK Studies

There have been few previous population based studies in the UK. A study in Leicester (Burden et al.,1992) looked at the rates of acceptance onto RRT of Asians with diabetic nephropathy. The renal unit serves a discrete catchment population, and so it is valid to derive population rates. Moreover there were studies in the area to determine ethnic status and diabetic prevalence during the period under study (1977-88). There were differences in the characteristics of the diabetic populations. In Whites there was a 1:1 sex ratio and a 4:1 ratio of IDDM to NIDDM, in Asians there was a 9:1 male preponderance and all cases were NIDDM. The estimated relative risk for diabetic nephropathy amongst diabetic Asians compared with diabetic Whites was 13.6 and in the general population the risk was 10.1 (Table 10). Not only do Asians have a higher prevalence of diabetes (specifically NIDDM) but this data suggests that Asians with diabetes may be more susceptible to renal damage than White diabetics. Other evidence supports this, for example studies in diabetic clinics have found a higher prevalence of proteinuria in Asians unexplained by glycaemic control or hypertension (Samanta et al., 1986; Allawi et al., 1988).

Table 10. **Annual Rates of End Stage Renal Failure Per 100000 Person Years in Leicester.**

	General population	Diabetics
Caucasians	2.3	35.6
Asians	23.3	486.6

Burden et al., 1992.

Previous surveys of DHA acceptance rates in South East Thames and North West Thames Regions have shown wide variations, with the highest levels found in those districts with a large ethnic population (Melia, Beech, Swan, 1991; Roderick, 1992). This finding is of course confounded by the siting of renal units in these or neighbouring districts. A review of acceptances onto RRT during 1987-91 from Hammersmith and Fulham, an inner London borough which has a high prevalence of Blacks, found an estimated acceptance rate of 129 pm for Blacks (Sethi, 1993).

Some renal units have analysed the ethnic profile of their patients on RRT. A review of 771 acceptances to the Charing Cross RRT programme from 1968 to 1990 showed that 79% were White, 12.7 % from the Indian subcontinent (Asian) and 7.2% AfroCaribbean. The ethnic groups were over-represented (according to the 1981 Census) but Charing Cross is close to areas with a high prevalence of ethnic minority populations. There was an over-representation of hypertensive nephropathy in AfroCaribbeans and of diabetes in Asians (Pazanias,et al. 1992), Table 11. Polycystic kidney disease was almost all confined to Caucasians.

Table 11 **Ethnic Distribution by Underlying Cause Charing Cross Unit, 1968-90**
Percent (Number)

Cause	AfroCaribbeans n=55	Asians n=107	Caucasian n=609
Hypertension	42 (23)	14 (15)	13 (80)
Diabetes	7 (4)	17 (18)	5 (28)
Unknown	2 (1)	21 (22)	9 (53)
Polycystic kidney	2 (1)	3 (3)	12 (75)
All other	47 (26)	45 (49)	61 (373)

A study at the King's Hospital Renal Unit of patients with diabetic nephropathy accepted for RRT between 1974-86 showed that Asians and AfroCaribbeans had a much higher proportion of NIIDM (Grenfell et al., 1988). The pattern of acceptance had changed during this period leading to an increase in the proportion of NIDDM patients.

Conclusions

The literature suggests that Asians and Blacks in the UK may be expected to have a greater incidence of ESRF and hence need for RRT, particularly secondary to hypertension and NIDDM. Primary and secondary prevention measures may reduce the incidence of ESRF (as well as cardiovascular disease) and this is particularly important in Asians and Black communities. The implementation of the Health of the Nation Strategy is therefore a significant development.

1.2.5 **Observed Acceptance and Stock Rates for Ethnic Groups in the Thames Regions**

Method

We have been able to perform population based analysis of ethnic risks using the 1991 Census denominators and the ethnic breakdown of patients treated in the units in the four Regions. The acceptance and stock rates for the four Thames Regions have been calculated, using the ethnic groupings, White, Asian, Black and Other.

The cross-boundary flow has been taken into account by including data from surrounding units (Cambridge, Oxford, RAF Halton, Portsmouth, Ipswich). The net flow is small and is assumed to be White.

Results

The stock (or prevalence) rate for adults for each ethnic group is shown in Table 12 and Figures 17-19. Overall stock rates are increased threefold in Asians and Blacks, this is particularly found for dialysis in Blacks suggesting a reduced rate of transplantation (probably reflecting different tissue types). The total stock rate is 18% higher than the White's only rate.

Adult acceptances onto RRT and rates for each ethnic group are:

	White	Asian	Black	Other
Average number accepted 1991-2 (%)	743 (74)	123 (12)	101 (10)	36 (4)
Annual rate pm	74.4	237.5	236.8	244.6

There is a threefold increased risk in Blacks and Asians.

We only have available at the time of writing an age ethnic breakdown of patients accepted from some of the units (Table 13). The age specific acceptance rates been calculated by applying this breakdown to all new patients, this assumes that it would not alter if all units were included. The risk increases with age and is similar for Asians and Blacks (Table 14).

One factor which may partly account for these increased rates is better access as the ethnic minority populations live closer to the renal units. Previous studies have shown the inverse relationship between acceptance rate and distance from central London (Dalziel 1987). Analysis of acceptance rates for Greater London DHAs (whose populations are all within 30 minutes driving time from renal units) by the proportion of ethnic minorities shows a high positive correlation (Figure 20). This suggests that there is a strong relationship between ethnicity and acceptance rates. Moreover access is not likely to be a major factor in the under 55s where rates in Asians and Blacks are increased three fold. For Blacks the risk estimates would be consistent with the findings in the US (Table 9). To further separate the effects of access and ethnic need on acceptance rates DHA based rates are needed but these are not derivable from the data obtained so far.

The variation in the ethnic profile by renal unit is shown in figures 21-23. There is considerable variation reflecting largely the ethnic mix of the local DHAs of each unit.

1.2.6   Expected Proportions with End-stage Renal Failure

To allow for the younger age distribution of Asians and Blacks the expected numbers of patients with advanced chronic renal failure for the Thames Regions have been calculated assuming that the age specific rates are equal in all ethnic groups (Table 15, Figure 24). The estimates are based on the age and ethnic distribution of the population at the 1991 Census, and the age specific rates for advanced chronic renal failure derived from the McGeown and Feest data.

The expected percentages would be 94.1% in Whites, 3.4%% in Asians and 2.6% in Blacks. These compare with the observed new acceptances onto RRT of 74%, 12% and 10% respectively. This clearly illustrates the excess risk in these groups.

1.2.7   Estimates of DHA Population Need

The proportion of Asians and Blacks for each DHA was given a range of weighting of 1.5, 2.0, 3.0 and 4.0 to reflect possible relative risks of ESRF (Table 16). The estimates of need for each DHA and RHA were then calculated for each weighting, based on an underlying population need of 80 per million (the Renal Association estimate).

At a weighting of 1.5 some DHAs have an estimated population need of over 90 per million (pm) (Ealing, Parkside, City and Hackney, Newham, Tower Hamlets and Camberwell) reflecting their high ethnic populations. Overall, the need for the Thames Regions would be 83.5 pm. At a weighting of four however these districts would have risks of over 140 pm. The overall need would be 100 pm, being highest north of the river (North West Thames 109 pm, North East Thames 107 pm).

It is difficult to know which is the most appropriate estimate of risk, but these seem reasonable estimates bearing in mind the US data and the current ethnic risk estimates in the under 55s. For the ethnic groups, as for Caucasians, the risks increase with age but the rate of increase may be greater. As the ethnic populations age their need for RRT will increase.

The implications for the size of the eventual steady state position can be modelled using the techniques described in Appendix B. Tableau 5 has an acceptance rate of 80 per million (35pm low, 20pm medium and 25pm high risk), and a constraint on transplant supply of 30 pm. This model predicts a steady state of 11638 patients overall with 7417 on dialysis. If however an acceptance rate of 100pm is modelled and it is assumed for illustration that the additional 20 pm are a mix of medium and high risk patients (ie a mix of diabetics and/or patients over 55), the steady state increases by 14% to 13304 and the dialysis stock by 23% to 9083.

A DHA with a population of half a million with an acceptance of 80 pm would expect a steady state of 414 (stock rate 828pm), if the acceptance is 100 pm the stock increases to 473 (stock rate 946pm) and if the acceptance rate is 140pm the stock would increase to 592 (stock rate 1184pm). Again these calculations assume the additional patients are a mix of medium and high risk patients.

1.3.   GEOGRAPHICAL DISTRIBUTION

The DHA of residence of patients in each renal unit has been mapped to allow DHA based analysis of stock (ie prevalence) and acceptance. Rates are given as both adult rates (adult cases/adult population) and total rates (adult cases/total population). The child cases have not been mapped but are very few at DHA level (0-3 for both acceptance and stock), and their impact on overall rates is small.

1.3.1   Stock of Patients on RRT (Prevalence)

Table 17 shows the number, adult and total stock rates for each DHA's residents (wherever treated) and an indirectly standardised adult rate using the 'all Thames' rate as a standard (set at 100). Figures 27-29 map these adult stock rates for dialysis, transplants and all modalities for each DHA (a key is included in Figures 25-26).

The adult stock rate is 506pm of which 47% is dialysis and 53% transplants. The adult rates per million for the Shires, Greater and Inner London are 384, 583 and 713 respectively.

Stock rates are significantly higher in some London DHAs especially in Harrow, Haringey, Newham, Camberwell and West Lambeth. This reflects both the high prevalence of ethnic minorities and the access to central London units. Some Shire DHAs have very low rates reflecting historical inequity in access to RRT.

The total stock rate in the Thames Regions is 412 pm (excluding child cases), if the 21 children on dialysis and 108 with transplants are included the total rate is 421 pm. Most DHAs except for the outer shires have total stock rates above the 1991 UK figure of 354 per million (EDTA).

There is some cross boundary flow into and out of the Thames Regions (Table 18). 2.7% (1 in 37) of residents are treated in units outside the four Thames Regions. The net flows are 40 dialysis out, 143 transplants in, overall 103 patients transfer in.

Figures 30-50 show the geographical distribution by DHA of all RRT patients for each unit (note this has not been performed at electoral ward level, within each DHA the location is randomly assigned).

1.3.2 **Adult New Patients Accepted 1991-2**

This analysis is based on the new acceptances to each unit. Some units include transfers in from other units and patients returning to dialysis from transplantation as new patients. These groups are not large and where possible they have been excluded from the 'new patient analysis'. It has not been possible to include data from the London, St Mary's, Lister, Royal Free, St Bartholomew's, Southend and Brighton and so the results presented here will give very slightly higher new patient acceptance rates.

Table 19 and Figure 51 shows the average annual adult and total population rates during 1991-2 for each DHA. The adult rate is 87pm and the total population rate is 70.5pm, this compares with the national estimate of need of 80 per million. It varies from 110 in the inner London, to 82 in outer London and only 51 in the shires. If the 36 child cases were included the total rate rises to 73.5pm.

There is a wide variation with total rates of over 100 per million in some London DHAs and significantly low rates in some shires (North Bedfordshire, Mid-Essex, North-East Essex, West Essex, Maidstone). Rates are higher in the northern Regions; total rates per million are North West Thames 82, North East Thames 68, South East Thames 66 and South West Thames 66.

1.3.3 **Travel Times**

We have performed preliminary analysis of the 30 minute drive times to both current and potential renal units (Appendix E).

1.4. **HOSPITALISATION ANALYSIS**

We have not performed detailed analysis of routine hospitalisation data but have relied on the units' returns. A 'nephrology consultant episode' may include: all types of nephrology admissions (eg acute, chronic dialysis complication, transplantation); maintenance dialysis if they are classified as day cases; and general medicine if the consultant has a combined appointment. There may also be problems with the completeness of ascertainment. It is therefore a crude and imprecise indicator of overall workload.

Nevertheless the variation in hospitalisation by DHA follows a similar pattern to the acceptance and stock rate data described above.

SECTION 2: ACUTE RENAL FAILURE

2.1   INTRODUCTION

Acute renal failure (ARF) describes an episode of renal failure occurring acutely, severe enough to influence patient morbidity and survival, which may need specialist advice and management, and may have workload and planning implications. There are many causes of ARF. It may occur de novo due to intrinsic disease of the kidneys but more often occurs as part of other morbid conditions such as a severe trauma, post-operative complications, severe burns, severe prolonged hypotension due to haemorrhage, sepsis, and after a wide variety renal insults including urinary tract obstruction. Acute renal failure was once a relatively common sequel of severe childbirth complications, but this has now become rare. It may still occur and may be a index of poor medical care in the community.

Patients with ARF are often severely ill and there may be failure of more than one organ system. They require high quality medical and nursing care in specialised units, where there are facilities for dialysis (haemodialysis, peritoneal dialysis), haemofiltration, and respiratory support if needed. A small number may need plasma exchange.

2.2   POPULATION NEED FOR ACUTE RENAL FAILURE THERAPY

Kumar, Hill and McGeown (1973) reported the wide-ranging causes of ARF and that it is common amongst the elderly. The incidence of ARF rises with increasing age, being rare in childhood. In a recent prospective study (Feest, Round and Hamad, 1993) the age related annual incidence rose from 17.1 per million population in adults aged under 50, to 949 in the 80-89 age group, 72% of the patients being over 70. The annual incidence of ARF in males was more than 2.5 times that in females, and remained significantly higher when cases of prostatic disease were excluded.

Earlier studies of ARF were renal unit based and patients who were not referred for specialist nephrologist's opinion were not included, therefore do not give a true reflection of patient need. Feest, Round and Hamad (1993) point out that acute severe ARF in the community is at least twice as high as that reported in renal unit based studies. Their prospective study of a Devon population is unique in providing information on which to base planning for provision of services for treatment of ARF. They report that 140.5 (95% confidence limits 116.9-171.9) per million total population develop ARF yearly, the figure for the total adult population being 172.4 (95% confidence limits 144.1-205.5). The age related incidence rose from 50 to 949 (in 80-89 age group) per million yearly. Prostatic disease was the commonest cause of ARF, accounting for 25% of cases, and had the best prognosis. Older patients have less renal reserve and may have diseased kidneys already and thus be more susceptible to further insults than those with normal kidneys. As the numbers of the elderly increase in the population so will the incidence of acute severe ARF.

2.3   PROVISION OF SERVICES

The renal units were asked to make returns of the number of patients with ARF for 1991 and 1992, separating them into those treated on ICU, and those not treated on ICU, provide the information in the form requested and gave approximate numbers, or a range. The approximate current workload for patients treated with dialysis or haemofiltration shown in Figure 12 in Appendix H. The data reflects the fact that policy for the treatment of ARF varies from hospital to hospital. Some have beds reserved for the treatment of ARF within the unit where they manage all patients except those needing ventilation; some do not have beds for this purpose and admit all patients with ARF to ICU. Of the patients treated in ICU, particularly those with multiple trauma, the episode of ARF (while life-threatening in itself and requiring treatment) may be only a part of the management of the patient and may not be mentioned in the final diagnosis nor indexed as a case of ARF.

Some, but not all, of the patients with ARF require dialysis or haemofiltration, perhaps repeated over a period of days or weeks. This may be given by renal unit staff in whichever area they are being treated, or by ICU staff, according to the policy of the hospital. The nephrologists continue to be involved in giving advice and these often very ill patients takes up considerable amounts of their time. Patients are referred from other specialities within the hospital with acutely impaired renal function due to a variety of causes, including electrolyte disturbances, for advice from the nephrologists.

Hospitals with major accident and emergency, cardiac surgery, major vascular surgery departments will have significantly more patients with ARF. Plasma exchange may be used for the treatment of acute parenchymal renal disease (eg Goodpasture's syndrome; vasculitis), or myeloma. This very expensive treatment is usually provided by acute nephrology service, but the extent to which it is used varies. It is not used at all in some units. The centres where it is used extensively are Hammersmith and the Royal Free (Figure 8 Appendix H). The number of treatment sessions vary from 0 to 373.

2.4   OUTCOME OF TREATMENT FOR ARF

The outcome of treatment for ARF depends on the cause of the renal failure, and in the very severe cases how many other organs are affected. If kidneys only fail the mortality may be as low as 10%, though as already noted many patients, particularly the older, may have residual impairment of renal function and require long term follow-up. If both kidneys and lungs are affected and the patient requires ventilation, the mortality is about 50%, rising to above 80% if inotropes are also needed, and to over 90% if liver failure is also present

2.5   INCIDENCE OF ARF

The various factors discussed above show the difficulty in arriving at an estimate of the number of cases of ARF likely to occur per million population (pmp) yearly. The number was estimated at 50pmp in the Renal Association Report (1991), but the Report referred to the very severe cases, often with failure of more than one organ system. The true number who would benefit from referral is considerably greater. Feest's study included patients not referred for specialist opinion, not all of whom might have benefited had one been obtained. After scrutinising the patients' notes they suggested a potential referral rate to nephrologists of 70 pmp (confidence limits 53.4 - 89.3) or 85.4 (65.5 - 109.5) per million adults yearly. Their estimate of 70 pmp total population seems to be a reasonable approximation.

Feest et al.'s study under-estimate ARF in that it did not include patients with acute rapidly progressive renal failure whose renal function does not recover, though they may have received many treatments with plasma exchange. Their population of patients with ARF included patients with mild chronic renal failure (CRF) with acute (or chronic deterioration of renal function who showed some recovery. Follow-up at two years showed that with one exception these patients did not deteriorate further to require long term RRT; however some died in who CRF may have been a factor. Many of Feest's patients did not make a full recovery, possibly because the ARF itself was associated with some degree of permanent damage. The elderly (72% of their patients) have less renal reserve and are less able to make a full recovery after an acute insult. Kjellstrand, Ebben and Davin (1981) showed that incomplete recovery from acute tubular necrosis (a more restrictive diagnosis of ARF) was common after the age of 55. Some of the older may have already impaired renal function and thus more susceptible to further insults than those with normal kidneys. If the renal function does not recover completely such patients require follow-up as they may become future patients for renal support, which has implications for revenue provision, especially for staff.

2.6 BED REQUIREMENTS FOR TREATMENT OF ACUTE RENAL FAILURE

The duration of support required by patients with acute renal failure is very variable, may be from one to six weeks, or even longer. About 60% of the patients maybe treated in the renal unit the remainder including those requiring ventilation being in ICU. It may be assumed that 42 pmp may be treated in the renal unit for four weeks as inpatients per year (168 bed weeks), which would require the provision of three to four beds for this purpose. A similar usage of beds may be expected in the ICU, although the severe cases of trauma and post-operative ARF will be treated there because of the need for ventilation.

2.7 ETHNIC MIX ON THE INCIDENCE OF ARF

The effect of admixture of ethnic populations on the incidence of ARF has not been studied. However Feest showed that 94.4% of cases of ARF in their population (predominantly caucasian) occurred over the age of 49. This suggests that at present the relatively young population of non-Caucasian races does not contribute significant numbers of patients with ARF (unless excess incidence of ARF is a market for poor medical care). The numbers of cases of ARF in non-Caucasians can be expected to increase in future with increasing numbers of the ageing in their population.

2.8   AUDIT AND QUALITY OF OUTCOME

The management of renal disease lends itself to audit and this is being developed and encouraged by the Renal Association and the Royal College of Physicians. Outcome measures require to be studied prospectively with a careful analysis of the case mix in question and are not thought presently to be good comparators between individual units.

ACKNOWLEDGEMENTS

The Chronic Renal Failure section was written by:

Dr P Roderick, North West Thames RHA.
Mr I Jones, Queen Mary and Westfield/East London and City DHA.
Dr V Raleigh, Institute of Public Health, Surrey University, Guildford.
Professor M McGeown, Belfast University.

We thank Ms A Simmons of North West Thames RHA Information Department, and the Institute of Public Health, Guildford for producing the maps, and Dr T Feest, Southmead Hospital for advice.

The Acute Renal Failure section was written by Professor M McGeown, Belfast University.

REFERENCES

Adelstein AM, Marmot MG. The Health of Migrants in England and Wales. In Ethnic Factors in Health and Disease, ed Cruickshank JK, Beevers DG. London, Wright, 1989.

Allawi J, Rao PV, Gilbert R, Scott G, Jarrett RJ, Keen H. Viberti GC, Mather HM. Microalbuminuria in non-insulin dependent diabetics; its prevalence in Indian as compared with Europid patients. Br Med J 1988; 296: 462-4.

Balarajan R, Bulusu L. Mortality Among Migrants in England and Wales, 1978-83. In Mortality and Geography: a review in the mid-1980s, England and Wales. Ed Britten M, OPCS, Series DS no 9, pps 103-21 (see Appendix tables). London: HMSO, 1990.

Balarajan R, Bulusu L, Adelstein AM, Shukla V. Patterns of mortality among migrants in England and Wales from the Indian subcontinent. Br Med J 1984; 289:1185-7.

Balarajan R. Ethnic differences in mortality from ischaemic heart disease and cerebrovascular disease in England and Wales. Br Med J 1991;302:560-4.

Beckles GLA, Miller GJ, Kirkwood BR, Alexis SD, Carson DC, Byam NTA. High total and cardiovascular disease mortality in adults of Indian descent in Trinidad, unexplained by major coronary risk factors. Lancet 1986;i:1298-301.

Bodansky HJ, Staines A, Stephenson C, Haigh D, Cartwright R. Evidence for an environmental effect on the aetiology of insulin dependent diabetes in a transmigratory population. Br Med J 1992; 304: 1020-2.

Brancati F, Whittle J, Whelton P, Seidler A, Klag M. The excess incidence of diabetic end stage renal disease among blacks. JAMA1992;268:3079-84.

Burden AC, McNally P, Feehally J, Walls J. Increased incidence of end stage renal failure secondary to diabetes mellitus in Asian ethnic groups in the United Kingdom. Diabetic Medicine 1992;9:641-5.

Cowie CC, Port FK, Wolfe RA, Savage PJ, Hawthorne VM. Disparities between incidence of diabetic end stage renal disease by diabetic type. Diabetes 1990;321:1074-79.

Cruickshank J, Cooper J, Burnett M, MacDuff J, Dubra U. Ethnic differences in fasting C-peptide and insulin in relation to glucose tolerance and blood pressure. Lancet 1991;338:842-7.

Cruickshank J, Jackson S, Beevers G, Bannan L, Beevers M, Stewart V. Similarity of blood pressure in blacks, whites, and Asians in England: the Birmingham Factory Study. Journal of Hypertension 1985;3:365-71.

Cruickshank J, Beevers DG, Osbourne VL, Haynes RA, Corlett JCR, Selby S. Heart attack, stroke, diabetes and hypertension in West Indians, Asians and whites in Birmingham, England. Br Med J 1980;281:1108.

Dalziel M,Garrett C. Intraregional variation in the treatment of end-stage renal failure. Br Med J 1987;294:1382-3.

Donaldson LJ, Taylor JB. Patterns of Asian and non-Asian morbidity in hospitals. Br Med J 1983;286:949-51.

Drury PL, Watkins PJ, Viberti G-C, Walker J. Diabetic nephropathy. Br Med Bull 1989;45:127-147.

Easterling RE. Racial factors in the incidence of causation of end stage renal failure. Trans Am Soc Artif Int. Organs. 1977;23:28-32.

Eggers PW, Connerton R, McMullan M. The Medicare experience of end stage renal disease. Trends in incidence, prevalence and survival. Health Care Finance Rev 1984;5:69-88.

Editorial. Coronary heart disease in Indians overseas. Lancet 1986;i:1307-8.

Feehally J, Burden AC, Mayberry JF et al. Disease variations in Asians in Leicester. Quarterly Journal of Medicine 1993;86:263-9.

Feest TG, Mistry CD, Grimes DS, Mallick NP. Incidence of advanced chronic renal failure and the need for end stage replacement treatment. Br Med J 1990;301:897-900.

Feest, TG, Round, A, Hamad, S. Incidence of acute severe renal failure in adults: results of a community based study. Br Med J 1993;306:481-3

Ferguson R, Grim C, Opgenorth TJ. The epidemiology of end stage renal disease: the six year South Central Los Angeles experience 1980-5. Am J Public Health 1987;77:864-5.

Grenfell A, Bewick M, Parsons V, Snowden S, Taube D, Watkins PJ. Non-insulin dependent diabetes and renal replacement therapy. Diabetic Medicine 1988;5:172-6.

Gupta OP, Joshi MH, Dave SK. Prevalence of diabetes in India. In Advances in Metabolic Disorders. Ed Miller M, Bennett PH,. Academic Press, New York, , 1978.

Hiatt RA, Friedman DG. Characteristics of patients referred for treatment of and stage renal disease in a defined population. Am J Public Health 1982;72:829-33.

Hypertension Detection and Follow-up Program Cooperative Group Blood pressure studies in 14 communities: a two stage screen for hypertension. JAMA 1977;237:2385.

Keil JE, Weinrich MC, Keil BW, Britt RP, Hollis Y. Hypertension in a population sample of female Punjabi Indians in Southall. Journal of Epidemiology and Community Health 1980;34:45-47.

Kjellstrand, CM, Ebben, J, Davin T. Time of death, recovery of renal functions, development of chronic renal failure and need for chronic haemodialysis in patients with acute renal failure. Trans Amer Soc Artif Int Organs 1981;27:45-50

Kumar R, Hill, C, McGeown, M.G. Acute renal failure in the elderly. Lancet 1973;1:90-91

McClellan W, Tuttle E, Issa A. Racial differences in the incidence of hypertensive end stage renal disease (ERSD) are not entirely explained by differences in the prevalence of hypertension. Am J Kidney Dis 1988;4:285-90.

McGeown MG. Prevalence of advanced renal failure in Northern Ireland. Br Med J 1990;301:900-3.

McKeigue PM, Marmot MG, Syndercombe Court YD, Cottier DE, Ramhan S, Riemersma RA. Diabetes, hyperinsulinaemia, and coronary risk factors in Bangleshis in East London. British Heart Journal 1988;60:390-6.

McKeigue PM, Shah B, Marmot MG. Relation of central obesity and insulin resistance with high diabetes prevalence and cardiovascular risk in South Asians. Lancet 1991;337:382-6.

Marmot MG, Adelstein AM, Bulusu L. Immigrant mortality in England and Wales 1970-78: causes of death by country of birth OPCS. London: HMSO, 1984.

Mather HM, Keen H. The Southall diabetes survey: prevalence of known diabetes in Asians and Europeans. Br Med J 1985;291:1081-4.

Mather HW, Verma NPS, Metha SP, Madhu S, Keen H. The prevalence of known diabetes in Indians in New Delhi and London. Journal of Medical Association of Thailand 1987;70:54-8.

Mauser J, KappClark J, Coles B, Menduke H. An areawide survey of treated end stage renal failure. Am J Public Health 1978;68:166-9.

Melia J, Beech R, Swan T. Incidence of advanced renal failure. Br med J. 1991;301:51-2.

Odugbesan O, Rowe B, Fletcher J, Walford S, Barnett AH. Diabetes in the UK West Indian community: the Wolverhampton Study. Diabetic Medicine 1989;6:46-58.

Omar MAK, Seedat MA, Dyer RB, Rajput MC, Motala AA, Joubert SM. The prevalence of diabetes mellitus in a large group of South African Indians. South African Medical Journal 1985;67:924-6.

Pazianas M, Eastwood J, MacRae K, Phillips M. Racial origin and primary renal diagnosis in 771 patients with end stage renal disease. Nephrol Dial Transplant 1991;6:931-5.

Perneger TV, Klag MJ, Feldman HI, Whelton PK. Projections of hypertension related renal disease in middleaged residents of the United States. JAMA 1993;269:1272-77.

Pugh JA, Stern M, Haffner S, Eifler C, Zapata M. Excess incidence of treatment of end-stage renal disease in Mexican Americans. Am J Epidemiol 1988;127:135-44.

Report of the British Diabetic Ass, the Renal Ass, & the Research Unit of the Royal College of Physicians: Care of diabetics with end stage renal failure, 1988;5:79-84.

Ramachandran A, Jali MV, Mohan V, Snehalatha C, Viswanathan M. High prevalence of diabetes in an urban population in south India. Br Med J 1988 297:587-90.

Roberta J, Maurer K. Blood pressure levels of persons 6-74 years, United States 1972-74. National Health Centre for Health Statistics Series 11, no 203; Washington, 1977.

Roderick P. Personal communication. 1993

Rostand SG, Kirk K, Rutsky E, Pate B. Racial differences in the incidence of treatment of end- stage renal disease. N Engl J Med 1982;306:1276-9.

Samanta A, Burden AC, Feehally J, Walls J. Diabetic renal disease: differences between Asians and white patients. Br Med J 1986;293:366-7.

Samanta A, Burden AC, Fent B. Comparative prevalence of no-insulin diabetes mellitus in Asian and white Caucasian adults. Diabetes Res Clin Pract 1987;4:1-6.

Sethi, D. Personal communication, 1993.

Shulman NB, Dallas Hall W. Renal vascular disease in African-Americans and other racial minorities. Circulation 1991;83:1477-8.

Simmons D, Williams DRR, Powell MJ. Prevalence of diabetes in a predominantly Asian community; preliminary findings of the Coventry diabetes study. Br Med J 1989;298:18-21.

Sugimoto T, Rosansky S. The incidence of treated end stage renal disease in the Eastern United States 1973-9. Am J Public Health US Renal Data System USRDS 1989. Annual report Bethesda Maryland Ma National Institutes of Diabetic Medicine and Digestive and Kidney Diseases. 1989.

Weller J, Wu S, Ferguson W. End-stage renal disease in Michigan. Am J Neprol 1985;5:84-95.

Whelton PK, Klag M. Hypertension as a risk factor for renal disease. Review of clinical and epidemiological evidence. Hypertension 1989;13:Suppl:1 19-27.

Whittle JC, Whelton PK, Seidler A, Klag M. Does racial variation in risk factors explain black-white differences in the incidence of hypertensive end-stage renal disease. <u>Arch Int Med</u> 1991;151:1359-64.

Zimmet P, Taylor R, Ram P et al. Prevalence of diabetes and impaired glucose tolerance in the biracial (Melanesian and Indian) population of Fiji; a rural - urban comparison. <u>Am Journal of Epidemiology</u> 1983;118:673-88.

TABLE 3

PROVISIONAL REBASED MID-1991 POPULATION ESTIMATES

	Males						Females						Grand Total	Under 15 %	65 & over %	75 & over %	85 & over %
	0–14	15–44	45–64	65–74	75+	Total	0–14	15–44	45–64	65–74	75+	Total		%	%	%	%
North Bedfordshire	25400	58400	26800	8700	5300	124600	24100	55200	26400	10000	9400	125100	249700	19.8	13.4	5.9	1.4
South Bedfordshire	32100	87100	26300	8700	5000	142200	30800	64800	27900	9800	9300	142600	284800	22.1	11.5	5.0	1.1
East & North Hertfordshire	47900	110500	53600	17600	10200	239800	44800	105700	54100	20700	18600	243900	483700	19.2	13.9	6.0	1.3
NW Hertfordshire	25900	56500	28300	9600	5600	128800	24300	56600	28300	11300	10400	131900	260700	19.2	14.2	6.1	1.4
SW Hertfordshire	23400	59300	28200	9500	6000	119000	22400	52500	26600	11500	11000	124000	243000	18.8	15.6	7.0	1.6
Barnet	28400	66600	28900	10400	8300	142600	27200	68500	30800	13500	15500	155500	298100	18.7	16.0	8.0	1.9
Harrow	19900	45700	21100	6600	5300	98600	18800	45300	21800	8300	10100	104300	202900	19.1	14.9	7.6	1.8
Hillingdon	22800	55200	24300	8200	5400	115700	21700	52900	24600	10300	10100	119600	235300	18.8	14.4	6.6	1.4
Hounslow & Spelthorne	28500	71100	31400	10200	6400	147500	26800	68200	31400	12200	11900	151500	299000	18.5	13.6	6.1	1.4
Ealing	27700	67200	27000	8800	6000	136700	26000	68200	27500	10700	10900	143300	280000	19.2	13.0	6.0	1.4
Riverside	19500	74600	28700	9100	6100	138100	19500	79800	29100	11700	12300	152200	290300	13.5	13.5	6.3	1.4
Parkside	39200	105000	43400	13300	8800	209700	37100	110000	43500	15900	16300	222800	432500	17.6	12.6	5.8	1.3
NWT Total	340500	833700	370000	120700	78400	1743300	323500	828500	373000	145900	145800	1816700	3560000	18.7	13.8	6.3	1.4
Basildon & Thurrock	30900	87300	28900	10500	5000	143500	29100	66500	30600	12700	9500	148400	291900	20.6	12.9	5.0	1.0
Mid Essex	29800	67300	32300	10200	6500	146100	28400	64600	31500	12200	11800	148500	294600	19.8	13.8	6.2	1.4
North East Essex	27700	63900	32800	14500	10400	149300	26600	61100	33600	18000	18200	157500	306800	17.7	19.9	9.3	2.2
West Essex	24800	56900	28900	10300	5900	127800	23200	55100	30400	12200	10300	131200	259000	18.5	14.9	6.3	1.3
Southend	30700	68700	35500	13700	9500	158100	29000	67800	36400	17200	17800	168200	326300	18.3	17.8	8.4	2.0
Barking, Havering & Brentw	43400	98500	48800	19400	10300	217500	40700	94300	51600	23600	19700	229900	447400	18.8	16.3	6.7	1.4
Hampstead	8100	24900	10000	3400	2500	48900	7700	28000	10700	4500	5200	56100	105000	15.0	14.9	7.3	1.7
City & Hackney	21200	44600	15600	5700	3400	90600	20100	47400	16300	6400	6400	96800	187400	22.0	11.7	5.2	1.1
Newham	26300	52300	18400	6600	3800	107400	24800	51300	18400	7900	7300	109700	217100	23.5	11.8	5.1	1.1
Tower Hamlets	20800	37400	15100	5700	2900	81900	19400	37700	14000	6200	5700	83000	164900	24.4	12.4	5.2	1.1
Enfield	25500	59100	27000	9000	6200	126800	24200	59000	27500	11300	12800	134800	261600	19.0	15.0	7.3	1.6
Haringey	19800	53000	18700	5600	3700	100800	19200	53500	19200	6800	7500	106200	207000	18.8	11.4	5.4	1.4
Redbridge	22100	51700	23500	8600	5800	111700	21300	51000	24300	10600	11100	118300	230000	18.9	15.7	7.3	1.7
Waltham Forest	21700	51000	19700	6800	5100	104400	20400	51800	20200	8700	10300	111400	215800	19.5	14.4	7.1	1.7
Bloomsbury & Islington	21400	59800	22800	8000	4700	116300	21100	63700	22800	9600	9200	126200	242500	17.5	13.0	5.7	1.3
NET Total	374200	853200	380100	138100	85700	1831300	355200	852800	387300	167900	162800	1926000	3757300	19.4	14.8	6.6	1.5
Brighton	25500	68500	30800	13200	10300	148100	24300	67000	32600	17600	21300	162800	310900	16.0	20.1	10.2	2.5
Eastbourne	20600	42500	24700	12100	10600	110400	19400	43900	27200	16200	19900	126600	237000	16.9	24.8	12.8	3.3
Hastings	14700	30000	17300	8900	7400	78300	14400	30700	21600	8900	14600	90300	168600	17.3	25.3	13.0	3.5
SE Kent	28000	57100	29400	12100	8300	132900	26100	54900	30300	14400	15500	140700	273600	18.5	18.8	8.7	2.1
Canterbury & Thanet	27900	58500	31200	15300	10900	144800	26900	57400	32600	19300	20400	158600	303400	17.8	21.7	10.3	2.5
Dartford & Gravesham	22100	50300	25000	8000	4500	109900	20800	48300	25800	9600	8400	113100	223000	19.4	13.7	5.8	1.3
Maidstone	20100	45000	29200	7000	4300	105600	19300	43800	29800	9800	8200	107800	201100	19.3	13.9	6.2	1.4
Medway	36100	78900	34200	11000	6300	168500	34300	75300	33600	13600	11700	166400	334900	21.0	12.7	5.4	1.1
Tunbridge Wells	18600	42400	23300	7900	5300	97500	17900	42000	24300	11700	10900	105100	202600	18.0	16.8	8.0	2.1
Bexley	21100	48500	23500	8000	5000	106100	20500	47800	24400	10900	9400	111900	218000	19.1	14.8	6.6	1.4
Greenwich	22700	47400	16300	7800	4800	101800	21700	48000	20200	10000	9100	110100	211900	21.0	14.9	6.6	1.4
Bromley	28000	62500	32700	11900	7300	140400	24700	63000	34800	15000	14900	152400	292800	17.3	16.8	7.6	1.7
West Lambeth	14700	41800	13300	4900	3000	77700	14200	43700	14000	5900	5900	83700	161400	17.9	12.2	5.5	1.2
Camberwell	22500	52500	18700	6800	4000	104500	21400	56600	19600	8400	7500	113500	218000	20.1	12.2	5.3	1.1
Lewisham & N Southwark	32100	77000	28200	11500	7000	158600	31000	81500	30400	14000	14000	170900	327700	19.3	14.2	6.4	1.4
SET Total	350700	803900	375300	146200	98900	1775000	334200	806800	391900	185100	191600	1909900	3684900	18.6	16.9	7.9	1.9
North West Surrey	18600	48500	23700	8000	5400	105200	18600	47300	23900	9600	10100	109600	214800	17.9	15.4	7.2	1.8
West Surrey & NE Hants	28400	70300	31100	8100	5100	143000	26500	63300	30200	9900	10100	140000	283000	19.4	11.7	5.4	1.3
South West Surrey	17200	41800	20800	7100	5300	92200	16000	39800	21600	8900	10000	96300	188500	17.6	16.6	8.1	2.0
Mid Surrey	15400	33900	20500	7200	5300	82300	14100	33300	21000	9100	9800	87300	169300	17.4	18.4	8.9	2.1
East Surrey	17300	41000	21800	7500	5200	92800	16700	39800	22200	9100	9800	97600	190400	17.9	16.6	7.9	1.9
Chichester	14900	32900	18800	9500	7900	85000	13900	32700	21600	12600	13900	94700	179700	16.0	24.4	12.1	3.0
Mid Downs	28000	64300	30300	10300	6400	140300	26600	62600	31300	12700	12200	145400	285700	19.5	14.6	6.5	1.6
Worthing	20600	45500	25600	12700	11100	115700	19800	44800	28100	17400	22400	132600	248300	16.3	25.6	13.5	3.6
Croydon	31200	73400	32200	10300	6700	153800	29700	74000	33600	13000	13300	163600	317400	19.2	13.6	6.3	1.5
Kingston & Esher	16300	42200	19000	6700	4900	89100	15600	41200	19400	8700	9400	94300	183400	17.4	16.2	7.8	1.7
Rich, Twick & Roe	18900	52200	23300	8400	6200	109000	18200	55100	24600	11600	12400	121900	230900	16.1	16.7	8.1	1.8
Wandsworth	15000	52000	15900	5400	3700	92000	14700	53400	16600	6700	7900	99200	191200	15.5	12.4	6.1	1.5
Merton & Sutton	31700	78100	34100	11800	8400	164100	29900	78300	35500	15600	17500	176700	340800	18.0	15.6	7.6	1.8
SWT Total	275500	676100	318300	113000	81600	1464500	260400	633800	329400	144700	176700	1558900	3023400	17.7	16.5	7.9	1.9
Thames RHAs Total	1340900	3166900	1443700	518000	344600	6814100	1273300	3153800	1481800	643600	659000	7211500	14025600	18.6	15.4	7.2	1.7

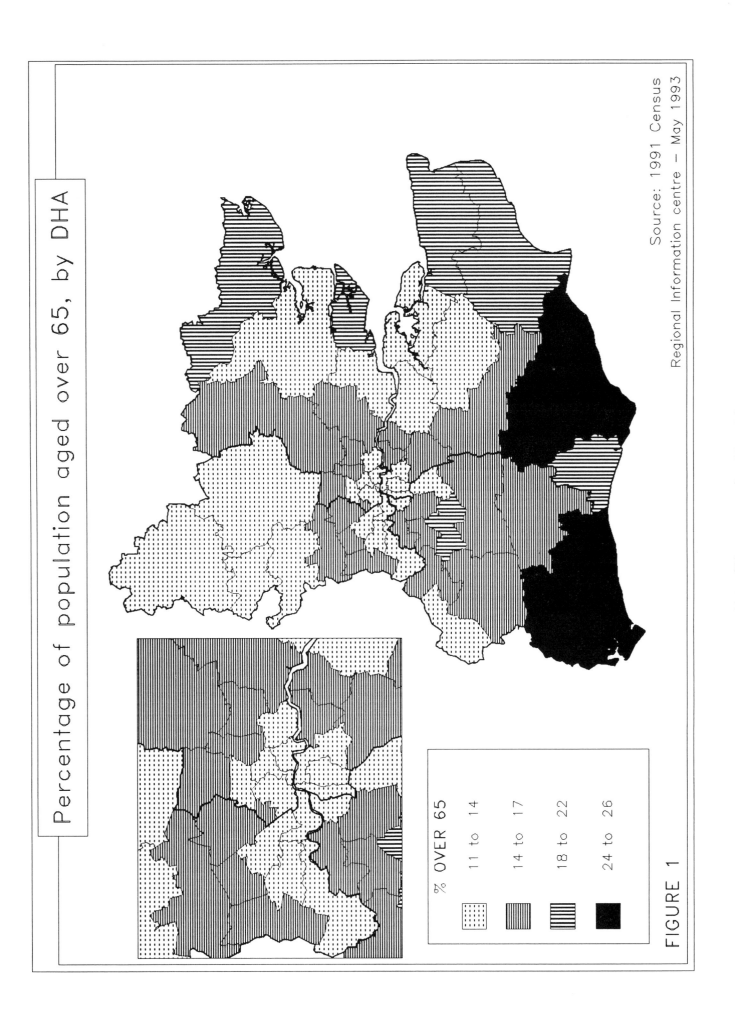

Percentage of population aged over 65, by DHA

Source: 1991 Census
Regional Information centre – May 1993

% OVER 65

11 to 14

14 to 17

18 to 22

24 to 26

FIGURE 1

TABLE 4 COMPARISON BETWEEN 1991 POPULATION ESTIMATES AND 1996 PROJECTIONS.

DHAs	1991 POP ESTIMATE	1996 POP PROJECTION	% DIFFERENCE IN '91 & 96 POPULATION	OVER 65 1991 ESTIMATE	OVER65 1996 PROJECTION	% DIFFERENCE IN '91 & 96 OVER 65	ABSOLUTE DIFFERENCE
NORTH BEDFORDSHIRE	249738	268426	7	33400	35796	7	2396
SOUTH BEDFORDSHIRE	284806	287868	1	32800	36923	13	4123
EAST & NORTH HERTFORDSHIRE	483659	491080	2	67100	74245	11	7145
NORTH WEST HERTFORDSHIRE	260788	264058	1	36900	40502	10	3602
SOUTH WEST HERTFORDSHIRE	242941	247829	2	38000	37406	-2	-594
BARNET	298145	309643	4	47700	41957	-12	-5743
HARROW	202924	199958	-1	30300	28679	-5	-1621
HILLINGDON	235231	239119	2	34000	34100	0	100
HOUNSLOW AND SPELTHORNE	299086	280927	-6	40700	39728	-2	-972
EALING	280031	287649	3	36400	36735	1	335
RIVERSIDE	290507	282609	-3	39200	37440	-4	-1760
PARKSIDE	432571	376149	-13	54300	46702	-14	-7598
NWT Total	3560427	3535315	-1	490800	490213	-0	-587
Basildon & Thurrock	291900	282556	-3	37700	40979	9	3279
Mid Essex	294600	304608	3	40700	43147	6	2447
North East Essex	306800	343891	12	61100	64543	6	3443
West Essex	259000	256188	-1	38700	41686	8	2986
Southend	326300	323449	-1	58200	56558	-3	-1642
Barking, Havering & Brentwood	447400	440576	-2	73000	72610	-1	-390
Hampstead	105000	104349	-1	15600	14817	-5	-783
City & Hackney	187400	196580	5	21900	22822	4	922
Newham	217100	217107	0	25600	24095	-6	-1505
Tower Hamlets	164900	175198	6	20500	19145	-7	-1355
Enfield	261600	271994	4	39300	38557	-2	-743
Haringey	207000	181142	-12	23600	21741	-8	-1859
Redbridge	230000	232360	1	36100	35355	-2	-745
Waltham Forest	215800	209857	-3	31000	28766	-7	-2234
Bloomsbury & Islington	242500	300758	24	31500	39836	26	8336
NET Total	3757300	3840613	2	554500	564657	2	10157
Brighton	310900	301520	-3	62400	57668	-8	-4732
Eastbourne	237000	265687	12	58700	62167	6	3467
Hastings	166600	180925	7	42600	44651	5	2051
SE Kent	273600	286948	5	51300	49914	-3	-1386
Canterbury & Thanet	303400	319537	5	65900	65042	-1	-858
Dartford & Gravesham	223000	200745	-10	30500	31148	2	648
Maidstone	201100	200389	-0	28000	30019	7	2019
Medway	334900	377557	13	42600	47401	11	4801
Tunbridge Wells	202600	188382	-7	34100	33636	-1	-464
Bexley	218000	215798	-1	32200	30482	-5	-1718
Greenwich	211900	223237	5	31600	30114	-5	-1486
Bromley	292800	308877	5	49100	49156	0	56
West Lambeth	161400	156492	-3	19700	19258	-2	-442
Camberwell	218000	204790	-6	26700	25100	-6	-1600
Lewisham & N Southwark	327700	318551	-3	46500	46474	-0	-26
SET Total	3684900	3749435	2	621900	622230	0	330
North West Surrey	214800	207961	-3	33100	33153	0	53
West Surrey & NE Hants	283000	282605	-0	33200	36486	10	3286
South West Surrey	188500	180052	-4	31300	32160	3	860
Mid Surrey	169300	171998	2	31100	28702	-8	-2398
East Surrey	190400	184110	-3	31600	29223	-8	-2377
Chichester	179700	198791	11	43900	45692	4	1792
Mid Downs	285700	287265	1	41600	42956	3	1356
Worthing	248300	256836	3	63600	66309	4	2709
Croydon	317400	319345	1	43300	40901	-6	-2399
Kingston & Esher	183400	181451	-1	29700	29209	-2	-491
Rich, Twick & Roe	230900	235537	2	38600	37498	-3	-1102
Wandsworth	191200	177171	-7	23700	20824	-12	-2876
Merton & Sutton	340800	331335	-3	53300	50520	-5	-2780
SWT Total	3023400	3014457	-0	498000	493633	-1	
Thames RHAs Total	14026027	14139820	1	2165200	2170733	0	5533

FIGURE 2

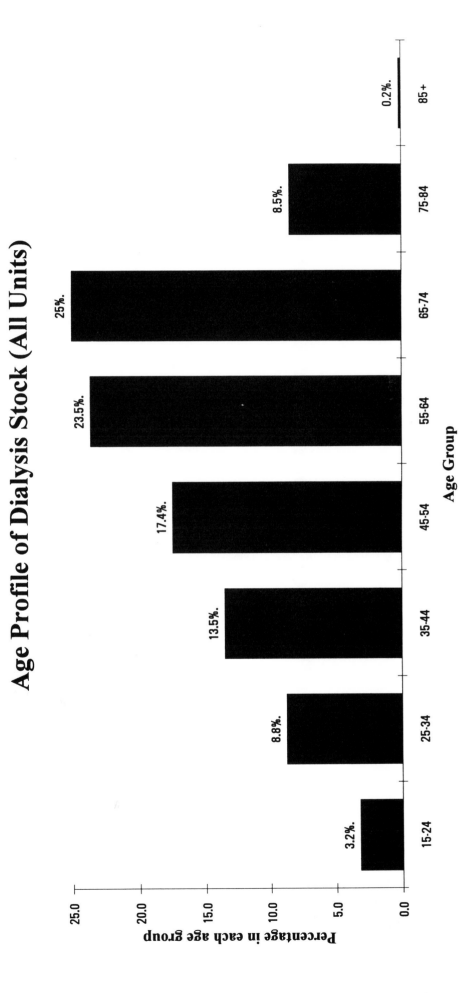

Age Profile of Dialysis Stock (All Units)

FIGURE 3

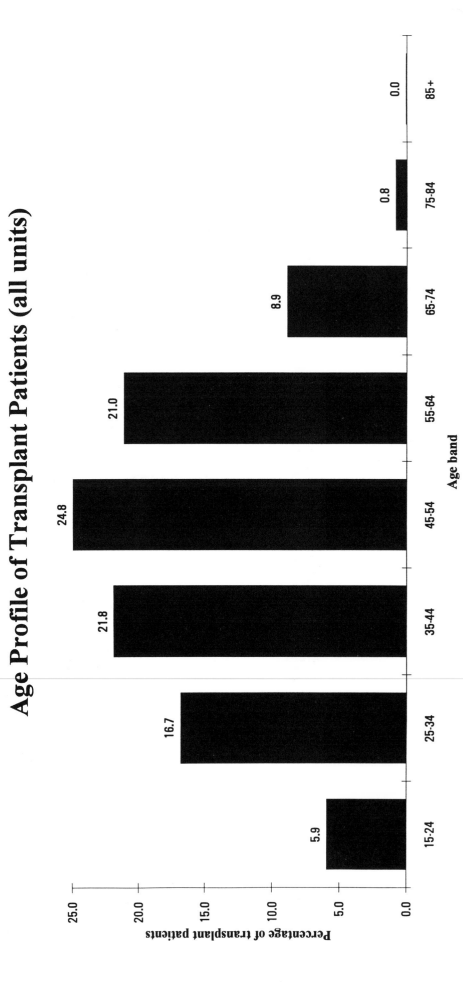

Age Profile of Transplant Patients (all units)

FIGURE 4

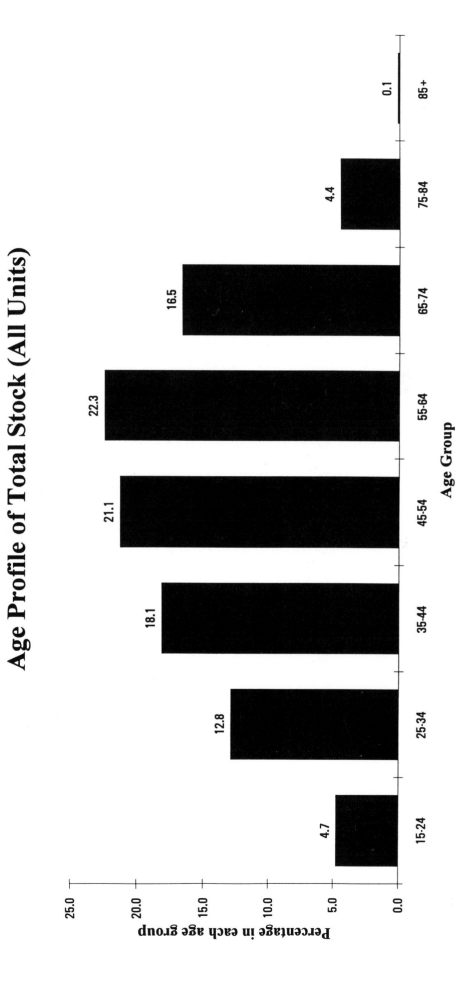

Age Profile of Total Stock (All Units)

FIGURE 5

Age Profile of New Patients in 1992 (all units)

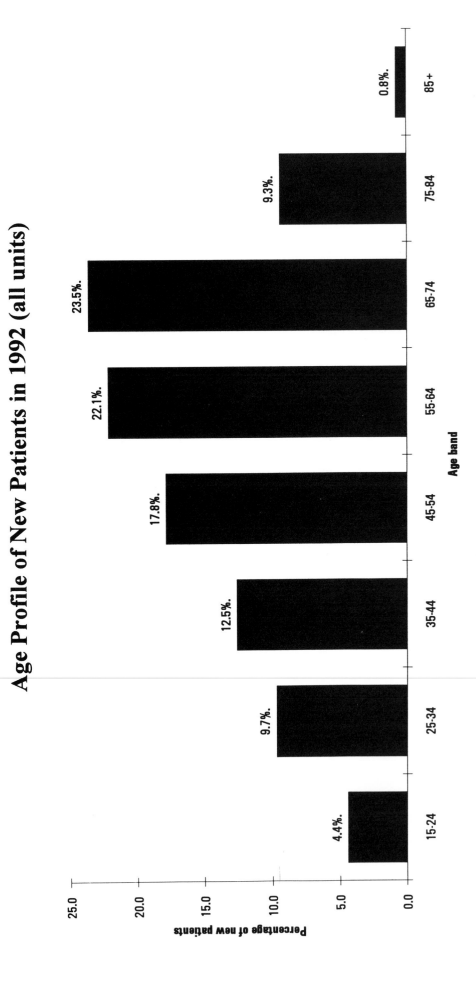

TABLE 5

AETIOLOGY OF END STAGE RENAL FAILURE

EDTA 1991

	PERCENT
Glomerulonephritis	15.0
Pyelonephritis	12.3
Nephropathy	0.5
Polycystic Kidney	8.1
Hereditary	1.8
Renovascular[1]	13.6
Diabetes Mellitus	14.8
Multisystem	6.6
Miscellaneous	1.5
Other	1.6
Unknown	24.3

[1] mainly hypertension

TABLE 6   **POPULATION PROFILE OF THE THAMES RHAS BY ETHNICITY AND AGE (1991 CENSUS).**

	Total	White	Black Caribbean	Black African	Black other	Indian	Pakistani	Bangladeshi	Chinese	Other Asian	Other
All ages	13770790	12210198	313181	171980	92114	409307	114784	99147	74933	133588	151558
0-4	918216	755336	23878	21066	17701	34670	13235	14753	5067	10147	22363
5-9	829813	677697	22291	15193	13979	37973	13786	15029	5284	10232	18349
10-14	791115	6576	19428	12057	10903	34874	13130	13955	5345	9186	14567
15	152786	129121	3734	2221	1928	6010	2098	2599	1085	1596	2394
16-17	324598	278467	7109	4278	3446	11546	4179	5402	2171	3230	4770
18-19	358136	308988	8603	4977	3752	12050	4561	4041	2529	3799	4836
20-24	1084688	938520	30126	19581	10859	32914	11086	8035	8091	11806	13670
25-29	1231996	1062174	40146	28018	11795	36676	9007	5684	9033	13888	15575
30-34	1077082	923360	31377	22412	6440	41454	9672	6152	8584	14990	12641
35-39	932658	809819	19935	13537	2989	38948	8649	5560	7796	15281	10144
40-44	1001487	906951	13682	9387	2081	30358	6202	3150	6561	14601	8514
45-49	827610	753220	16928	6826	1640	22088	5199	3066	3609	8852	6182
50-54	730034	652787	23094	5650	1402	21883	5726	5015	3162	6323	4992
55-59	686294	625918	21158	3015	1089	17560	3953	3463	2440	3874	3824
60-64	669026	627348	15413	1791	852	12173	2216	2044	1647	2390	3152
65-69	637574	612911	8559	975	544	8056	1088	647	1072	1530	2192
70-74	527381	513338	4255	490	330	5039	537	313	691	912	1476
75-79	456448	448720	2141	262	210	2780	232	133	416	569	985
80-84	313319	309610	848	129	95	1415	129	63	220	245	565
85 & over	220529	218243	476	115	79	840	99	43	130	137	367

FIGURE 6

AGE PROFILE OF TOTAL STOCK IN EACH UNIT

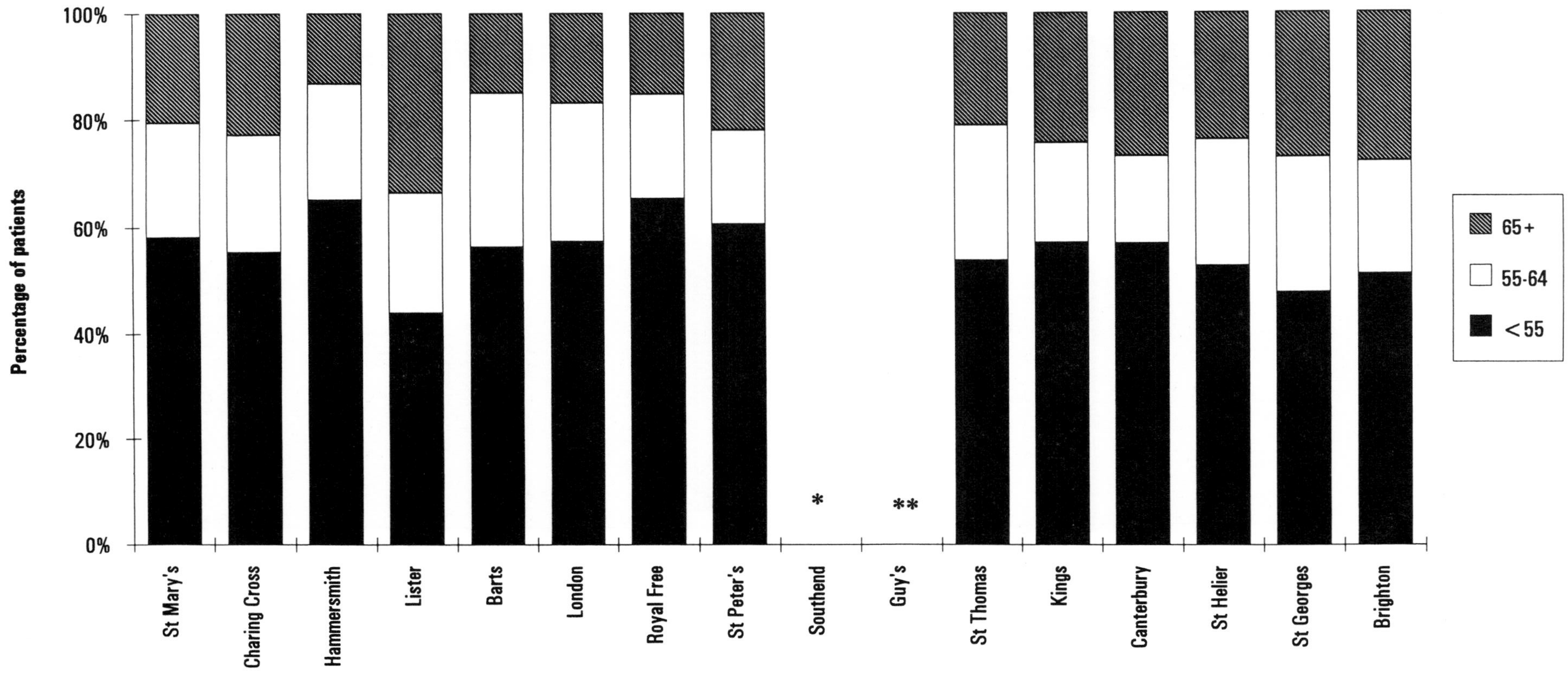

Percentage of patients

Legend:
- 65+
- 55-64
- <55

* Data in different age format

** Data unavailable

FIGURE 7

Numbers of persons Asian or Black
Greater and inner London

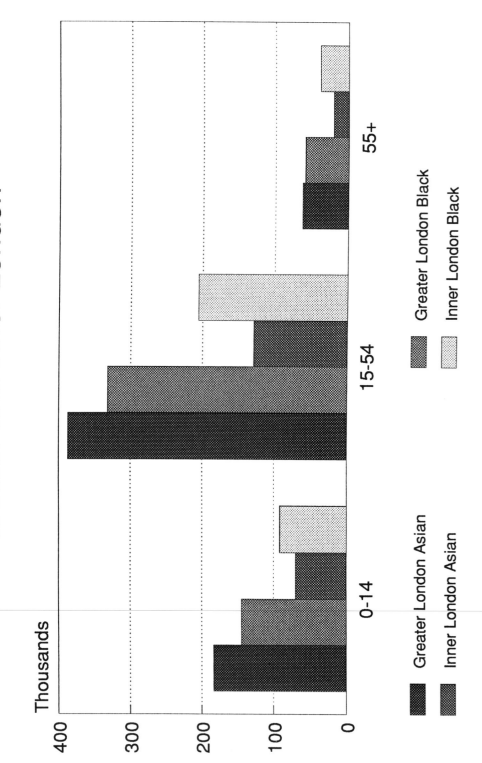

Thousands

Greater London Asian

Inner London Asian

Greater London Black

Inner London Black

Source 1991 census

TABLE 7

ETHNIC ORIGIN OF THE POPULATION IN GREATER LONDON

	% WHITE	% ASIAN	% BLACK	% OTHER
Inner London				
0 - 54	70.4	10.2	15.3	4.1
55 - 64	80.4	6.3	11.6	1.7
65+	93.3	2.0	3.8	0.9
Outer London				
0 - 54	80.0	11.8	5.7	2.6
55 - 64	88.5	6.7	3.6	1.2
65+	96.2	2.4	0.9	0.6
Greater London				
0 - 54	76.2	11.2	9.4	3.2
55 - 64	85.6	6.6	6.5	1.4
65+	95.2	2.2	1.9	0.7

FIGURE 8

Number of persons Asian or Black
By Regional Health Authority

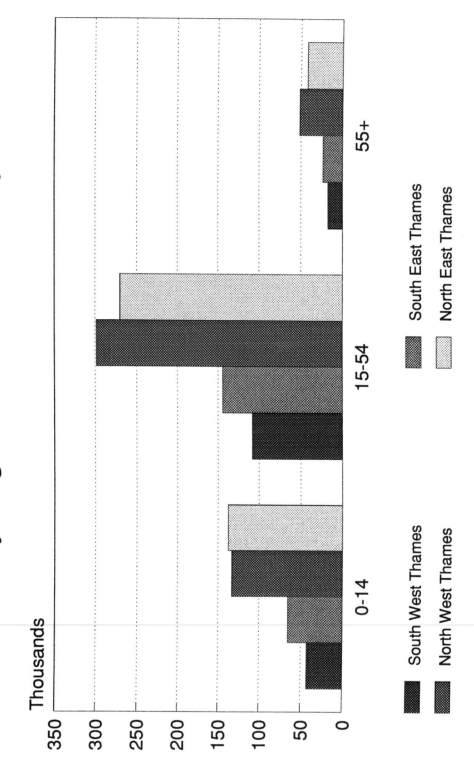

Thousands

South West Thames
North West Thames

South East Thames
North East Thames

1991 census

FIGURE 9

AGE DISTRIBUTION OF POPULATION BY ETHNIC ORIGIN

Greater London

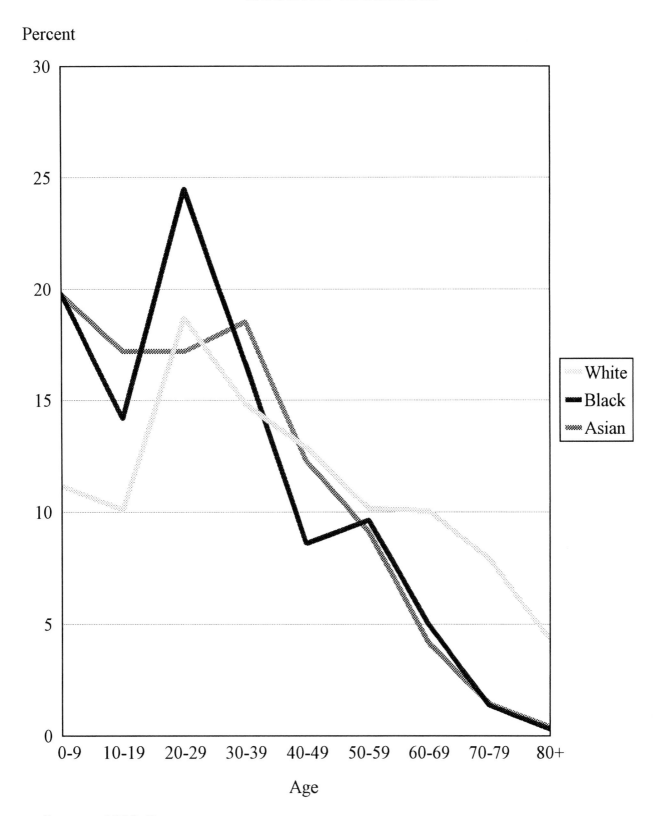

Source: 1991 Census

FIGURE 10   Percent of the total borough population aged 0-14 that is
            Asian or Black: Greater London

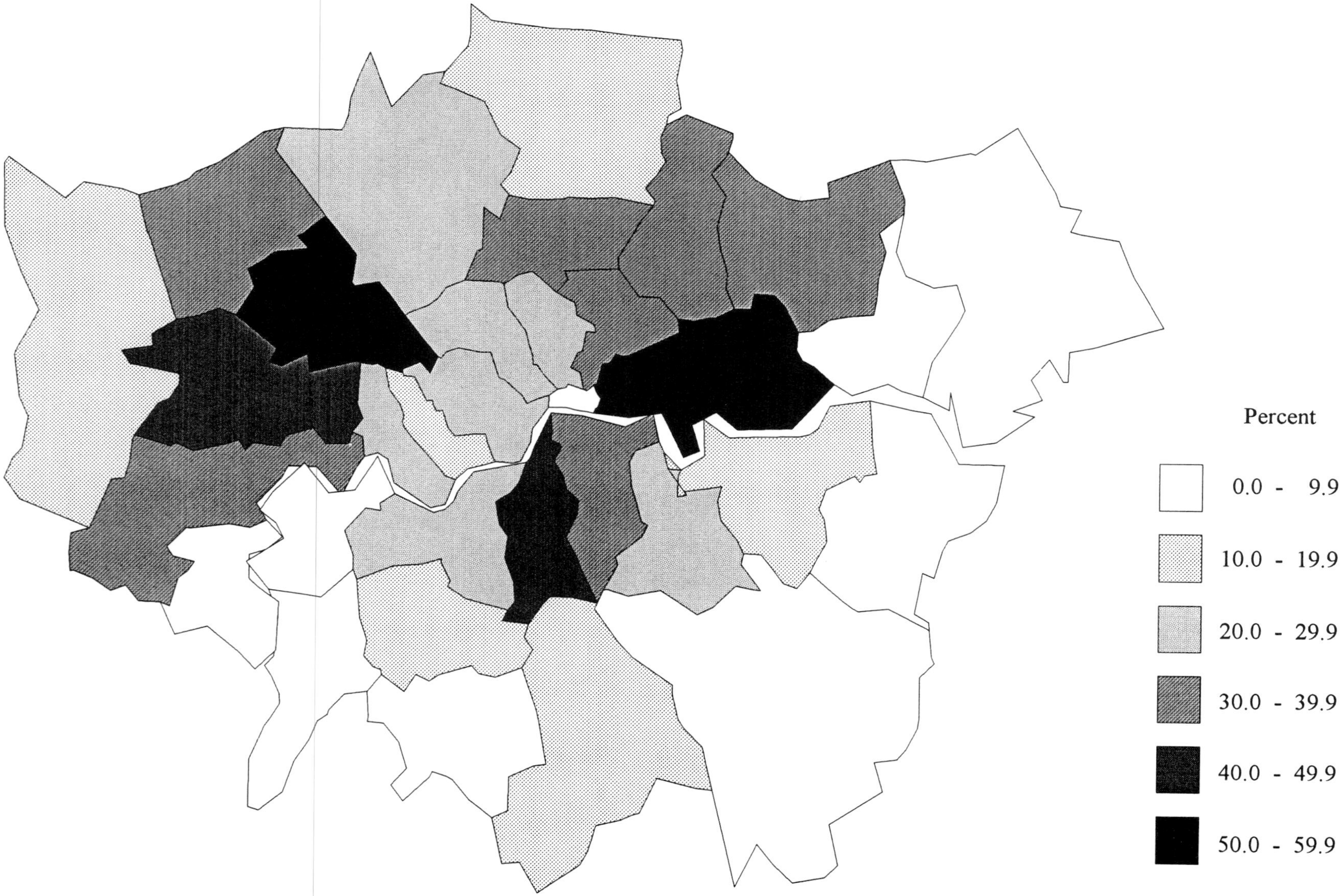

Percent

0.0 - 9.9

10.0 - 19.9

20.0 - 29.9

30.0 - 39.9

40.0 - 49.9

50.0 - 59.9

Source: 1991 Census   *Produced by the Institute of Public Health, University of Surrey*

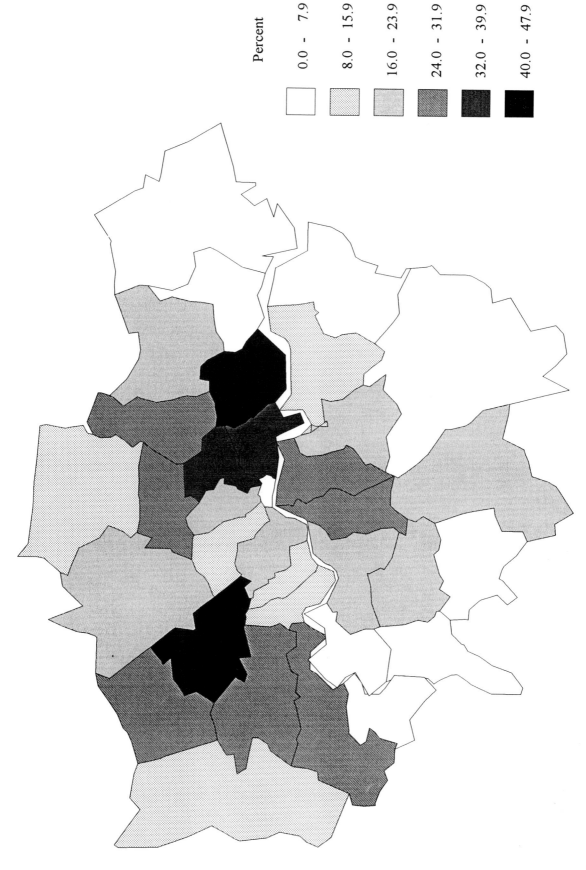

FIGURE 11   Percent of the total borough population aged 15-54 that is Asian or Black: Greater London

Percent

0.0 - 7.9
8.0 - 15.9
16.0 - 23.9
24.0 - 31.9
32.0 - 39.9
40.0 - 47.9

Source: 1991 Census   *Produced by the Institute of Public Health, University of Surrey*

FIGURE 12 Percent of the total borough population aged 55-64 that is Asian or Black: Greater London

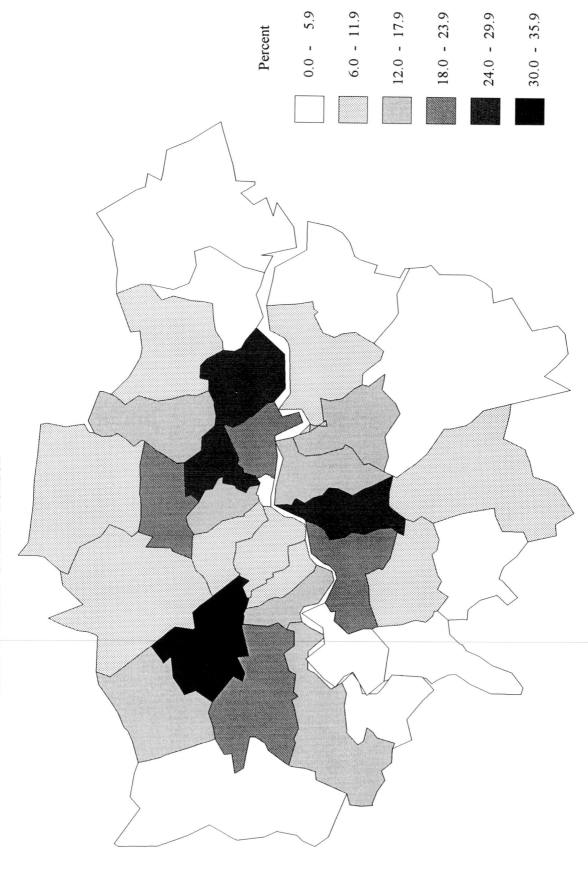

Percent

0.0 - 5.9
6.0 - 11.9
12.0 - 17.9
18.0 - 23.9
24.0 - 29.9
30.0 - 35.9

Source: 1991 Census

Produced by the Institute of Public Health, University of Surrey

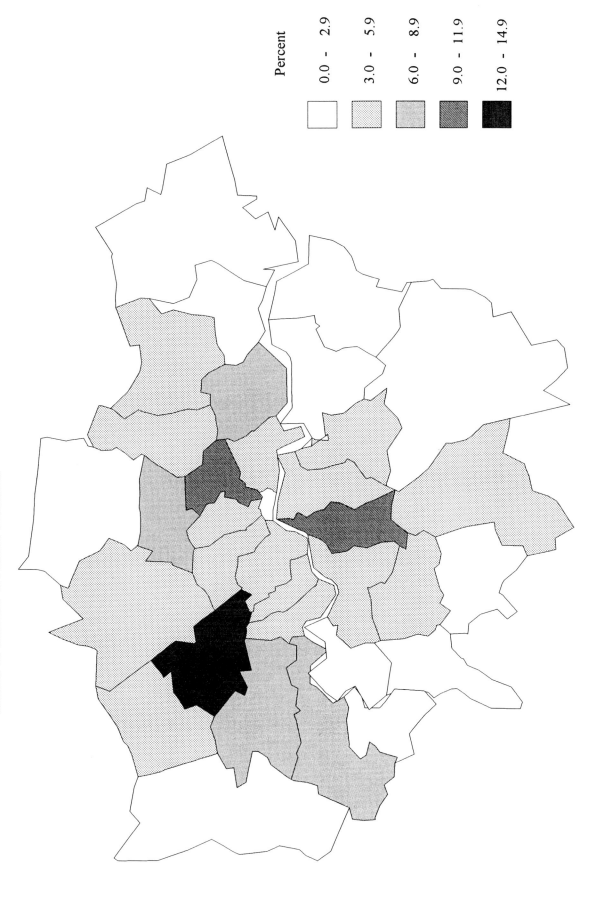

FIGURE 13   Percent of the total borough population aged 65+ that is Asian or Black: Greater London

Percent

0.0 - 2.9

3.0 - 5.9

6.0 - 8.9

9.0 - 11.9

12.0 - 14.9

Source: 1991 Census   *Produced by the Institute of Public Health, University of Surrey*

FIGURE 14

ETHNIC COMPOSITION OF THE POPULATION

Greater London

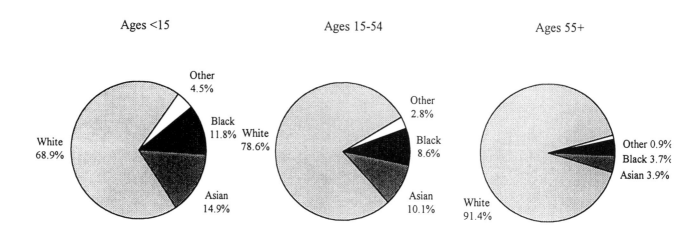

Inner London

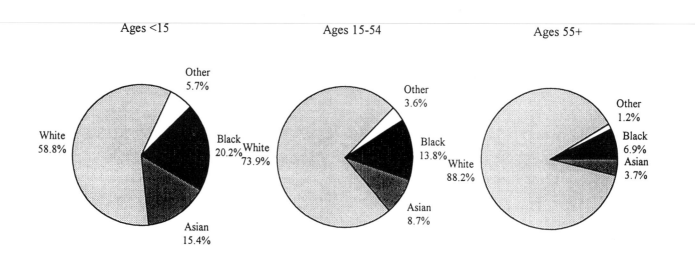

Source: 1991 Census

FIGURE 15

ETHNIC COMPOSITION OF THE POPULATION

North West Thames Regional Health Authority

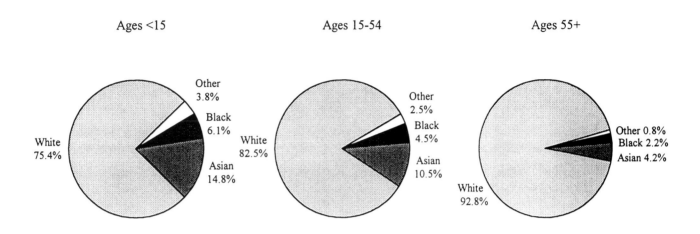

North East Thames Regional Health Authority

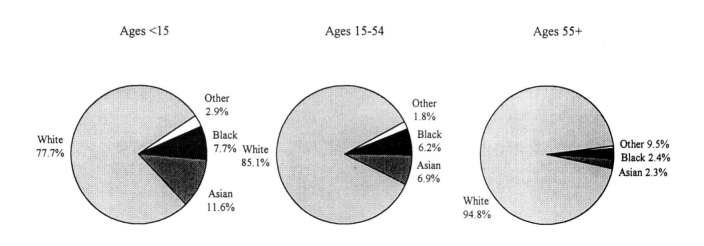

Source: 1991 Census

FIGURE 16

ETHNIC COMPOSITION OF THE POPULATION

South West Thames Regional Health Authority

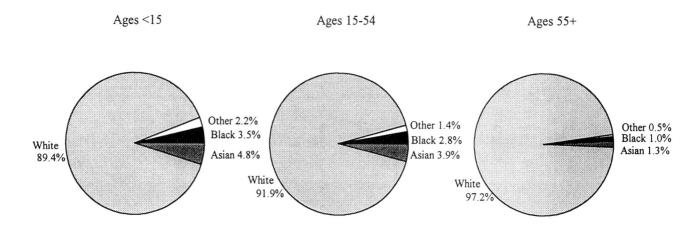

Ages <15   Ages 15-54   Ages 55+

South East Thames Regional Health Authority

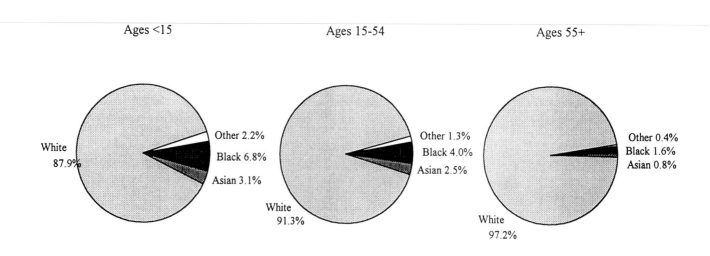

Ages <15   Ages 15-54   Ages 55+

Source: 1991 Census

TABLE 9

RELATIVE RISKS OF END STAGE RENAL FAILURE IN BLACKS IN THE UNITED STATES

PLACE	YEAR	NUMBER OF CASES	ALL CAUSES	HYPER-TENSION	DIABETES	GLOMERULO-NEPRITIS	OTHER	INTERSTITIAL NEPHRITIS	UN-KNOWN	POLY-CYSTIC KIDNEYS
Alabama	74-78	296	4.2	17.7	3.4	3.3	1.2	3.3	3.8	0.8
Delaware	73-74	345	M 4.3[1] F 6.6							
Michigan	73-75	711	3.8	16.9	3.3	2.7	1.8 (all)			
Michigan	74-81	7000	4.3	10.9	3.8	1.7				
Eastern US	73-80	88968	M 2.1 F 2.5	M 7.0 F 6.0	M 2.0 F 3.0	1.5				
Texas	78-84	9691	4.4[1]	10.9	4.3	2.6	2.1		3.9	
US	80	9310	2.8	6.6	2.9	1.9				
Georgia	79-83	3049	2.9	8.4						
California	80-85	1000	2.9	4.4	2.6	3.3	1.1 (all)			2.1
Maryland	80-85	534		M 7.4 F 9.9						
US	84	26736	3.8	7.7	3.7	2.6				1.2
US	87	33578	3.8	6.6	3.8	2.3				

[1] = age adjusted

TABLE 12

TABLE 12

ETHNIC BREAKDOWN OF RENAL REPLACEMENT THERAPY STOCK

ADULTS, DECEMBER 1992

	WHITE	BLACKS	ASIANS	OTHER	TOTAL
Dialysis					
Number (%)	1996 (74.2)	308 (11.5)	315 (11.7)	70 (2.6)	2689
Rate per million	199.8	745.8	610.5	437.5	242.7
Transplant					
Number (%)	2174 (78.3)	188 (6.8)	334 (12.0)	81 (2.9)	2777
Rate per million	217.6	455.2	647.3	506.3	250.7
All Modalities					
Number (%)	4170 (76.3)	496 (9.1)	649 (11.9)	151 (2.8)	5466
Rate per million	417.4	1201.0	1257.8	943.8	493.4

TABLE 13

AGE AND ETHNIC PROFILE OF PATIENTS ACCEPTED

ONTO RRT[1] 1991-92

PERCENT (NUMBER)		
WHITE	ASIAN	BLACK
AGE		
15-54 46.9 (402)	51.9 (55)	55.0 (71)
55-64 19.3 (166)	30.2 (32)	27.1 (35)
65+ 33.7 (289)	17.9 (19)	17.8 (23)
100 (857)	100 (106)	100 (129)

[1] Based on individual patient analysis from:

Charing Cross
Hammersmith
Royal Free
St Thomas's
St George's
King's
St Helier's
Canterbury
Guy's

TABLE 14

AGE AND ETHNIC PROFILE OF PATIENTS ACCEPTED

ONTO RENAL REPLACEMENT THERAPY 1991-92 AVERAGE

	WHITE	ASIAN	BLACK
AGE			
15-54			
Number	348	64	56
Rate	51.5	137.8	155.2
Relative rate	1.0	2.68	3.01
55-64			
Number	143	37	27
Rate	114.4	794.9	631.9
Relative rate	1.0	6.95	5.52
65+			
Number	250	22	18
Rate	119.1	887.5	921.6
Relative rate	1.0	7.45	7.74
TOTAL			
Number	743	123	101
Rate	74.4	237.5	236.8
Relative rate	1.0	3.19	3.18

FIGURE 17

Ethnicity of dialysis stock (all units)

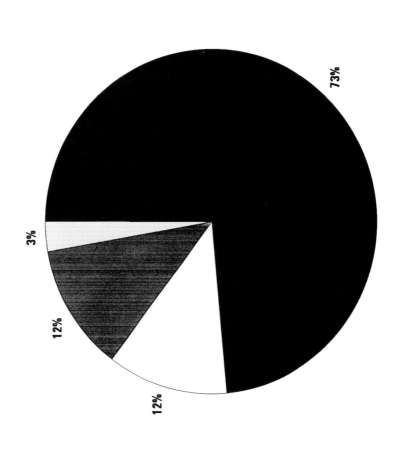

FIGURE 18

Ethnicity of Transplant stock (all units)

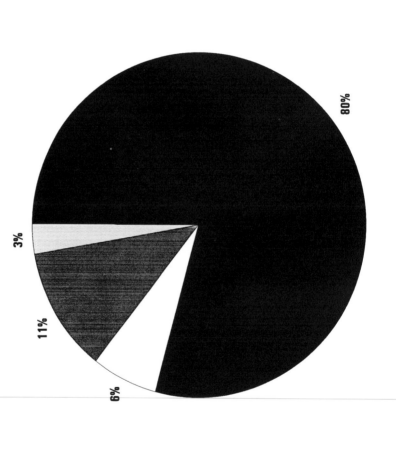

■	White
□	Black
▓	Asian
░	Other

FIGURE 19

Ethnicity of Total Stock (all units)

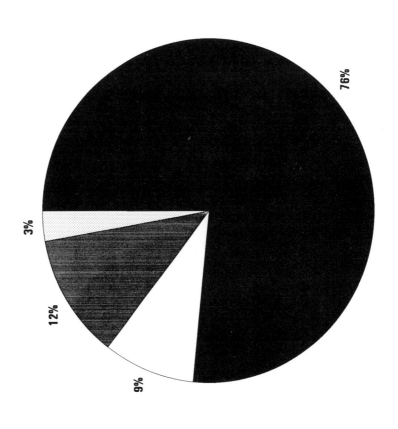

76%

9%

12%

3%

White
Black
Asian
Other

FIGURE 20

Scatterplot of dialysis rate with
% of population non-white

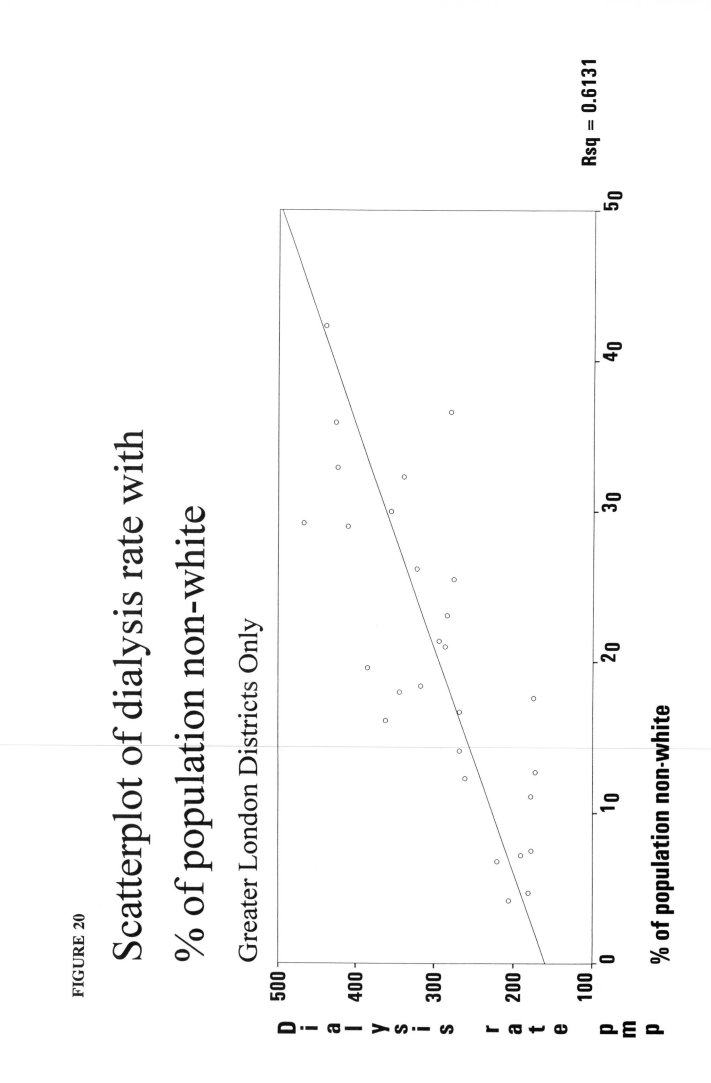

Greater London Districts Only

Rsq = 0.6131

% of population non-white

FIGURE 21

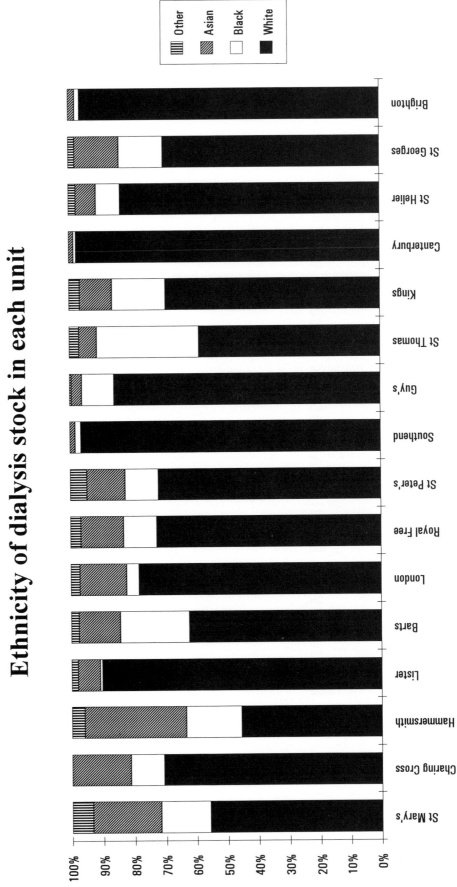

Ethnicity of dialysis stock in each unit

FIGURE 22

Ethnicity of Transplant stock in each unit

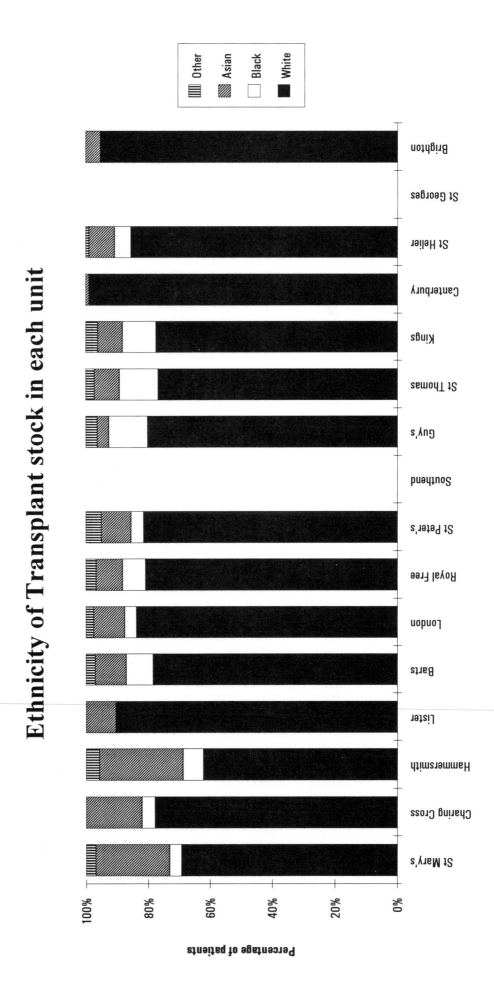

FIGURE 23

Ethnicity of new patients in each unit

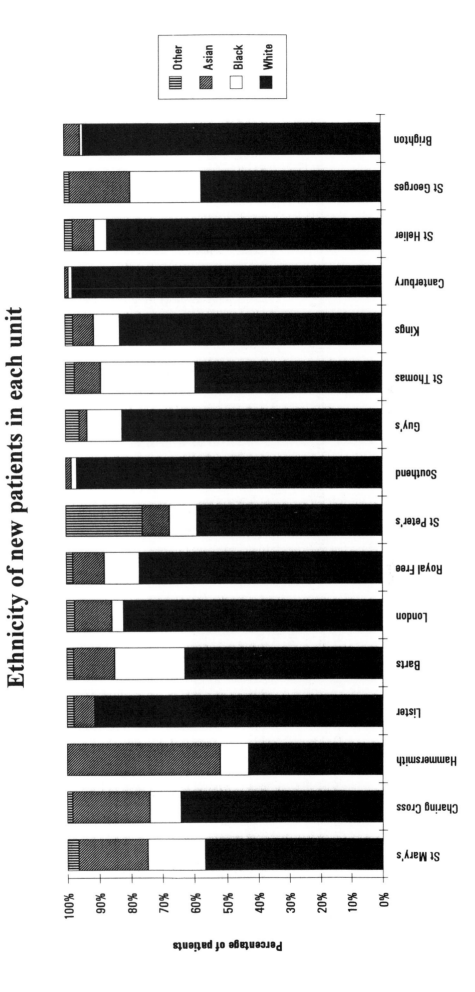

TABLE 15

CHRONIC RENAL FAILURE: EXPECTED NUMBERS FOR 4 THAMES RHAS

	Age distribution of population of 4 Thames RHAs: 1991 census			Chronic renal failure: incidence per million+	Chronic renal failure: expected numbers++				Chronic renal failure: expected numbers++ percent distribution			
	White	Black*	Asians**		White	Black	Asian	Total	White	Black	Asian	Total
Total	12210198	577275	756826		1348.5	37.2	48.0	1433.8	94.1	2.6	3.4	100.0
0-19	2807279	196544	282081	20	56.1	3.9	5.6	65.7	85.4	6.0	8.6	100.0
20-39	3733873	237215	269802	37	138.2	8.8	10.0	156.9	88.0	5.6	6.4	100.0
40-49	1660171	50544	93516	90	149.4	4.5	8.4	162.4	92.0	2.8	5.2	100.0
50-59	1278705	55408	67797	185	236.6	10.3	12.5	259.4	91.2	4.0	4.8	100.0
60-69	1240259	28134	30144	243	301.4	6.8	7.3	315.5	95.5	2.2	2.3	100.0
70-79	962058	7688	10515	296	284.8	2.3	3.1	290.2	98.1	0.8	1.1	100.0
80+	527853	1742	2971	345	182.1	0.6	1.0	183.7	99.1	0.3	0.6	100.0

* Includes Caribbeans, Africans, and Black Other

** Includes Indians, Pakistanis, Bangladeshis, and Other Asians

+ Rates derived by pooling McGeown and Feest data, except for age groups 20-39 and 40-49 where the McGeown rates were used because the Feest data were only available for the aggregate 20-49 age group

++ Assuming all ethnic groups have the same age-specific chronic renal failure rates

FIGURE 24

CHRONIC RENAL FAILURE

Expected numbers by ethnic origin*

4 Thames RHAs

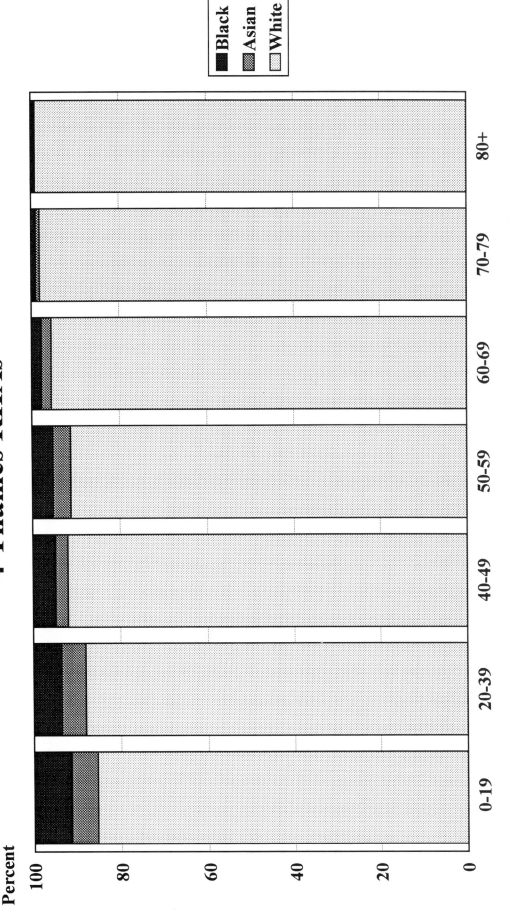

*Based on 1991 census and assuming all ethnic groups have the same age-specific
chronic renal failure rates (pooled McGeown/Feest incidence rates)*

TABLE 16

DISTRICT AND REGIONAL ACCEPTANCE RATES FOR RENAL REPLACEMENT THERAPY AFTER ADJUSTMENT FOR ETHNIC MINORITY RISK.

80 per million taken as baseline Caucasian estimate

Ethnic Minority Relative Risk

	1.5	2.0	3.0	4.0
North Bedfordshire	82.2	84.4	88.7	93.1
South Bedfordshire	84.6	89.2	98.4	107.6
East & North Hertfordshire	80.9	81.7	83.4	85.1
NW Hertfordshire	81.0	82.0	84.0	86.0
SW Hertfordshire	81.7	83.4	86.9	90.3
Barnet	84.8	89.7	99.4	109.1
Harrow	88.5	97.0	114.0	131.0
Hillingdon	83.8	87.7	95.3	103.0
Hounslow & Spelthorne	85.8	91.6	103.2	114.7
Ealing	90.5	100.9	121.8	142.7
Riverside	83.8	87.7	95.4	103.1
Parkside	91.0	102.0	123.9	145.9
NWT Total	84.9	89.8	99.7	109.5
Basildon & Thurrock	80.6	81.1	82.2	83.3
Mid Essex	80.4	80.7	81.4	82.2
North East Essex	80.3	80.5	81.0	81.5
West Essex	80.6	81.1	82.2	83.4
Southend	80.4	80.8	81.7	82.5
Barking Havering & Brentwoo	81.3	82.5	85.0	87.5
Hampstead	83.5	87.1	94.2	101.3
City & Hackney	91.1	102.1	124.3	146.4
Newham	94.9	109.7	139.4	169.1
Tower Hamlets	92.7	105.5	130.9	156.4
Enfield	84.4	88.7	97.5	106.2
Haringey	89.2	98.4	116.8	135.2
Redbridge	87.3	94.5	109.0	123.6
Waltham Forest	88.7	97.4	114.8	132.2
Bloomsbury & Islington	85.7	91.4	102.8	114.1
NET Total	84.5	89.0	98.0	106.9

Ethnic Minority Relative Risk

	1.5	2.0	3.0	4.0
Brighton	80.5	81.0	82.0	83.0
Eastbourne	80.2	80.4	80.9	81.3
Hastings	80.3	80.5	81.1	81.6
SE Kent	80.2	80.5	81.0	81.5
Canterbury & Thanet	80.2	80.5	80.9	81.4
Dartford & Gravesham	81.7	83.4	86.9	90.3
Maidstone	80.3	80.7	81.3	82.0
Medway	81.0	82.1	84.1	86.2
Tunbridge Wells	80.2	80.4	80.9	81.3
Bexley	81.6	83.2	86.5	89.7
Greenwich	83.8	87.6	95.3	102.9
Bromley	81.2	82.3	84.7	87.0
West Lambeth	89.7	99.5	118.9	138.4
Camberwell	90.1	100.3	120.6	140.9
Lewisham & N Southwark	86.9	93.8	107.6	121.4
SET Total	82.4	84.8	89.6	94.3
North West Surrey	80.9	81.9	83.8	85.6
West Surrey & NE Hants	80.4	80.9	81.8	82.7
South West Surrey	80.3	80.6	81.2	81.8
Mid Surrey	80.7	81.3	82.6	84.0
East Surrey	80.4	80.9	81.7	82.6
Chichester	80.2	80.4	80.7	81.1
Mid Downs	81.0	81.9	83.9	85.8
Worthing	80.2	80.4	80.9	81.3
Croydon	85.4	90.9	101.7	112.6
Kingston & Esher	81.4	82.8	85.6	88.4
Rich, Twick & Roe	81.7	83.3	86.6	90.0
Wandsworth	87.5	95.0	110.0	125.0
Merton & Sutton	82.9	85.8	91.6	97.4
SWT Total	81.9	83.8	87.6	91.4
Thames RHAs Total	83.5	87.0	94.0	100.9

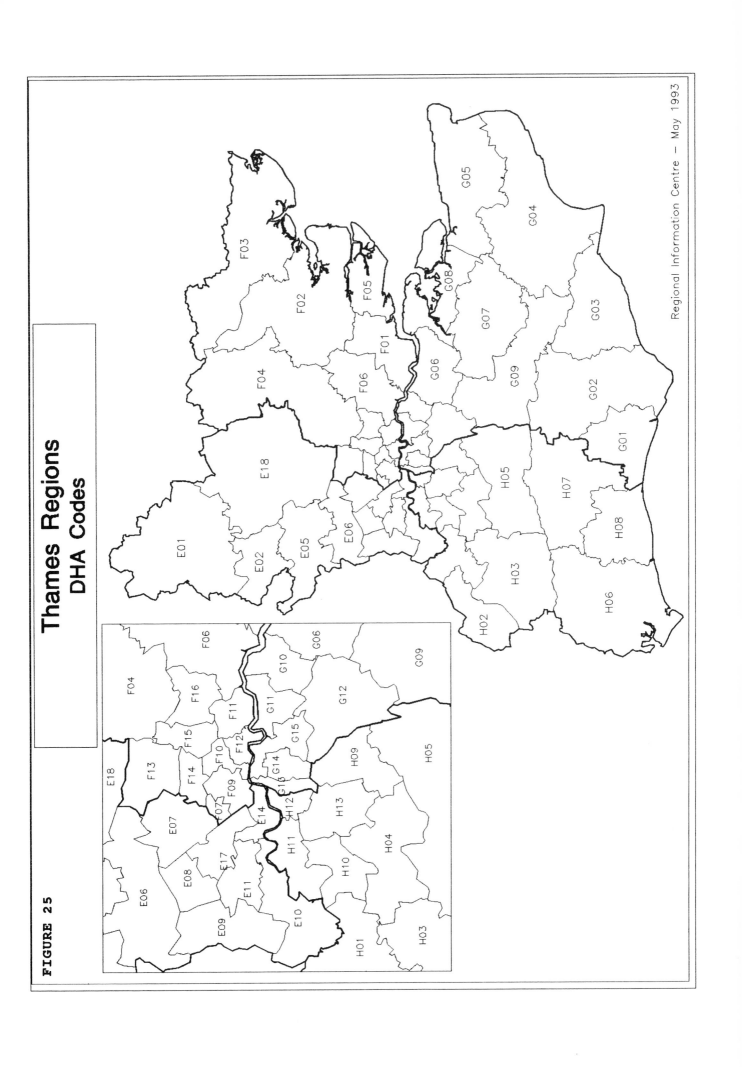

FIGURE 25

Thames Regions
DHA Codes

Regional Information Centre — May 1993

FIGURE 26

Thames Regions – DHA Codes

DHA Code	District
E01	North Bedfordshire
E02	South Bedfordshire
E05	North West Hertfordshire
E06	South West Hertfordshire
E07	Barnet
E08	Harrow
E09	Hillingdon
E10	Hounslow & Spelthorne
E11	Ealing
E14	Riverside
E17	Parkside
E18	East & North Hertfordshire
F01	Basildon & Thurrock
F02	Mid Essex
F03	North East Essex
F04	West Essex
F05	Southend
F06	Barking Havering & Brentwood
F07	Hampsted
F09	Bloomsbury & Islington
F10	City & Hackney
F11	Newham
F12	Tower Hamlets
F13	Enfield
F14	Haringey
F15	Redbridge
F16	Waltham Forest
G01	Brighton
G02	Eastbourne
G03	Hastings
G04	South East Kent
G05	Canterbury & Thanet
G06	Dartford & Gravesham
G07	Maidstone
G08	Medway
G09	Tunbridge Wells
G10	Bexley
G11	Greenwich
G12	Bromley
G13	West Lambeth
G14	Camberwell
G15	Lewisham & North Southwark
H01	North West Surrey
H02	West Surrey & North East Hants
H03	South West Surrey
H04	Mid Surrey
H05	East Surrey
H06	Chichester
H07	Mid Downs
H08	Worthing
H09	Croydon
H10	Kingston & Esher
H11	Richmond Twickenham & Roehampton
H12	Wandsworth
H13	Merton & Sutton

TABLE 17

ADULT AND TOTAL STOCK RATES OF RENAL REPLACEMENT THERAPY BY DISTRICT OF RESIDENCE. END 1992.

Stock of Patients by district of residence	Popn	Dialysis	Adult Rate	Transplant	Adult Rate	Total	Adult Rate	Standardised Thames Rate	Standardised Thames Rate	Standardised Thames Rate	Total Popn	Total Stock Rate pmp
District of Residence	18+	Stock	Per Million	Stock	Per Million	Stock	Per Million	Dialysis	Tx	Total Stock		(Total Popn)
North Bedfordshire	200200	37	184.8	6	30.0	43	214.8	78.1	11.1	42.4	249700	172.2
South Bedfordshire	221900	56	252.4	38	171.2	94	423.6	106.7	63.5	83.7	284800	330.1
East&North Hertfordshire	391000	96	245.5	57	145.8	153	391.3	103.8	64.1	77.3	483700	316.3
NW Hertfordshire	210600	41	194.7	58	275.4	99	470.1	82.3	102.1	92.8	260700	379.7
SW Hertfordshire	197200	45	228.2	30	152.1	75	380.3	96.4	56.4	75.1	243000	308.6
Barnet	242500	77	317.5	81	334.0	158	651.5	134.2	123.8	128.7	298100	530.0
Harrow	164200	53	322.8	117	712.5	170	1035.3	136.4	264.2	204.5	202900	837.9
Hillingdon	191000	50	261.8	61	319.4	111	581.2	110.6	118.4	114.8	235300	471.7
Hounslow&Spelthorpe	243700	84	344.7	85	348.8	169	693.5	145.7	129.3	137.0	299000	565.2
Ealing	226300	77	340.3	73	322.6	150	662.8	143.8	119.6	130.9	280000	535.7
Riverside	251200	91	362.3	75	298.6	166	660.8	153.1	110.7	130.5	290300	571.8
Parkside	356200	152	426.7	80	224.6	232	651.3	180.4	83.3	128.8	432500	536.4
NORTH WEST THAMES	2896000	859	296.6	761	262.8	1620	559.4	125.4	97.4	110.5	3560000	455.1
Basildon&Thurrock	231900	46	198.4	59	254.4	105	452.8	83.8	94.3	89.4	291900	359.7
Mid Essex	236400	29	122.7	55	232.7	84	355.3	51.8	86.3	70.2	294600	285.1
North East Essex	252500	40	158.4	53	209.9	93	368.3	67.0	77.8	72.7	306800	303.1
West Essex	211000	37	175.4	52	246.4	89	421.8	74.1	91.4	83.3	259000	343.6
Southend	266600	61	228.8	40	150.0	101	378.8	96.7	55.6	74.8	326300	309.5
Barking Havering&Btwood	363300	75	206.4	94	258.7	169	465.2	87.3	95.9	91.9	447400	377.7
Hampstead	89200	24	269.1	24	269.1	48	538.1	113.7	99.8	106.3	105000	457.1
City&Hackney	146100	62	424.4	50	342.2	112	766.6	179.4	126.9	151.4	187400	597.7
Newham	166000	73	439.8	67	403.6	140	843.4	185.9	149.7	166.6	217100	644.9
Tower Hamlets	124700	35	280.7	31	248.6	66	529.3	118.6	92.2	104.5	164900	400.2
Enfield	211900	57	269.0	57	269.0	114	538.0	113.7	99.7	106.3	261600	435.8
Haringey	168000	69	410.7	68	404.8	137	815.5	173.6	150.1	161.1	207000	661.8
Redbridge	186600	55	294.7	55	294.7	110	589.5	124.6	109.3	116.4	230000	478.3
Waltham Forest	173700	48	276.3	68	391.5	116	667.8	116.8	145.2	131.9	215800	537.5
Bloomsbury&Islington	200000	77	385.0	71	355.0	148	740.0	162.7	131.6	146.2	242500	610.3
NORTH EAST THAMES	3027900	788	260.2	844	278.7	1632	539.0	110.0	103.4	106.5	3757300	434.4
Brighton	261100	45	172.3	46	176.2	91	348.5	72.8	65.3	68.8	310900	292.7
Eastbourne	197000	29	147.2	34	172.6	63	319.8	62.2	64.0	63.2	237000	265.8
Hastings	139500	24	172.0	22	157.7	46	329.7	72.7	58.5	65.1	168600	272.8
SE Kent	223000	35	157.0	38	170.4	73	327.4	66.3	63.2	64.7	273600	266.8
Canterbury&Thanet	249400	57	228.5	48	192.5	105	421.0	96.6	71.4	83.2	303400	346.1
Dartford&Gravesham	179800	43	239.2	67	372.6	110	611.8	101.1	138.2	120.8	223000	493.3
Maidstone	162300	19	117.1	33	203.3	52	320.4	49.5	75.4	63.3	201100	258.6
Medway	264800	46	173.8	57	215.4	103	389.3	73.5	79.9	76.9	334900	307.6
Tunbridge Wells	166100	27	162.6	40	240.8	67	403.4	68.7	89.3	79.7	202600	330.7
Bexley	176400	39	221.1	75	425.2	114	646.3	93.4	157.8	127.8	218000	522.9
Greenwich	167500	29	173.1	52	310.4	81	483.6	73.2	115.1	96.5	211900	382.3
Bromley	242100	44	181.7	83	342.8	127	524.6	76.8	127.1	103.8	292800	433.7
West Lambeth	132500	62	467.9	52	392.5	114	860.4	197.8	145.5	169.9	161400	706.3
Camberwell	174100	62	356.1	93	534.2	155	890.3	150.5	198.1	175.8	218000	711.0
Lewisham&North Southwark	264600	76	287.2	105	396.8	181	684.1	121.4	147.1	135.1	327700	552.3
SOUTH EAST THAMES	3000000	637	212.3	845	281.7	1482	494.0	89.7	104.4	97.6	3684900	402.2
North West Surrey	176400	38	215.4	40	226.8	78	442.2	91.0	84.1	87.3	214800	363.1
West Surrey&NE Hants	228100	29	127.1	54	236.7	83	363.9	53.7	87.8	71.9	283000	293.3
South West Surrey	155300	13	83.7	34	218.9	47	302.6	35.4	81.2	59.8	188500	249.3
Mid Surrey	139800	21	150.2	28	200.3	49	350.5	63.5	74.3	69.2	169300	289.4
East Surrey	156400	25	159.8	47	300.5	72	460.4	67.6	111.4	90.9	190400	378.2
Chichester	150900	16	106.0	29	192.2	45	298.2	44.8	71.3	58.9	179700	250.4
Mid Downs	230100	35	152.1	58	252.1	93	404.2	64.3	93.5	79.8	285700	325.5
Worthing	207900	34	163.5	47	226.1	81	389.6	69.1	83.8	77.0	248300	326.2
Croydon	256500	45	175.4	86	335.3	131	510.7	74.1	124.3	100.8	317400	412.7
Kingston&Esher	151500	27	178.2	36	237.6	63	415.8	75.3	88.1	82.1	183400	343.5
Rich Twick&Roe	193800	37	190.9	41	211.6	78	402.5	80.7	78.4	79.5	230900	337.8
Wandsworth	161500	46	284.8	50	309.6	96	594.4	120.4	114.8	117.4	191200	502.1
Merton&Sutton	279300	50	179.0	78	279.3	128	458.3	75.7	103.5	90.5	340800	375.6
SOUTH WEST THAMES	2487500	416	167.2	628	252.5	1044	419.7	70.7	93.6	82.9	3023400	345.3
Total	11411400	2700	236.6	3078	269.7	5778	506.3	100.0	100.0	100.0	14025600	412.0
Oxford RHA		39		101		140						
Wessex RHA		13		38		51						
East Anglia RHA		3		19		22						
Other RHA		7		36		43						
Total		2762		3272		6034						

	Adult	Adult	Adult Rate
	Popn	stock	pmp
Inner London	1976900	1410	713.2
Outer London	3727500	2174	583.2
Shires	5707000	2194	384.4
Total	11411400	5778	506.3

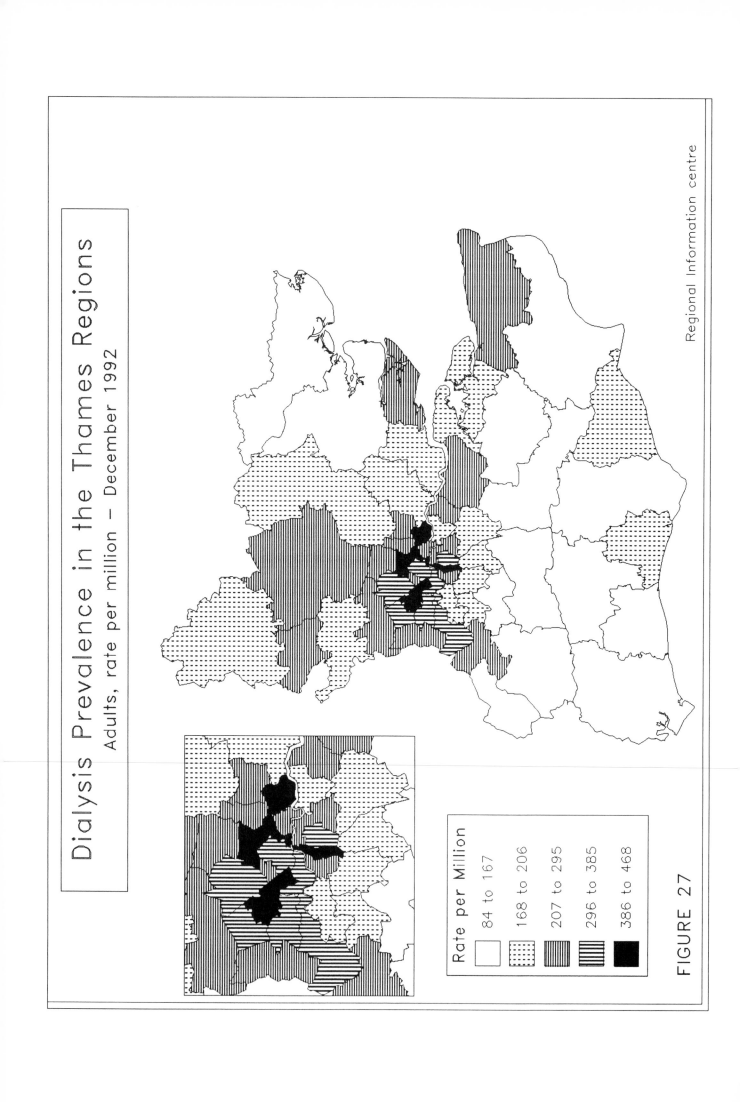

Dialysis Prevalence in the Thames Regions
Adults, rate per million – December 1992

Regional Information centre

Rate per Million

84 to 167
168 to 206
207 to 295
296 to 385
386 to 468

FIGURE 27

Renal Transplant Prevalence in the Thames Regions

Adults, rate per million – December 1992

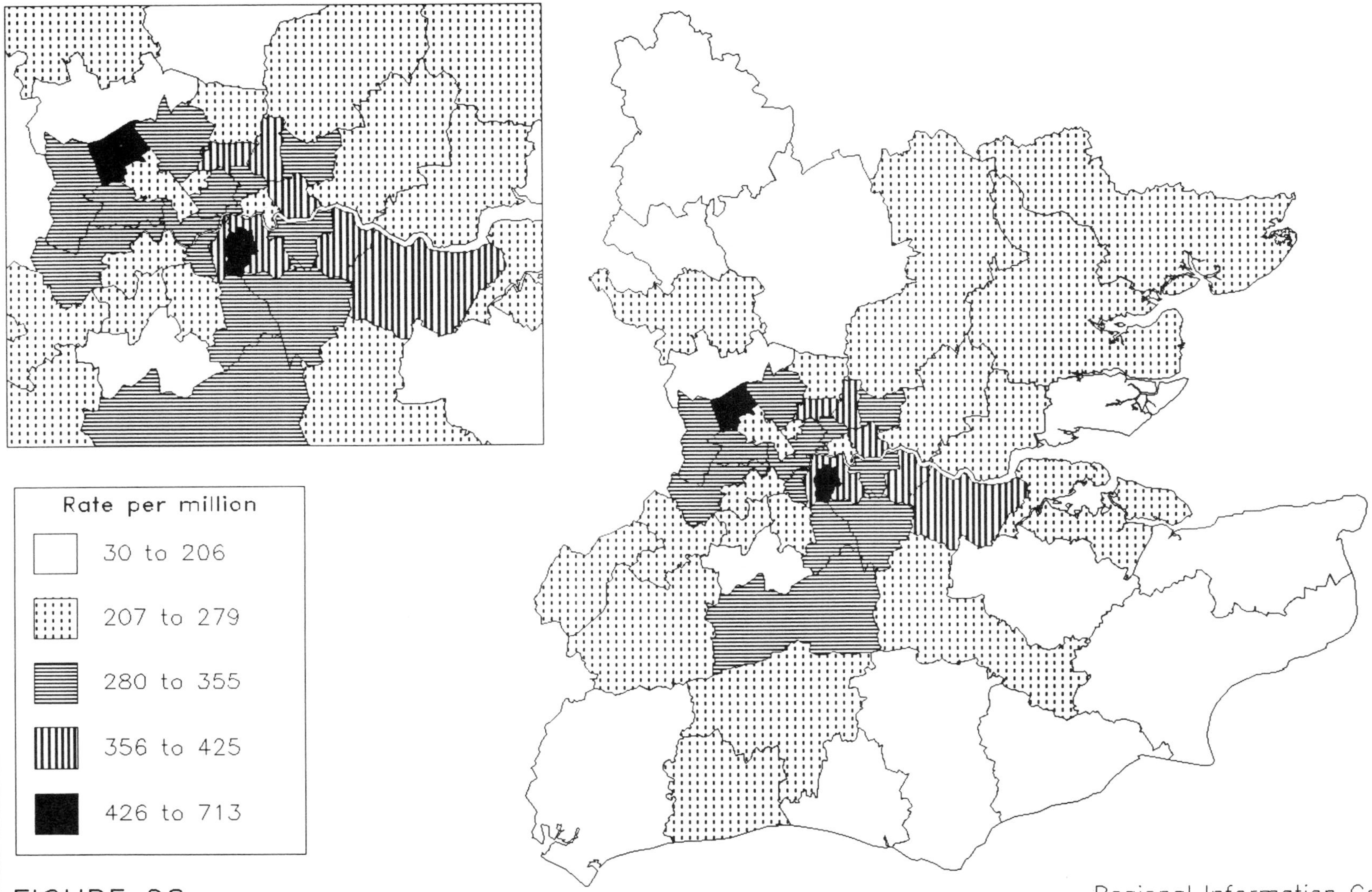

Rate per million

- 30 to 206
- 207 to 279
- 280 to 355
- 356 to 425
- 426 to 713

Regional Information Centre

FIGURE 28

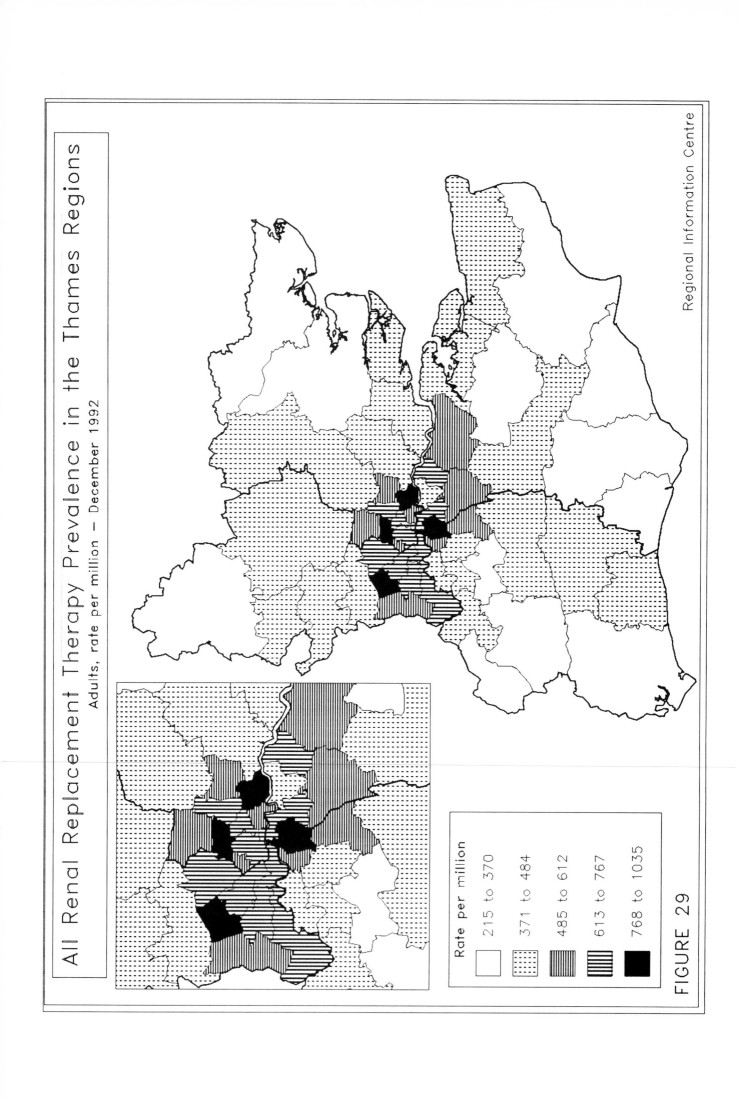

All Renal Replacement Therapy Prevalence in the Thames Regions

Adults, rate per million — December 1992

Regional Information Centre

Rate per million

- 215 to 370
- 371 to 484
- 485 to 612
- 613 to 767
- 768 to 1035

FIGURE 29

TABLE 18

CROSS BOUNDARY FLOWS INTO AND OUT OF THE 4 THAMES REGIONS FOR RENAL REPLACEMENT THERAPY

ADULTS, END 1992

	THAMES RESIDENTS TREATED IN 4 THAMES UNITS	THAMES RESIDENTS TREATED OUTSIDE 4 THAMES RHAS	NON-RESIDENTS TREATED IN 4 THAMES UNITS
Dialysis	2700	102	62
Transplant	3078	51	194
All patients	5778	153	256

97% of residents of Thames Regions treated in units in the 4 Thames Regions.

4% of patient treated in the Thames renal units are from other Regions.

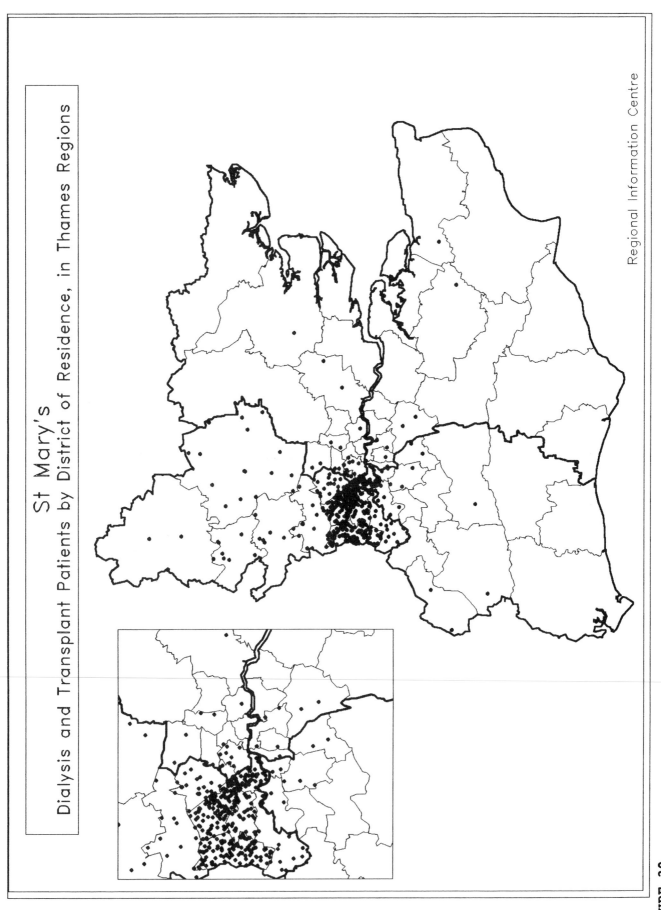

St Mary's

Dialysis and Transplant Patients by District of Residence, in Thames Regions

Regional Information Centre

FIGURE 30

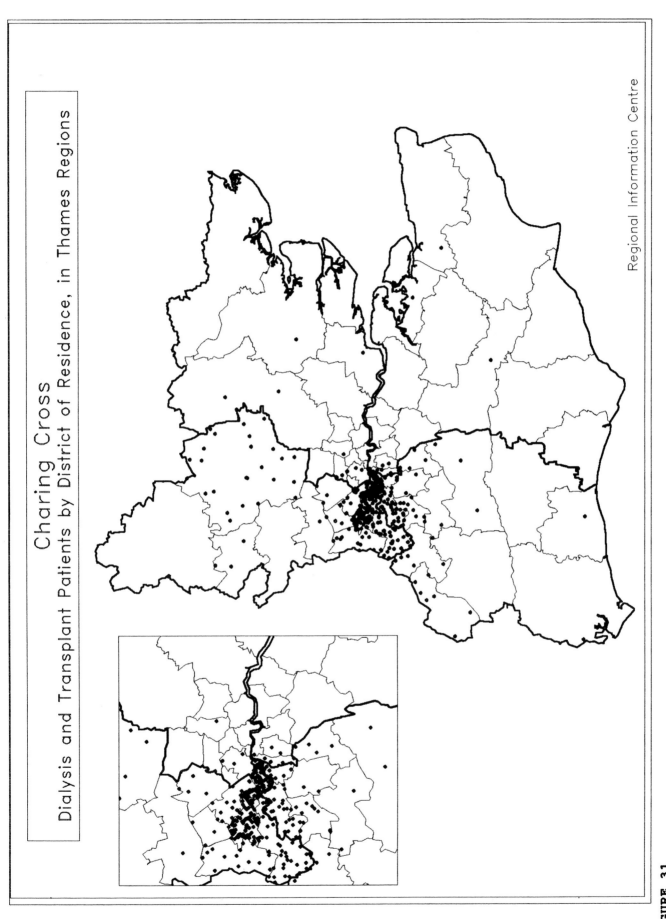

Charing Cross

Dialysis and Transplant Patients by District of Residence, in Thames Regions

Regional Information Centre

FIGURE 31

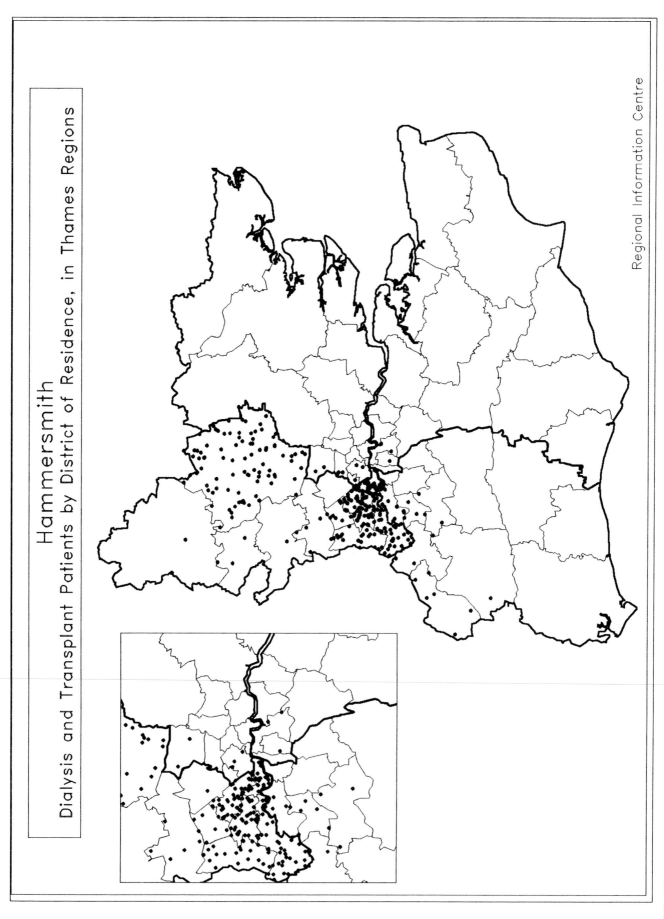

Hammersmith

Dialysis and Transplant Patients by District of Residence, in Thames Regions

Regional Information Centre

FIGURE 32

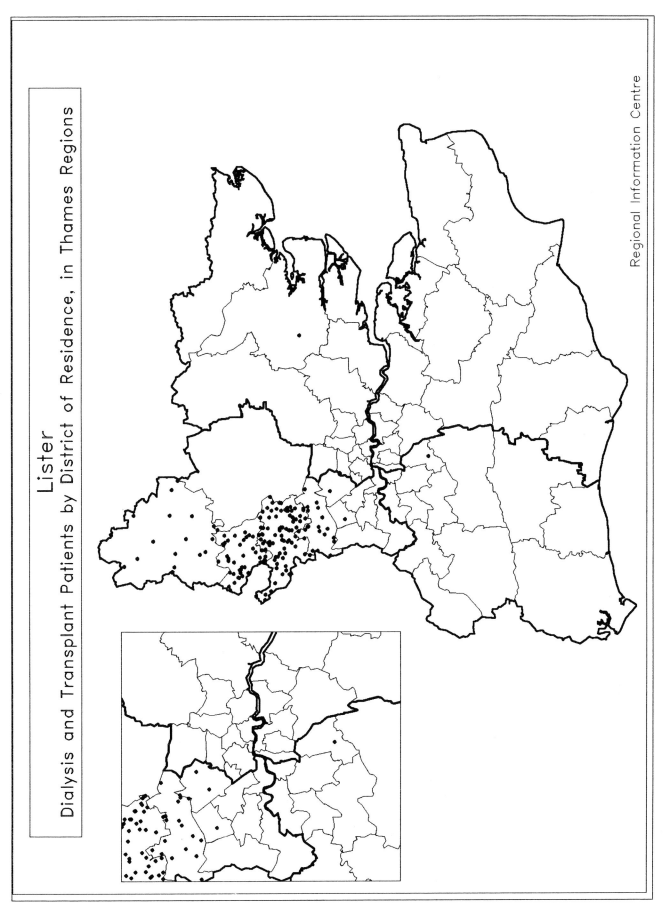

Lister
Dialysis and Transplant Patients by District of Residence, in Thames Regions

Regional Information Centre

FIGURE 33

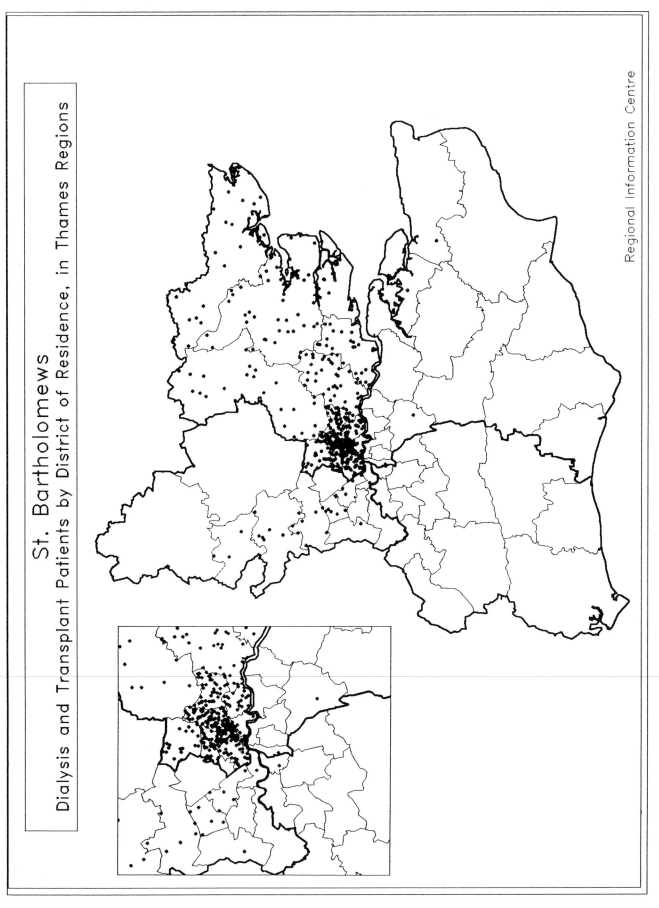

St. Bartholomews

Dialysis and Transplant Patients by District of Residence, in Thames Regions

Regional Information Centre

FIGURE 34

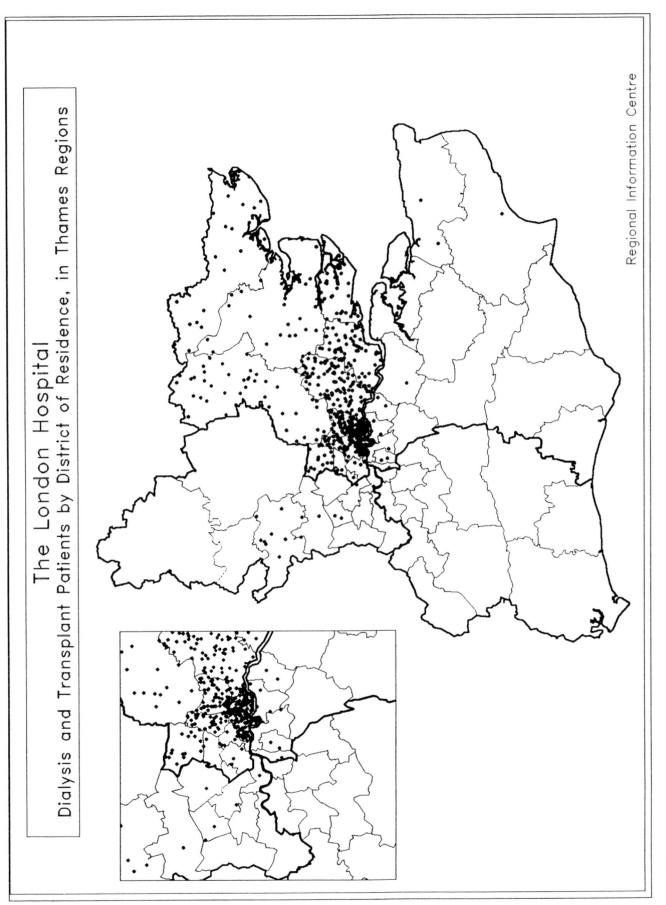

The London Hospital

Dialysis and Transplant Patients by District of Residence, in Thames Regions

Regional Information Centre

FIGURE 35

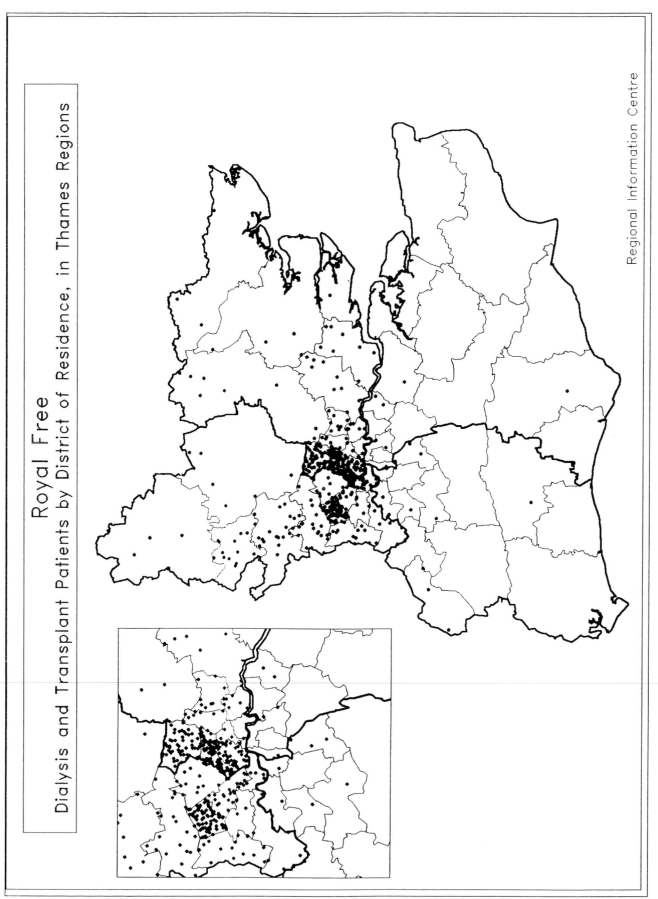

Royal Free

Dialysis and Transplant Patients by District of Residence, in Thames Regions

Regional Information Centre

FIGURE 36

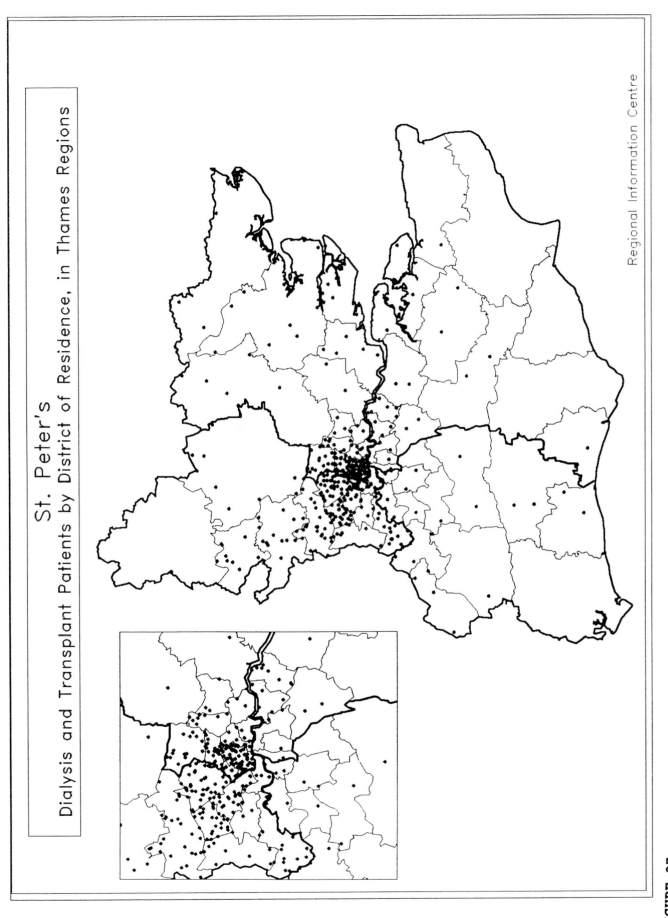

St. Peter's

Dialysis and Transplant Patients by District of Residence, in Thames Regions

Regional Information Centre

FIGURE 37

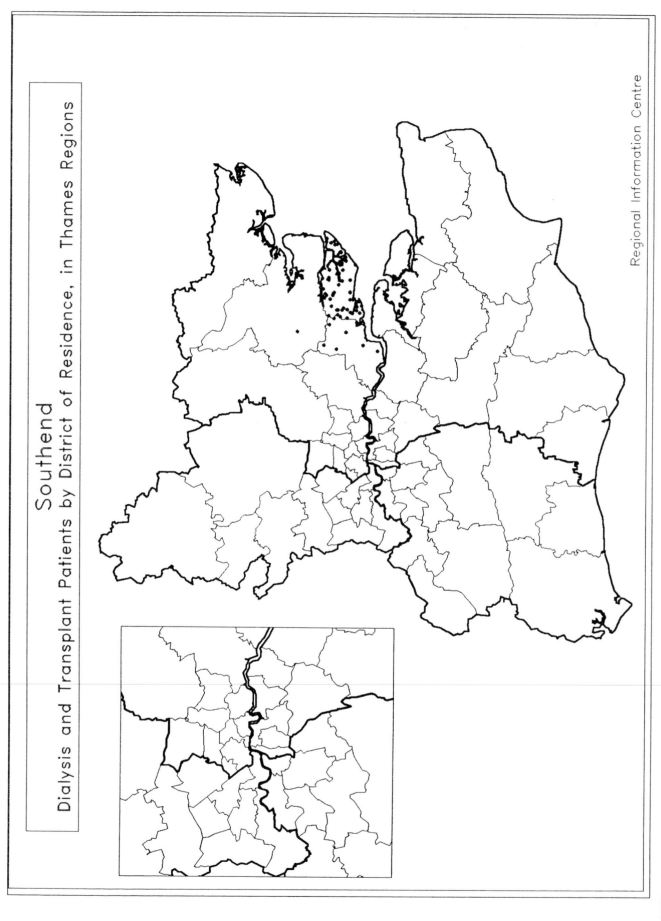

Southend

Dialysis and Transplant Patients by District of Residence, in Thames Regions

Regional Information Centre

FIGURE 38

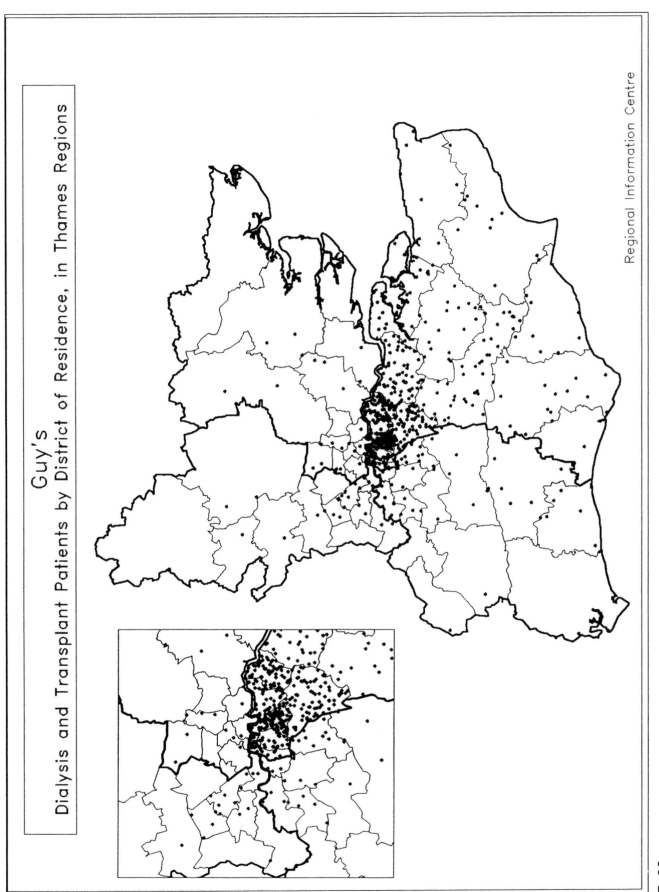

Guy's

Dialysis and Transplant Patients by District of Residence, in Thames Regions

Regional Information Centre

FIGURE 39

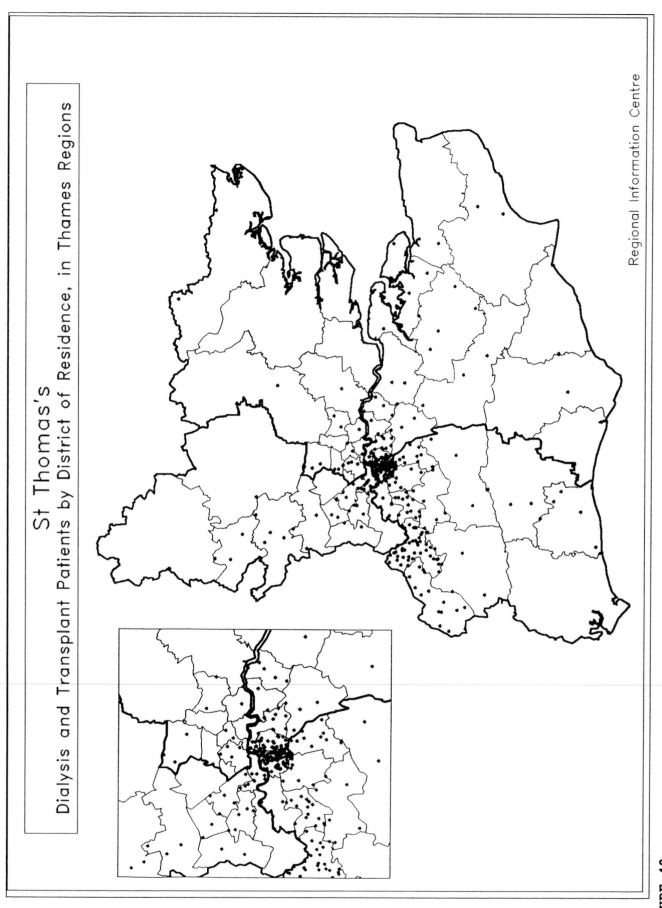

St Thomas's

Dialysis and Transplant Patients by District of Residence, in Thames Regions

Regional Information Centre

FIGURE 40

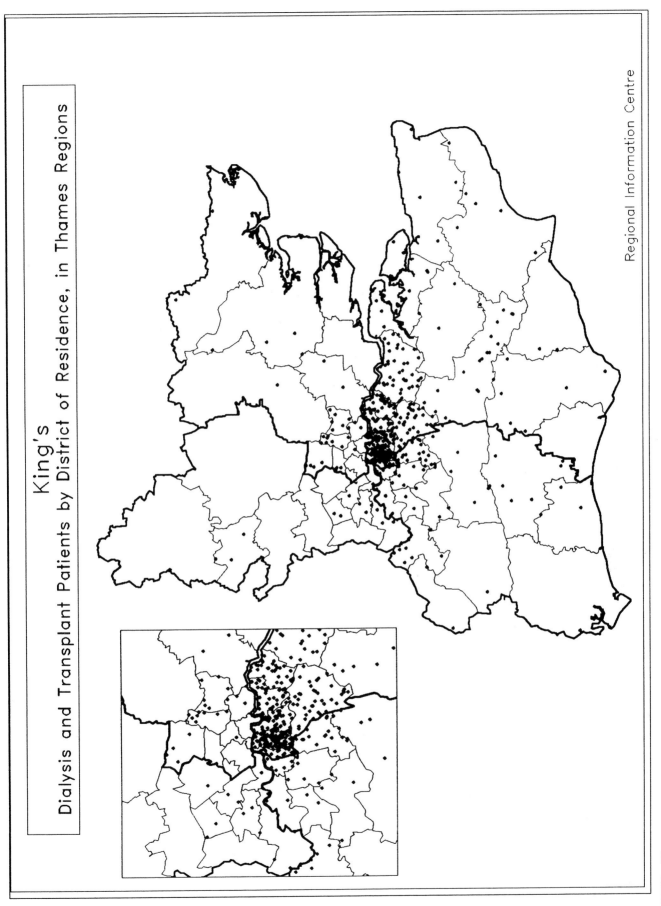

King's

Dialysis and Transplant Patients by District of Residence, in Thames Regions

Regional Information Centre

FIGURE 41

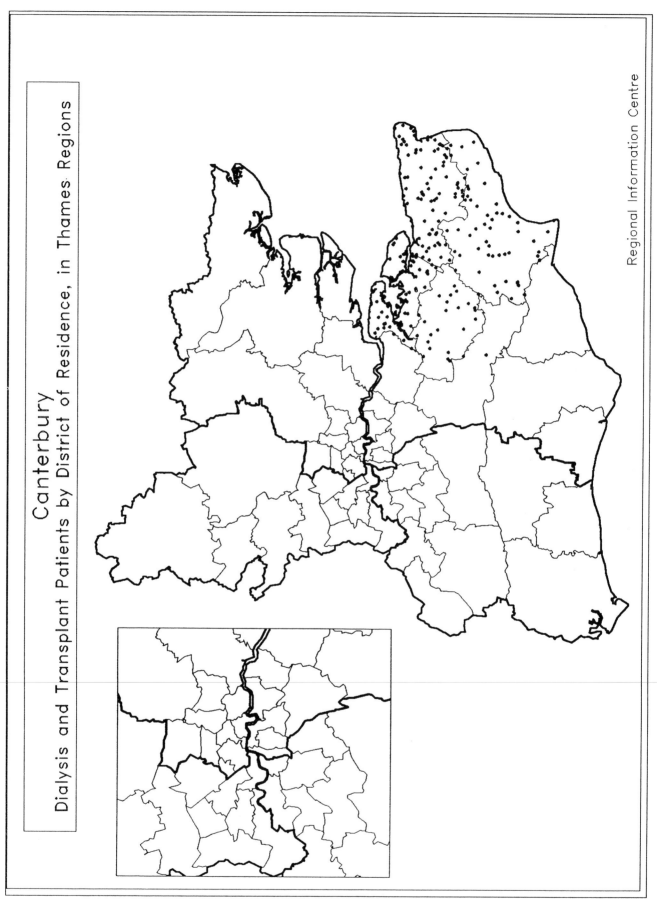

Canterbury

Dialysis and Transplant Patients by District of Residence, in Thames Regions

Regional Information Centre

FIGURE 42

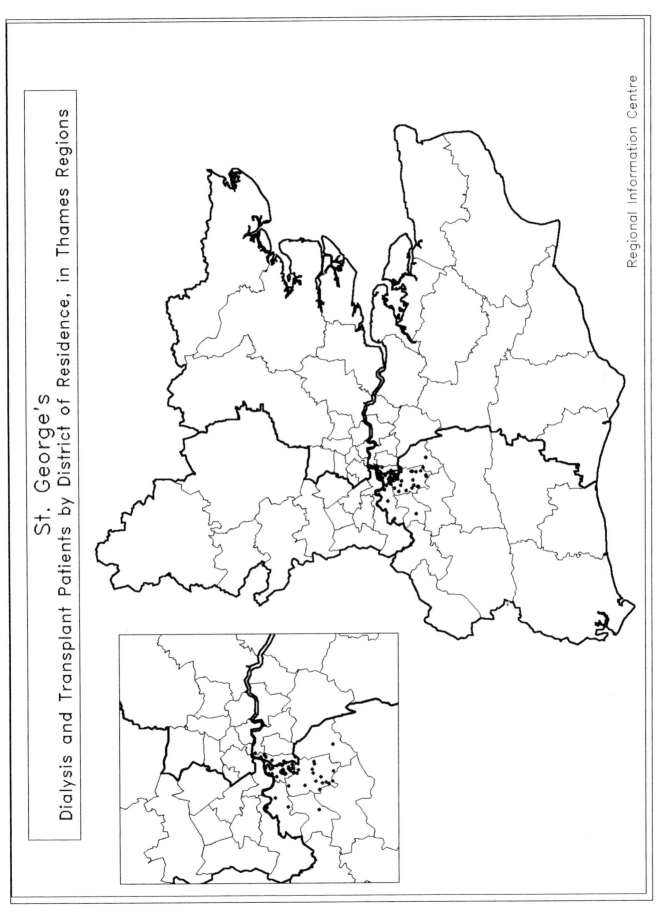

St. George's

Dialysis and Transplant Patients by District of Residence, in Thames Regions

Regional Information Centre

FIGURE 43

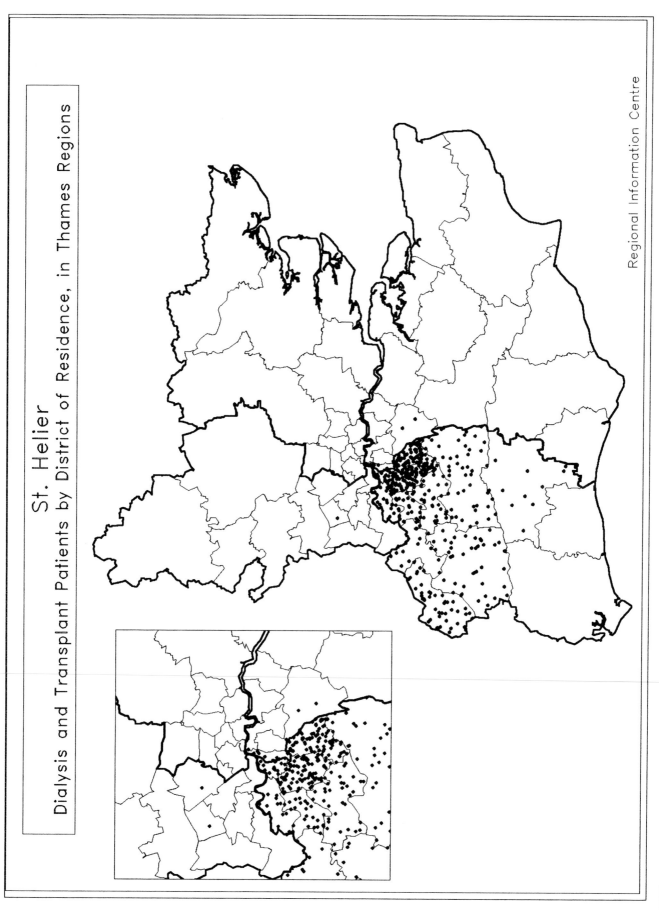

St. Helier

Dialysis and Transplant Patients by District of Residence, in Thames Regions

Regional Information Centre

FIGURE 44

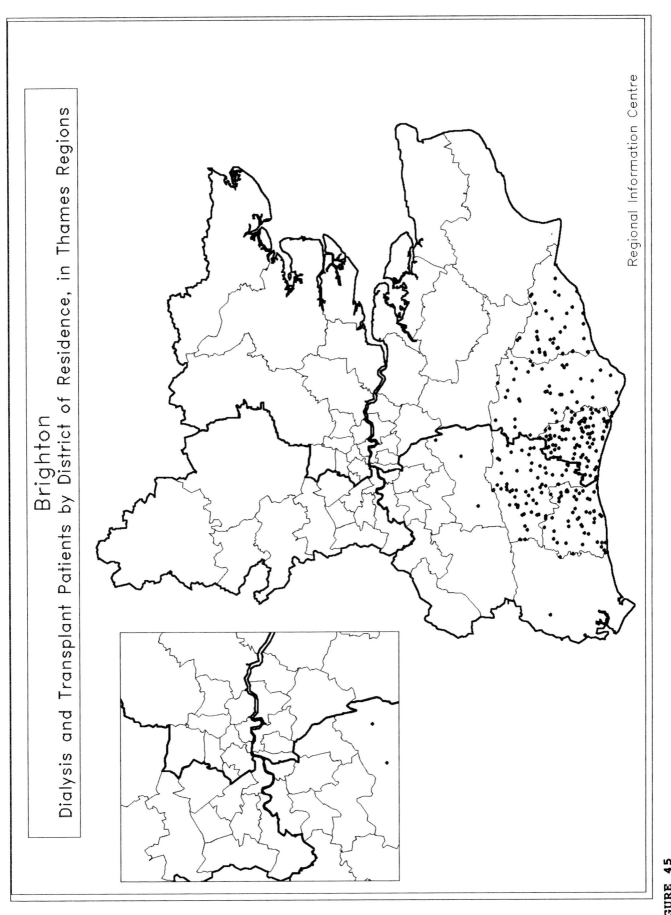

Brighton

Dialysis and Transplant Patients by District of Residence, in Thames Regions

Regional Information Centre

FIGURE 45

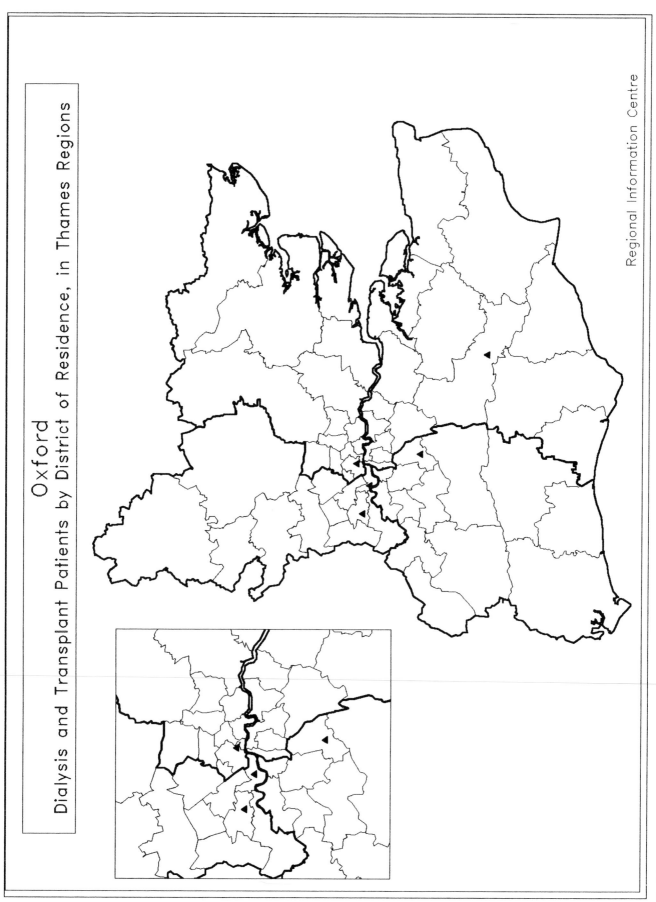

Oxford

Dialysis and Transplant Patients by District of Residence, in Thames Regions

Regional Information Centre

FIGURE 46

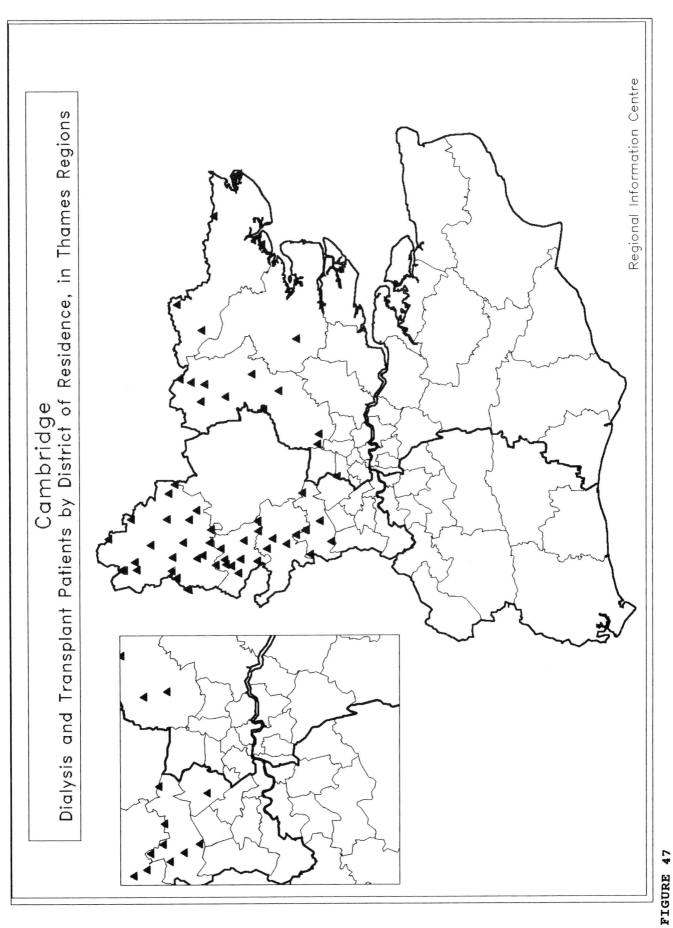

Cambridge

Dialysis and Transplant Patients by District of Residence, in Thames Regions

Regional Information Centre

FIGURE 47

Portsmouth

Dialysis and Transplant Patients by District of Residence, in Thames Regions

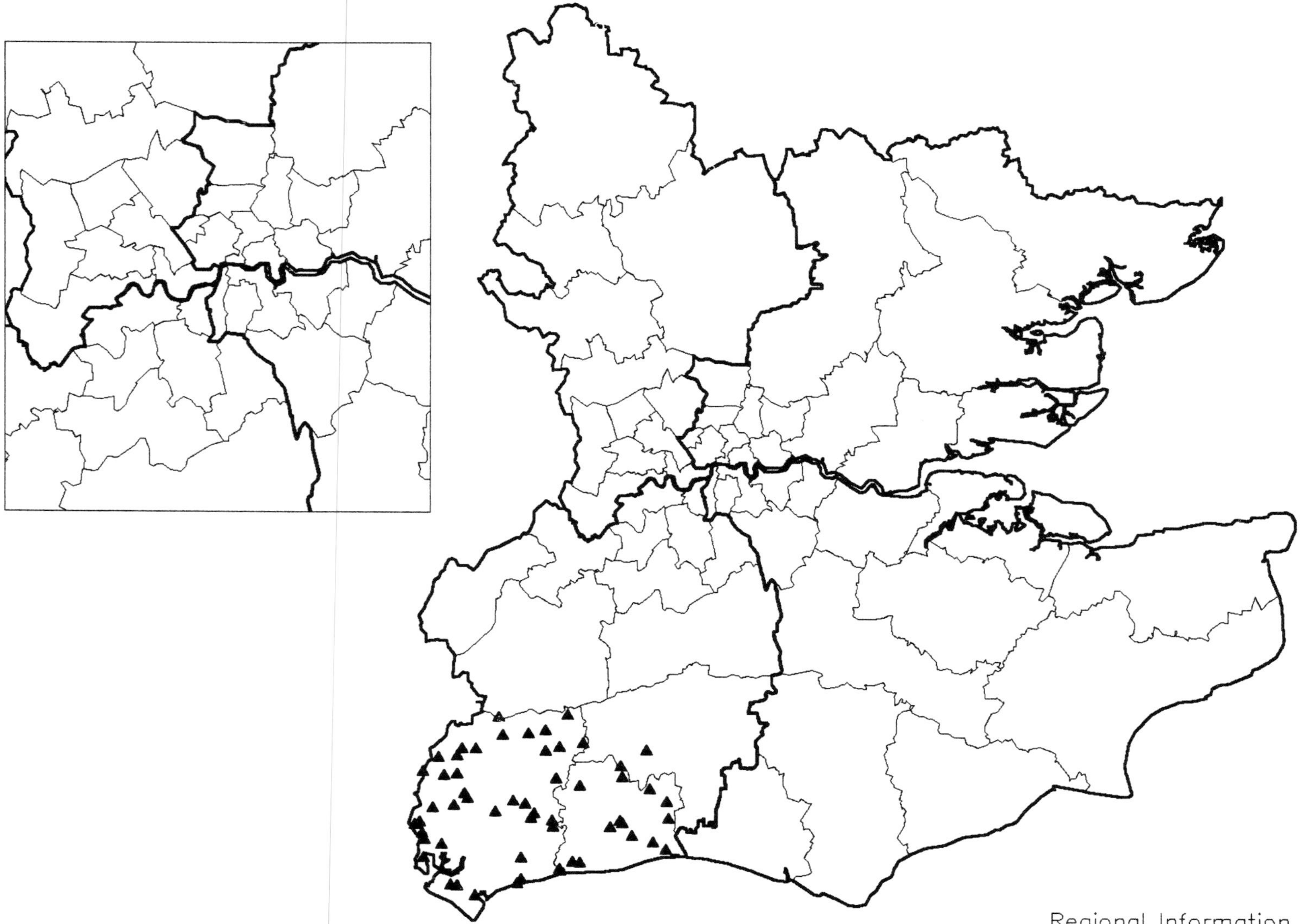

Regional Information Centre

FIGURE 48

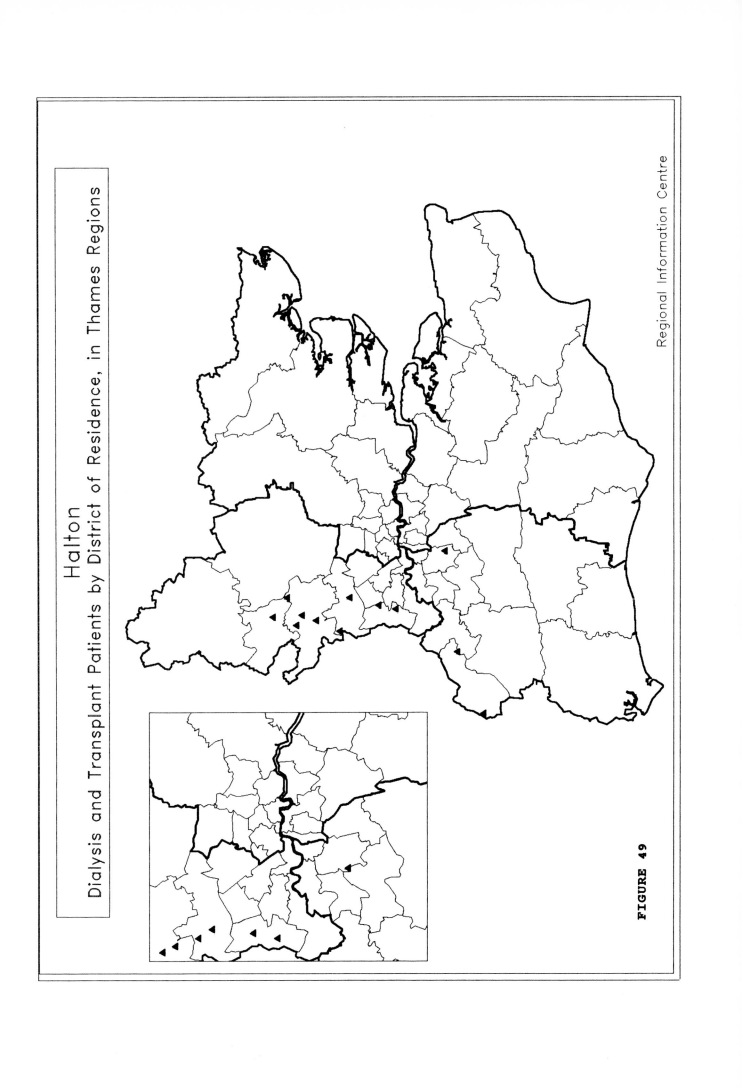

Halton

Dialysis and Transplant Patients by District of Residence, in Thames Regions

Regional Information Centre

FIGURE 49

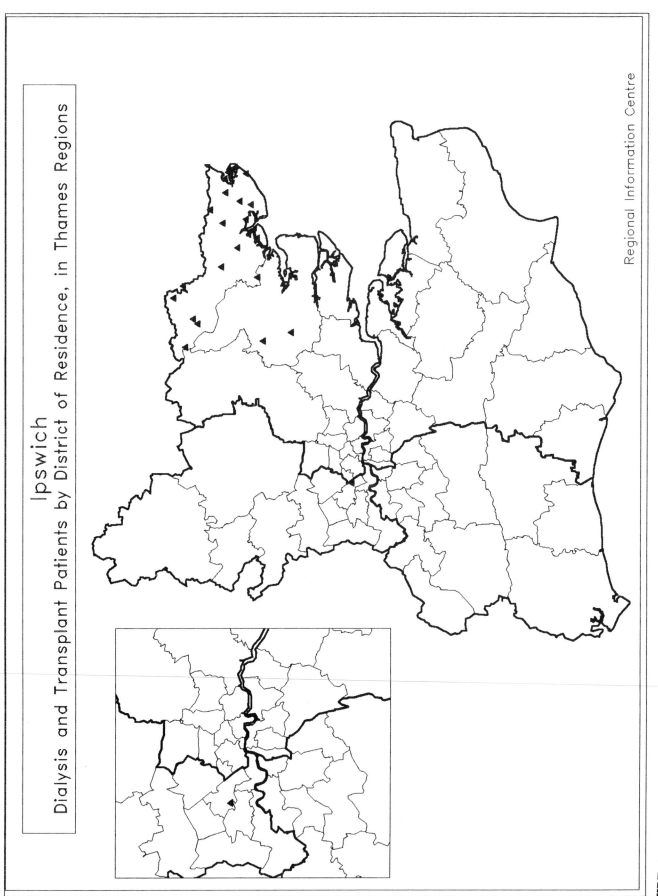

Ipswich

Dialysis and Transplant Patients by District of Residence, in Thames Regions

Regional Information Centre

FIGURE 50

TABLE 19

ACCEPTANCE ONTO RENAL REPLACEMENT THERAPY BY DISTRICT OF RESIDENCE. AVERAGE 1991-92.

New Patients 1991-92 by district of residence						
	New	16+	Adult	Standard	Total	Total
District of Residence	Patients	Popn	Rate pmp	Thames rate	Popn	Rate pmp
North Bedfordshire	20	200200	50.0	57.6	249700	40.0
South Bedfordshire	29	221900	65.3	75.4	284800	50.9
East&North Hertfordshire	51	391000	65.2	75.2	483700	52.7
NW Hertfordshire	33	210600	78.3	90.4	260700	63.3
SW Hertfordshire	34	197200	86.2	99.4	243000	70.0
Barnet	53	242500	109.3	126.0	298100	88.9
Harrow	53	164200	161.4	186.1	202900	130.6
Hillingdon	33	191000	86.4	99.6	235300	70.1
Hounslow&Spelthorne	53	243700	108.7	125.4	299000	88.6
Ealing	57	226300	125.9	145.3	280000	101.8
Riverside	58	251200	115.4	133.2	290300	99.9
Parkside	107	356200	150.2	173.2	432500	123.7
NORTH WEST THAMES	**581**	**2896000**	**100.3**	**115.7**	**3560000**	**81.6**
Basildon&Thurrock	32	231900	69.0	79.6	291900	54.8
Mid Essex	12	236400	25.4	29.3	294600	20.4
North East Essex	15	252500	29.7	34.3	306800	24.4
West Essex	17	211000	40.3	46.5	259000	32.8
Southend	45	266600	84.4	97.3	326300	69.0
Barking Havering&Btwood	48	363300	66.1	76.2	447400	53.6
Hampstead	20	89200	112.1	129.3	105000	95.2
City&Heckney	37	146100	126.6	146.1	187400	98.7
Newham	52	166000	156.6	180.7	217100	119.8
Tower Hamlets	26	124700	104.3	120.2	164900	78.8
Enfield	39	211900	92.0	106.1	261600	74.5
Haringey	36	168000	107.1	123.6	207000	87.0
Redbridge	47	186600	125.9	145.3	230000	102.2
Waltham Forest	40	173700	115.1	132.8	215800	92.7
Bloomsbury&Islington	46	200000	115.0	132.6	242500	94.8
NORTH EAST THAMES	**512**	**3027900**	**84.5**	**97.5**	**3757300**	**68.1**
Brighton	35	261100	67.0	77.3	310900	56.3
Eastbourne	21	197000	53.3	61.5	237000	44.3
Hastings	17	139500	60.9	70.3	168600	50.4
SE Kent	28	223000	62.8	72.4	273600	51.2
Canterbury&Thanet	34	249400	68.2	78.6	303400	56.0
Dartford&Gravesham	28	179800	77.9	89.8	223000	62.8
Maidstone	11	162300	33.9	39.1	201100	27.3
Medway	37	264600	69.9	80.6	334900	55.2
Tunbridge Wells	21	166100	63.2	72.9	202600	51.8
Bexley	27	176400	76.5	88.3	218000	61.9
Greenwich	19	167500	56.7	65.4	211900	44.8
Bromley	41	242100	84.7	97.7	292800	70.0
West Lambeth	38	132500	143.4	165.4	161400	117.7
Camberwell	57	174100	163.7	188.8	218000	130.7
Lewisham&North Southwark	74	264600	139.8	161.3	327700	112.9
SOUTH EAST THAMES	**488**	**3000000**	**81.3**	**93.8**	**3684900**	**66.2**
North West Surrey	23	176400	65.2	75.2	214800	53.5
West Surrey&NE Hants	27	228100	59.2	68.3	283000	47.7
South West Surrey	17	155300	54.7	63.1	188500	45.1
Mid Surrey	18	139800	64.4	74.3	169300	53.2
East Surrey	19	156400	60.7	70.1	190400	49.9
Chichester	20	150900	66.3	76.4	179700	55.6
Mid Downs	39	230100	84.7	97.7	285700	68.3
Worthing	30	207900	72.2	83.2	248300	60.4
Croydon	57	256500	111.1	128.2	317400	89.8
Kingston&Esher	35	151500	115.5	133.2	183400	95.4
Rich Twick&Roe	23	193800	59.3	68.4	230900	49.8
Wandsworth	43	161500	133.1	153.5	191200	112.4
Merton&Sutton	46	279300	82.3	95.0	340800	67.5
SOUTH WEST THAMES	**397**	**2487500**	**79.8**	**92.0**	**3023400**	**65.7**
Total	**1978**	**11411400**	**86.7**	**100.0**	**14025600**	**70.5**
Oxford RHA	23					
Wessex RHA	5					
East Anglia RHA	2					
Other RHA	17					
Total	**2025**					

	New	16+	Rate	Total	Rate	
	Patients	Popn	pmp	Popn	pmp	
Inner London	538	1976900	136.1	2433000	110.6	
Outer London	727	3727500	97.5	4577300	79.4	
Shires	713	5707000	62.5	7015300	50.8	
Total	1978	11411400	86.7	14025600	70.5	

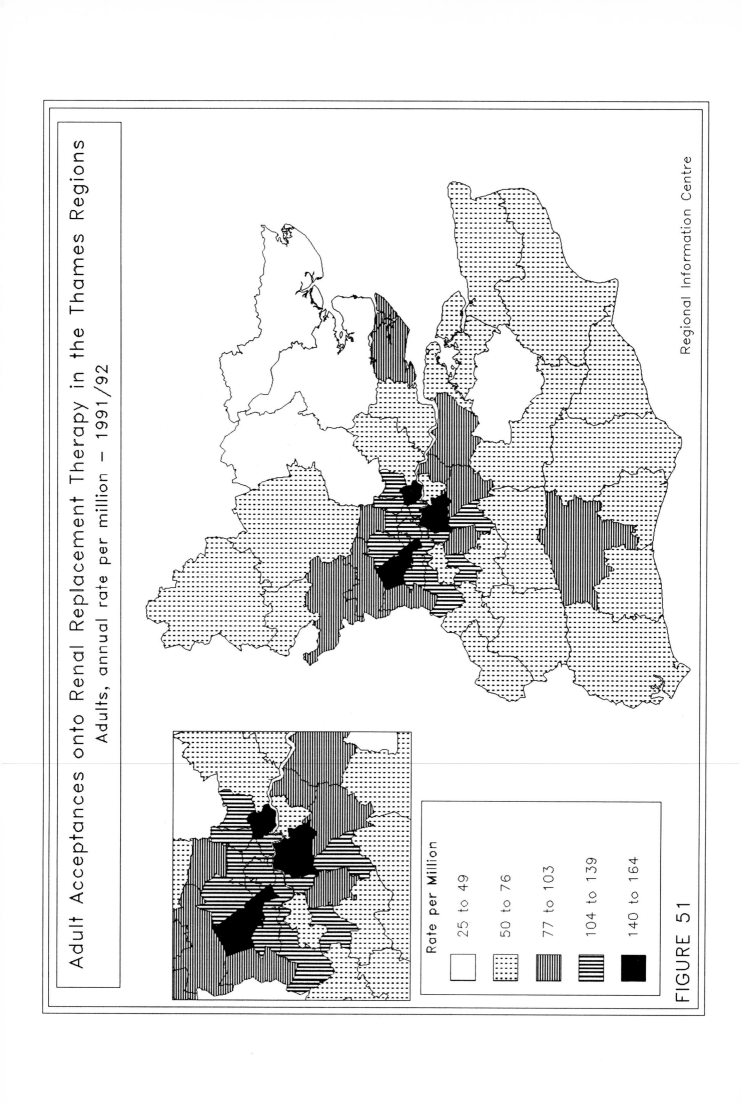

Adult Acceptances onto Renal Replacement Therapy in the Thames Regions
Adults, annual rate per million – 1991/92

Rate per Million

25 to 49
50 to 76
77 to 103
104 to 139
140 to 164

Regional Information Centre

FIGURE 51

Part I - Introduction

1. Models and Modelling

"The major challenge for Operation Research scientists working in the health field lies not in developing new and/or more sophisticated techniques, but in using what expertise they currently possess to make more of an impact on the delivery of health care".

"There is an urgent need for operation research and management scientists to devote their efforts to the design of decision systems that learn and adapt quickly and effectively - rather than the production of optimal decisions that don't".

"The aim should be to create a problem-solving relationship within which better models are likely to the built - the OR worker takes on the role of change agent, encouraging clients to find their own solutions, rather than trying to sell his own".

These quotes from Boldy, Ackoff and Pondy taken from the book *Operational Research Applied to the Health Services* (1981) struck resonance with the writer when he was completing previous work modelling renal services in the North Western RHA.

That work had been instigated after an indication by the NWRHA that they were intending to budget using the simple model by Pincherle (1). Although basic, it was totally understandable by planners and hence eminently usable. In searching for a 'closer approximation to reality' the writer explored the Markov chain models then in vogue (2). These had an inherent weakness in that the final stage of, say long-term dialysis, was modelled in such a way that the early survival probabilities produced an expected life rather longer than was considered reasonable. Also, a model of any degree of complexity produced a set of numerical arrays which would mean nothing to any other than the quantitative expert - planners would have to rely totally on others for the legitimacy of the results churned out on the computer. Pincherle's model could be calculated out on the back of an envelope using a pocket calculator - the planner was in full control. Hence, the Manchester model presented a picture one step up in complexity from Picherle's model, but decomposed the Markov chain into a series of simple stages in which a steady-state solution was still capable of being calculated on the proverbial envelope using a calculator. It achieved this by modelling a 'current minimum best set of working assumptions'. It was to be used to prepare long-term budget proposals, hence, the production of only a steady-state solution was not considered to be a limitation.

Simulation models (3) were considered but did not present the same opportunities for 'hands-on' understanding by non-specialist planners as the Manchester model.

The parameters used in the Manchester model (4) and its 'shape' were updated in the mid 1980's when it was used to produce estimates of national needs. The concept of a standard-risk intake (those aged 15 to under 55, with no coexisting disease) and high-risk intake (the 55 and over group plus any adult with diabetes) was introduced. The 'nuts and bolts' of how the model worked was again within the understanding of those who took part in its formulation.

The current version of the model has undergone a major transformation and

1

incorporates a variety of new features, following lengthy discussion with others in the Renal Working Party. For example,

It recognises the heavy constraint imposed by the low number of available organs

It allows an annual regraft rate of 16%

It accepts the realism of mixed mode treatment patterns and the limitations in the data relating to such patterns

It allows recognition of the spread in intake rates caused by non-homogeneous ethnic mixes

It presents its results for both steady-state and as a series of five-yearly 'wind-up' projections

It now uses annual treatment stages

It introduces a new "medium risk" category of patient.

At the request of the renal team much attention was given to the question of how scarce donor organs could be distributed between the original two risk groups. As a result, the high risk category has been split into two. A "medium risk" group of patients who are in the "younger of the older age-band; ie the 55-65 year olds - plus the younger adult diabetics", with the high risk group taking up the remainder. This was necessary because the Thames questionnaire returns indicated that over half the intake to the model would be over the age of 55 or diabetic. The essence of any model is to strike a balance between using a minimum number of modelled stages whilst also maintaining homogeneity between the characteristics of the patients in them.

The earlier quote by Pondy echoes the writer's view that this is, and should be, a model designed by a subgroup within the working party, where an important role of the modeller is to ensure that what is proposed is modellable in a sufficiently realistic way.

The request to provide five-year estimates of growth from current stock levels has meant that calculation is done by the original Markov chain methods. [The final long-term stages are computed in a different way to that used in the original models]. The incorporation of 'feedback' loops within the model to account for regrafts also means that the numerical arrays are too complex to reasonably process by calculator. However, the non-graft treatment streams are still amenable to simple checking by calculator, and, if the regraft loops are removed temporarily the remainder of the model is open for simple steady-state verification.

2. The Data

Much use has been made of data from the following sources:-

The questionnaire forms sent to each hospital as a part of the project

Computer tabulated processing of the European/UK EDTA patient register

The draft UKTSSA audit dated March 1993

Very late in the modelling exercise it was discovered that a certain amount of innocent double counting was present in the questionnaire returns from some hospitals for the numbers of patients in the new intakes in 1991 and 1992. The analysis of these returns had assumed the new intake to be those taken on a first mode of therapy in the end stage renal failure treatment process. In fact, some hospitals had included, as new intake, transfers from other units and patients whose grafts failed requiring a return to the dialysis programme. Thus, the 81 pmp new intake apparently seen in 1992 is likely to be less than this. Importantly for the model, the age structure of the new patients needs to be modified from those values gained directly from the questionnaire data. Midway during the task the hospitals were asked to state the proportion of diabetics in the under 55, and 55 and over groups in order to more accurately assess the "standard" and "high" risk needs. The few early responses showed great variation between the 1991 and 1992 intakes and in order to present results an overall figure of 15% adult diabetics under the age of 55 has been assumed for the new intake of patients.

Previous work on these models had used published EDTA patient statistics and survival data, tables and charts which would have been carefully studied and double-checked for any inconsistencies. It is unrealistic to assume that data freshly drawn from the central computer patient data base will have such solidity. In the time available, the best use has been made of a limited set of data.

It was surprising to find that some EDTA tables had to be derived from a response rate of less than 50%. The recent Report on Management of Renal Failure in Europe, XXII, 1991 provided background information on recent trends.

The UKTSS audit report served as a useful cross check that the data tables received were giving sensible results.

3. The Model

Each stage is to be modelled as a series of annual events. This both simplifies the concept and also neatly fits in with current thinking on life-cycle costing the renal treatment process.

In the original North West Region version of the model a constraint was not put on the number of donor organs entering the model. A target new intake of 40pmp was assumed, of whom 75% were transplantable. Thus, a little under 30 organs pmp per year were assumed (after some small loss in the waiting pool). At that time regrafts were less frequent than nowadays and none were assumed.

In the National run of the model, the intakes were split into a standard risk group (15-under 55 age band and no coexisting diseases) of 35pmp and alternatives of a 5, 10 or 15 pmp high risk group (55.0 and over + coexisting diseases). Of the standard risk category, 80% were deemed to be transplantable and would hopefully receive organs. 60% of the high risk category were assumed to be suitable for a transplant. Hence, a little under 28 standard risk first transplant organs + 3 for each multiple of 5 high risk patients were required to feed the new intake of patients each year. Again, no regrafts were assumed.

Unfortunately, there has not been the desired increase in the numbers of donor organs made available. The larger new intakes now proposed (80pmp and more) will not be able to receive a transplant in the numbers required. There is also a large stock of patients waiting for a suitable organ. There is a feeling that transplantation may have plateaued out to steady state at the current organ rate of approximately 30pmp per year. The Renal Association have set a target, thought to be achievable, of 40pmp donor organs per year.

The model will be run between two organ availability rates; 30pmp and 40pmp.

For reasons outlined earlier, three streams of patient intake are envisaged:

> 35pmp "**standard risk**" patients, 80% of whom are considered to be suitable for transplantation

> a new group of "**medium risk**" patients all of whom are suitable for transplantation - they will consist mainly of the "younger of the high risk age group", those a little over 55 and the younger adult diabetics who, by definition, are excluded from the standard risk group.

> This has been done because of the great number of much older patients being taken on who will now form the "**high risk**" group. This group is conveniently modelled in terms of small units of, say, 5pmp. Then a multiplying factor for this group can be used in order to model a range of different intake rates.

The new category of the "medium-risk" patient has been introduced in order to achieve a greater homogeneity in the survival characteristics of the patients in each of the three streams modelled.

4

Early runs of the model reveal that to satisfy the transplant needs of an annual intake of 80 pmp new patients, in the mix of 35pmp standard risk, 10 pmp medium risk and 35 high risk, some 34 organs would be required if no regrafts occurred. This number would increase to 39 if 16% regrafts were carried out.

A 16% regraft level has been introduced into the model.

4.0   Overview of the flow of treatment modelled

The flow is depicted in Figure 1. Graft candidates spend a typical time of one to two years in the waiting pool before receiving their graft. Hence, two separate one year stages represent the time spent in the pool. This is followed by a one year post-operative stage; the transplantee may die in this time, or suffer early failure of the graft necessitating return to dialysis, or emerge successfully from the year with the functioning graft. Hopefully, this will continue to function for many years, during each of which there is a chance of the graft continuing, failing or of the patient dying.

Whether the graft fails in the first year or much later, the flow then enters a one year "first year following failure" stage. It is a characteristic of renal statistics that the first year following any major change of therapy presents worse survival statistics than pertain beyond that year.

If the patient emerges from that year, he will then re-enter long term dialysis; in each successive year he may return to a post-operative regraft year or he may die. In line with observable figures, the post-operative regraft stage has slightly lower survival characteristics than are modelled in the year of the first graft.

The non-graft candidate has a simpler flow pattern. He simply enters a first year of dialysis in which he is trained and may have a routine operation to facilitate dialysis, and then is maintained year by year on dialysis.

The type of dialysis the patient receives is not considered in the flow diagram. Modern treatment uses a mixture of therapies to suit the individual needs at given times of any patient. The survival data describing "all" starting therapies has been used to provide the parameters for the model. Since it is likely that a fairly even mix between haemodialysis and peritoneal dialysis will be used in practice, the use of the "all mode" statistics is reasonable. Limited data tables separating survival on the two modes of dialysis indicates that, particularly for the medium and high risk groups, PD has better figures than the ALL modes data but HD has worse survivals.

How the overall dialysis numbers forecast by the model are assigned to haemodialysis or CAPD is then a matter for planners using the model. There is medical debate on what is the proper ratio of HD to PD for each risk group of patient.

5

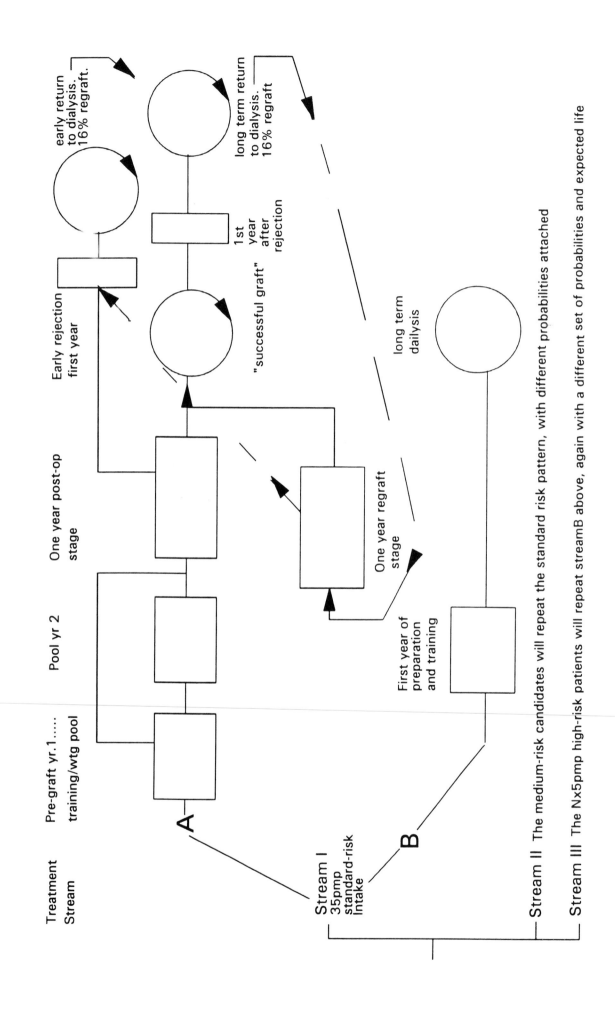

Treatment Stream

Pre-graft yr.1...... training/wtg pool

Pool yr 2

One year post-op stage

Early rejection first year

early return to dialysis. 16% regraft.

"successful graft"

1st year after rejection

long term return to dialysis. 16% regraft

long term dailysis

One year regraft stage

First year of preparation and training

A

B

Stream I 35pmp standard-risk Intake

Stream II The medium-risk candidates will repeat the standard risk pattern, with different probabilities attached

Stream III The Nx5pmp high-risk patients will repeat streamB above, again with a different set of probabilities and expected life

4.1   Summary of the parameters used in each stage

Ps=Patient survival   Gs=Graft survival   Pf=Graft failure probability

Standard Risk

Graft Candidates

1	Waiting Pool yr 1	Ps 0.94	0.5 are grafted in that year
2	Waiting Pool yr 2	Ps 0.96	
3	Post-op year	Ps 0.95	Gs 0.85
4	Regraft post-op year	Ps 0.95	Gs 0.63
5	Subsequent successful years on graft		Expected life 11.7 years Pr 0.6
6	Year 1 following an early graft failure	Ps 0.9	
7	Year 1 following a late graft failure	Ps 0.9	
8	Subsequent years on long term dialysis		

        Expected life 12.5 years from early graft failure, 7.5 years from late failure

Ungrafted

9	First year on dialysis	Ps 0.94
10	Expected life on long term renal dialysis 14.3 years	

Medium Risk

Graft Candidates

1	Waiting Pool yr 1	Ps 0.85	0.5 are grafted in that year
2	Waiting Pool yr 2	Ps 0.85	
3	Post-op year	Ps 0.88	Gs 0.77
4	Regraft post-op year	Ps 0.85	Gs 0.67
5	Subsequent successful years on graft		Expected life 10.1 years Pr 0.1
6	Year 1 following an early graft failure	Ps 0.85	
7	Year 1 following a late graft failure	Ps 0.85	
8	Subsequent years on long term dialysis		

        Expected life 7.5 years from early graft failure, 3.5 years from late failure

Ungrafted

9	First year on dialysis	Ps 0.83
10	Subsequent years on long term dialysis	Expected life 8.6 years

High Risk

Ungrafted

8	First year on dialysis	Ps 0.77
9	Subsequent years on long term dialysis	Expected life 3.5 years

7

Bibliography.

1
Pincherle G. Services for patients with chronic renal failure in England and Wales. *Health Trends* 1977. 9:41-44.

2
Farrow SC, Fisher DJH, Johnson DB. Statistical approach to planning an integrated haemodialysis/transplantation programme. *Brit. Med. J.* 1971. 2:671-676

West RR, Crosby DL, Jones JH. A mathematical model of an integrated haemodialysis and renal transplantation programme. *Brit. J. Prev. Soc. Med.* 1974. 28:149-155

Davies R, Johnson D, Farrow S. Planning patient care with a Markov model. *Operational Research Quarterly* 1975. 26,3:599-607.

SE Thames RHA. Renal Services. 1982.

3
Holmes DL. A simulation model of a renal dialysis and transplantation service. Trent RHA

Davies R. A study of a renal unit. *J. Opl. Res. Soc.* 1979.30:873-844

Bolger PG, Davies R. Simulation model for planning renal services in a district health authority. *Brit. Med. J.* 1992 305:605-608

4
Wood IT, Mallick NP, Moores B. A flexible model for planning facilities for patients with end-stage renal failure. *Brit. Med. J.* 1980. 281:575-577.

Wood IT, Mallick NP, Wing AJ Prediction of resources needed to achieve the national target for the treatment of renal failure. *Brit. Med. J.* 1987. 294:1467-1470.

Part II - Detailed examination of each stage of the model

5. The mean age of patient groups

5.1 Mean age of patients in the new intakes
Summaries from the questionnaire returns, based on age-mix only, are listed in Appendix 1.

The 15 to under 55s
mean age in 1991   38.45
mean age in 1992   39.12

The 55 and over group
mean age in 1991   67.13   52.1% of the total intake were in this group
mean age in 1992   68.16   54.6% of the total intake were in this group

A wide variation in the proportion of dialysis patients admitted is observed - these are listed at the foot of Appendix 1.
A minimum of 5% of new patients to a maximum of 25% were taken on with diabetes in 1991 to 1992.
In the stock the greatest variation was found at one hospital which had 4% of diabetic patients on haemodialysis compared with 26% of those on CAPD.

EDTA patient survival tables for all modes of new treatment commenced between 1985 and 1989 reveal that 15% of the adults were diabetic. Their average age was 41 years.

Applying this to the above age-mixes, the following ages will be used to model the typical age of the new patient at the commencement of treatment :-

Standard risk   38 years
Medium risk   50 years
High risk   65 years

The standard risk age has been reduced from the calculated mean because the latter figure may well be a little raised if some of the assumed new intake are, in fact, returning to the local unit from previous treatment. The figure of 38 years is only one year higher than the mean age used when the model was run in the mid eighties. This would imply that the standard risk group is a well established stable cohort.

In the medium risk category, half will be diabetic at approximately 40 years mean age, the other half non-diabetic aged between 55 and 65.

Again, in the high risk category, some of the intake will have "returned" and been counted as a new patient thus inflating the mean age.
It is noted that three hospitals in the sixteen tabled took on one or more new patients in the over 85 age group in 1992. None in that age group had been admitted in 1991.

The increase in apparent mean age of the new patients goes some way to explaining why the calculated mean age of the new intake is virtually the same as that of the stock.

5.2   Mean age of stock

Of the stock on transplant follow up
Based on age-mix only

The 15 to under 55s
mean age   40.06

The 55 and over group
mean age   63.25   31.6% of the total transplant stock were in this group

Of the stock on dialysis
Based on age-mix only

The 15 to under 55s
mean age   40.67

The 55 and over group
mean age   67.4   57.1% of the total dialysis stock were in this group

Six centres returned data allowing separation of the dialysis stock into haemodialysis and CAPD.

Of the stock on haemodialysis	**Of the stock on CAPD**
Based on age-mix only	
The 15 to under 55s	
mean age 39.29	mean age 36.0
The 55 and over group	
mean age 66.21	mean age 67.73
47.7% of the total were 55 or over	64.34% of the total were 55 or over

This high figure of 64% of older patients on CAPD perhaps reflects more a rationing of hospital dialysis stations in the Thames region than a deliberate treatment policy. Some members of the working group consider it to be too high a proportion and an equal split between haemodialysis and CAPD will be modelled for the high risk groups.

The amount of home haemodialysis carried out in the Thames regions is small - 8.3% for the standard risk group; a mere 3.4% for the high risk category. The team recommends it is not included in the model. The numbers on IPD are smaller still, at less than 0.5%, it too will be excluded. These facts are based on 1991 EDTA figures which arose from a 47% return and for which accurate diabetes numbers are known within the two age bands - these tables will be found in appendix 2.

Thus, the treatments modelled will be either haemodialysis or CAPD.

5.3   The stock mix in 1991

The same 1991 EDTA data indicated that of the stock,

standard risk group
19.9% were on haemodialysis   12.1% on PD   68.0% on transplant follow up

in the high risk group
27.1% were on haemodialysis   44.8% on PD   28.1% on transplant follow up

6.   Time spent by graft candidates whilst in the waiting pool

An expected wait of 1.5 years is experienced by to both standard and medium risk patients.

EDTA data sheet 93/1b reveals that, approximately, 50% wait for up to 1 year, 25% wait up to 2 years, 12.5% wait upto 3 years. The numbers are similar for both standard and higher risk patients as defined by under 55.0, and over 55.0 OR any adults with diabetes, respectively.

This process could be modelled by a simple circulating stage with an equal probability of exiting the pool, or waiting for another year; ie. a geometric series with $P_w = 0.5$.

However, this does not conveniently fit into the costing process - in which first year costs are necessarily higher than those incurred in following years. Alternative approaches are to model five serial 1 year stages in cascade to give a close model of reality, or, sufficiently, to model three serial stages which would cover 92% of those waiting (and modify stage 3 to make up the remainder).

An even simpler choice is to model only two cascaded 1 year stages of waiting, by which time almost 80% of patients have received their graft.

Using the last method, we can argue for standard risk patients -

Stage 1.   0.5 of those entering will be grafted by the end of that year.
            The All renal treatment patient survival rates indicate that 0.06 of those entering the year will die.

Stage 2.   Taking a further patient mortality of 0.04, of the remainder, all those waiting will receive a graft by the end of year 2

For the medium risk patient, both first and second stage patient mortalities of 0.15 apply. 0.5 will receive a graft by the end of the first year.

This simplified model will provide a sufficiently accurate number of 'those in the waiting pool' and of the costs incurred.

Deeper level discussion.

The use of data tabulated in annual increments tends to magnify the waiting time - they indicate a waiting time of 1.9 years.
If a geometric series is modelled by 3 month intervals, then the expected wait becomes only 1.6 years. If this is taken further down to monthly stages then the expected wait becomes 1.51 years. However, in the latter case, if few grafts are assumed to be done in the first three months in the pool, the expected waiting time increases back to 1.7 years. The introduction of annual mortality into the waiting pool equation also has the effect of reducing the expected waiting time by approximately 10%.

On balance, taking two 1 year stages, during which there is not insignificant mortality, adequately represents the expected waiting time of a little under 1.5 years.

7. Expected life on long-term modes of treatment

In a rapidly developing area of science, looking into the future obviously presents a challenge. The estimation of the expected life of a long-term renal treatment is no exception. Firstly, a long series of historical data does not fully reflect the most recent changes in technique. For example, the use of cyclosporin hardly entered into the data at the beginning of the eighties - now it is in full use - its effect is certainly to increase shorter term graft survival, however, its effect on long term survival (beyond 10 years) is less certain. Secondly, the method of preferred treatment may well change so that older data is less relevant to latest practice. Reports at the beginning of the eighties carried long series of patient survival tables for those permanently on "home" or "hospital" dialysis. Modern practice, particularly since the rapid growth of CAPD as a therapy, is to place the patient in more frequent changes of treatment and report each change to the central data registry. The use of CAPD spans both the type of patient who would have been considered suitable for independent dialysis (historically home haemodialysis or in a minimal care unit) and the patient suitable for dependent dialysis (as in hospital based dialysis). For most purposes this is of no consequence but for modelling resource needs such distinctions have some validity in producing a more finely structured model. Such data is not available for the present study.

Survival tables are most usually prepared by considering a specific mode of treatment as identified by the first mode of treatment given to a patient - and then, in the actuarial analysis of survival, "losing that patient to follow up" at the first change of treatment. For the present model the primary document used for the dialysis survival is to consider renal treatment as a whole from the tabled survivals for patients commencing on "any" treatment. Thus, eventual death provides the natural endpoint to the analysis.

Survival tables are processed for patients within specific age bands; usually in ten year spans from 25-34 up to 65-74.

A value for expected life may be estimated in two ways;

     1   By extracting the annual mortality for each ten year age band and fitting an exponential curve to these points. In this way a smooth annual series is generated which can be used to predict expected life. This method is preferred for the longer life span standard risk patient.

     2   More simply by inspecting the ten year survival span and calculating the area under the survival curve as given so far. Then adding an assumed tailing off to zero survival assumption. It is surprising how often the two approaches agree to within the limits inherent in the data. This method is particularly suitable for the high risk patient where the likely tailing off function has less effect on the total expected life.

7.1 The graft candidate patient streams

The model divides graft life into two phases.
Year 1
The first year commencing with the graft operation. Survival rates for this period can be taken from recent data. However, even this poses problems. Typically, one year graft survival is unit dependent and may vary over a wide range. Recent UKTSS data (the draft Renal Transplant Audit, March 1993) for UK centre first cadaveric grafts carried out between 1987 and 1991 indicated a variation in graft survival from 73% to 95% - both these extremes being from units performing a similar number of transplants. Over all the units the mean survival was 84% for this period. The mean patient survival for the same period was 91%.

In terms of age category, The same UKTSSA report identified the following one year survivals for UK first cadaveric grafts

| 19-55 age group | Patient survival 91% | Graft survival 78% |
| 55 and over | Patient survival 85% | Graft survival 80% |

Patient death increasingly becomes the reason for termination of a graft in the elderly rather than failure of the graft requiring a return to dialysis.

17.7% of the cadaveric grafts performed had been regrafts. For these, a one year first graft survival of 78% was contrasted with a 71% regraft graft survival. A patient survival for regrafts was not available from that source. EDTA Table 93/AA reveals that over the period 1978 - 1991, 13% of regrafts were given to medium risk patients, more to those aged 55 and over rather than to patients with diabetes; very few were given to anyone over 65.

The one year graft survivals used in the model arise from EDTA table, 93/10a, for first cadaver grafts carried out between 1989 and 1991

Graft survival
Standard risk patients   0.85   Medium risk patients   0.77
Corresponding patient survivals are 0.95 standard risk, 0.88 medium risk

Other EDTA survival tables reveal
Regraft graft survivals EDTA Table 93/9CC
Standard risk patients   0.63   Medium risk patients   0.67

Regraft patient survival (Data received by telephone call)
Standard risk patients   0.95   Medium risk patients   0.85

Three probabilities are entered into the model, patient survival, successful emergence from the post-operative year; the final proportion, for those whose grafts fail early, is then given by the value which makes the sum of the three probabilities equal to one.

These are the best available figures from data obtainable within the time scale of this study.

7.2 Expected life of the graft given its survival past the one year point

For the purposes of this model, an EDTA graft survival table, 93/7C, which included all first grafts performed in the UK between 1978 and 1991 was used. This wide span was felt to be necessary in order to provide age bands of reasonable sample size (particularly at the ten year point after grafting) and, further, in order to split survival rates into three subtables - 15-54s, over 55s, and those with diabetes. The last two groups of patients were to be included in the high risk category of patient. In the event, because of the impact of the results which emerged, the need for the medium risk category arose. Despite this lengthy data time span, only 26 patients in the age range of 65-75 years remain at the nine year point and diabetic numbers run out a year or two earlier.

The data appear in Table 1 and are depicted in Figure 2. Since survival past year 1 is assumed by definition, the data are standardised to the one year point for the subject of this examination. These rates are illustrated in Figure 3.

The expected life of a successful graft for the typical standard risk patient of mean age 38 at the commencement of treatment will be governed by their having spent a typical two years in the waiting pool and undergone a year of post-graft treatment; hence, that patient is by now 41 years of age. The expected life of the graft may be estimated by following the likely progress of a 41 year old, using available graft and patient survival data. Similarly, the expected life of a medium risk patient may be estimated from observing the progress of the typical patient of 50 years of age. However, that patient has already by now spent a total three years in the waiting pool and in the post-graft year. Hence, the progress of a 53 year old will be examined from the point one year after grafting.

The survivals are derived by averaging the patient mortality in each age band from year 2 to year 10 onwards - the high loss in year 1 is taken into account in the one year post-operative stage discussed in the previous section. This series of age-mortality points is fitted to an exponential curve series to project a smooth year by year series of mortality figures. The assumption is made that graft failure may be represented by an additional annual graft failure component which would be different in each age band. This is found by trial and error, matching each age band of the survival rates in EDTA Table 93/7C. A spreadsheet template is then used to estimate the effect of this compound failure pattern along an age trajectory. The expected life is summated as each year passes by simply adding successive annual survivals to compute the area under the survival curve [in fact, the trapezoids under the curve are added].

The progress of the typical 41 year old patient is depicted in Figure 4. **The graft in a standard risk patient is assumed to have an expected life of 11.7 years.** 63% of the total expected life is accounted for in the first ten years. The final 10% of expected life lies in the tail of the curve beyond the age of 61. This value of expected life is almost double the value computed ten years ago from data available at that time.

Similarly, a plot of the progress of the typical **medium-risk patient** starting from first anniversary of their graft at the age of 53 is depicted in Figure 5 - **an expected graft life of 10.1 years is predicted.** 72% of the expected life is accounted for in the first ten years. The survival rates for the adult diabetes closely match those for the 55-64 year old non-diabetic. [If carried out on the older "high-risk patient, the above analysis will show an expected graft life of only 6 years. Virtually all failures in this age range will result from patient death].

Inspection of the survival paths for each of the risk categories reveals why the simpler method of estimating expected life, by eyeballing an appropriate survival line, is a realistic method of estimating graft life. The area under that survival trajectory is the area of a simple triangle of base n years wide and height 1.

The estimation by spreadsheet of the annual renal component also allows estimation of the proportion of graft failures who will return to long term dialysis each year. This proportion may be taken as 0.6 for the standard risk patient and 0.10 for the medium-risk patient.

More than these proportions will return to dialysis from those whose grafts fail in the early years but fewer from failures in the later years. The single value entered into the model, taken at the expected life year, provides a reasonable compromise.

7.3   First year following graft failure and the return to long term dialysis

In the absence of awaited data on these survivals, older data is used. Namely, a first year patient survival of 0.9 is assumed for both early failures (those from the post-operative first year) and for failure to dialysis from the successful graft years. In the absence of more solid data, a survival of 0.85 will be assigned to the medium risk transplant stages.

7.4   The return to long term dialysis after graft failure

The expected life of those whose grafts fail and who after one year return to long term dialysis is discussed at the end of the next section.

In summary they are:-
Standard risk patient; 12.5 years for early graft failures, 7.5 years for late failures
Medium risk patient;   7.5 years for early graft failures, 3.5 years for late failures

Table 1 93/7C includes death with a functioning graft 1st CAD 79-91

						Years					
Age	0	1	2	3	4	5	6	7	8	9	10
35-44	97.8	71.68	67.1	62.4	58.9	55.9	52.8	50.1	47.3	45.00	43.00
45-54	97.7	70.24	65.32	61.3	56.00	52.1	49.06	44.96	41.676	38.577	34.368
55-64	97.8	70.8	65.1	60.00	54.5	50.00	46.00	40.00	36.3	34.9	30.8
65-74	99.2	70.6	65.00	59.7	51.8	47.4	39.6				

standardised values

	0	1	2	3	4	5	6	7	8	9	10
35-44	1	1	.9361	.8705	.8217	.7799	.7366	.6989	.6599	.6278	.5999
45-54	1	1	.9300	.8727	.7973	.7417	.6985	.6401	.5933	.5492	.4893
55-64	1	1	.9195	.8475	.7698	.7062	.6497	.5650	.5127	.4929	.4350
65-74	1	1	.9207	.8456	.7337	.6714	.5609				

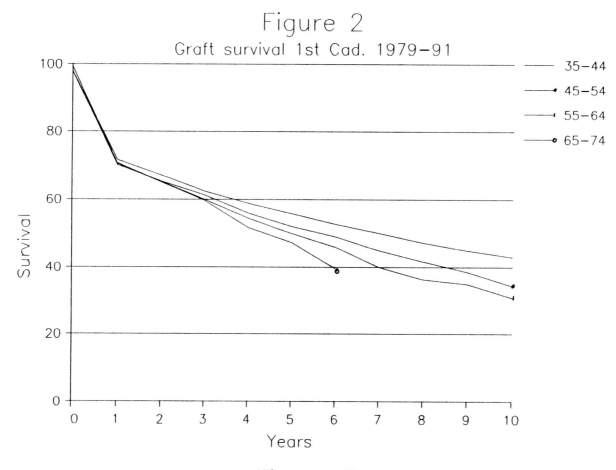

Figure 2
Graft survival 1st Cad. 1979–91

— 35–44
— 45–54
— 55–64
— 65–74

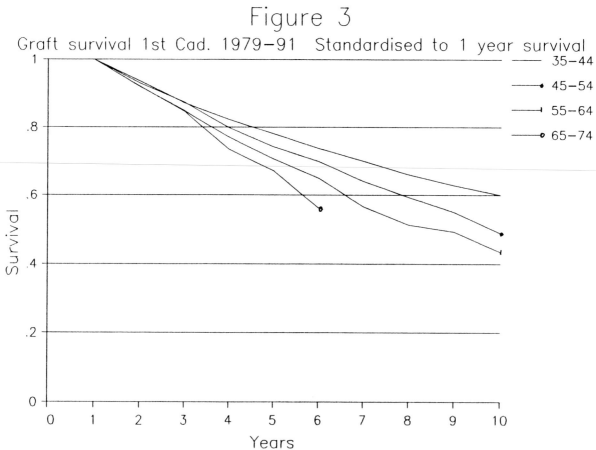

Figure 3
Graft survival 1st Cad. 1979–91 Standardised to 1 year survival

— 35–44
— 45–54
— 55–64
— 65–74

Figure 4
Graft survival 1978-91 data Standard risk

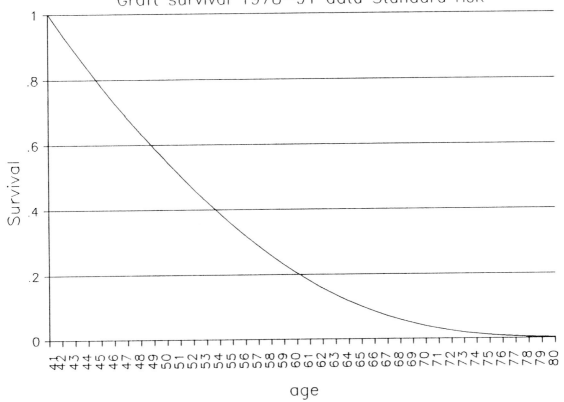

age

Figure 5
Graft Survival 1978-91 data Med risk

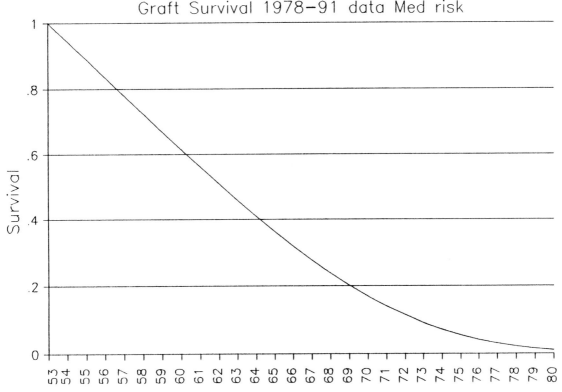

age

7.5 Expected life of patients on dialysis

In the absence of data which present a realistic picture of the survival patterns for those who spend "most of their time" on hospital dialysis or CAPD, the survival table for those starting on ANY treatment is utilised, EDTA Tables 93/4R and 93/4Q. In this table none are deemed to be "lost to follow up" (which tends to distort the survival rate) and patient death defines the end point.

This table includes all forms of HD and PD, and also those who are grafted, so it is not entirely applicable to dialysis only. However, the figures do reflect current therapy practice and their data will be used.

7.6 Survival through the first year in the renal treatment process
1985-89 EDTA data Table 93/4Q

For the patient of typical starting age, one year survival rates are:-

Standard risk   (39 years)   94%
Medium risk   (50 years)   83%   (81% for a 60 yr old, more for the diabetic)
High risk   (65 years)   77%   (Averaging the 55-64 and 65-74 age band first
                                                    year survival values)

7.7 Expected life on long term renal dialysis

Employing similar methods to those used in estimating expected graft life, the annual renal mortality is extracted for each age band. It is then fitted by an exponential curve series to generate a smooth year by year survival pattern. The expected life from any age, given survival to that age (preceded in the model by a one year "change of mode" stage) is then found by setting the survival clock to 1.0 at that age and then depreciating along the age scale. The pictorial effects of this are shown in Figures 6 to 8 for the standard-risk, medium risk and high risk patient.

Standard risk   (now 40 years)   **Expected life 14.3 years**
Medium risk   (now 51 years)   **Expected life 8.6 years**
High risk   (now 66 years)   **Expected life 3.5 years**

Although not strictly directly comparable, the expected life of the standard risk long term dialysis patient is some 50% longer than the value computed 10 years ago.

7.8 Expected life on dialysis following graft failure

Transplantees whose grafts fail after a long success time will start their return to dialysis at a later age. Adding the expected life of the graft (plus the post-operative year) to the mean age at grafting gives an approximation to that new dialysis starting age.

Such calculations then show the standard risk patient who carries a graft successfully for its expected life will have an expected life on dialysis of 12.5 years after failure in the first year of graft [given the successful completion of the first year following graft failure] and 7.5 years from a later failure. Corresponding estimates for the medium risk patient are 7.5 years and 3.5 years, respectively.

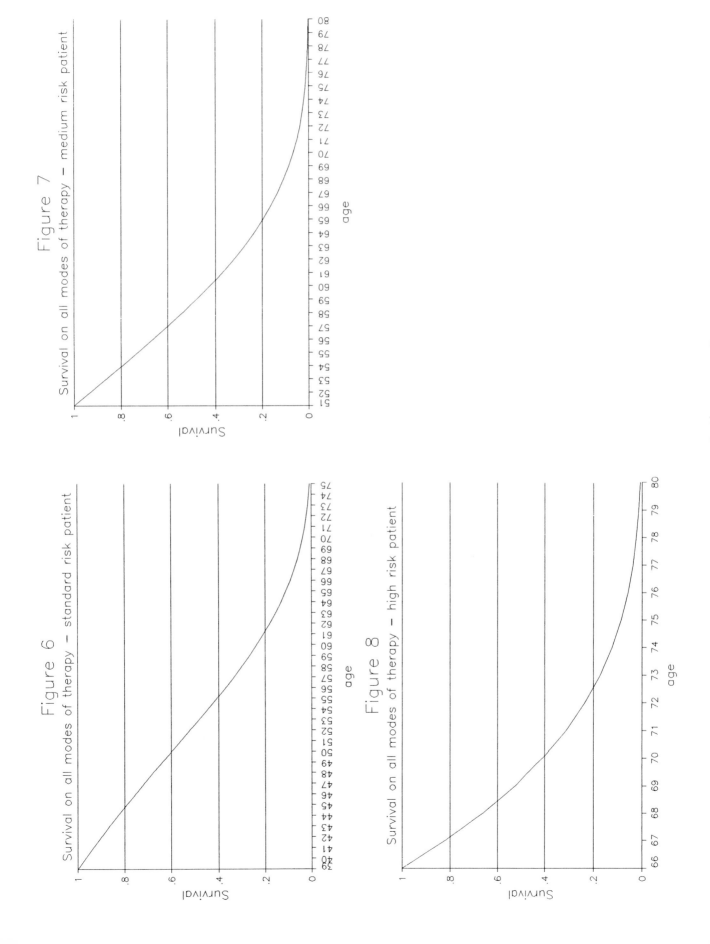

Figure 7

Survival on all modes of therapy — medium risk patient

Figure 6

Survival on all modes of therapy — standard risk patient

Figure 8

Survival on all modes of therapy — high risk patient

8.   Running the model

The appropriate probabilities, for each stream, are inserted into a conventional Markov matrix, which after subtraction from the identity matrix, is inverted to provide steady state numbers of people in each stage of therapy for unit input to that stream. Five such sets of arrays encompass the model and a fundamental Source Array results. From this array, the planning consequences of any set of intake assumptions are easily calculated.

The probabilities inserted into the array cells relating to long expected life spans in a Markov model are usually set at a value relating to the early years on that treatment. This tends to give an unrealistically long value of mean life. In this model, those cells are set to a probability which would produce the expected life previously calculated as described in section 7.

8.1   The format of the output Tableaux

Tableau 1 relates to a model in which no regrafts take place and is included to provide a starting set of figures to which the other tableaux can relate. The numbers in each column refer to the steady-state number of people on the mode of therapy for that column, for unit input per year (1pmp) into that stream.

When a 16% regraft rate is included, the resulting Source Array appears in Tableau 2. It is convenient to lump together some of the detailed stages - for example long term dialysis is given to those who are not grafted and survive the first year, to those whose grafts fail early and who survive that year and to those whose grafts fail late and survive that year. Similarly, it is convenient to group together those who are in a first year of dialysis training - and to aggregate those in the first year following graft failure. These numbers appear in the Aggregated Source Array.

Any planning mix of intake numbers can now be assigned to each stream to give overall steady-state numbers of people on therapy. The resultant array appears in the Standard Intake Array.

An overall Thames Estimate for the Thames regions is given by multiplying the last array by 14.03 million.

Lastly, the numbers of people in each cell of the standard array is presented in percentage terms in the Percentage Distribution Array.

A textual summary at the foot of each tableau provides an easily read statement of the results from above arrays. This concludes by noting that there will also need to be provision for hospital backup   for those with grafts returning to hospital and requiring   dialysis, and for the CAPD patient who may need a temporary stay in hospital.

19

8.2   Justification for the two intake mixes used.

The mix of 35pmp standard risk, 10 pmp medium risk and 25pmp high risk was chosen in order to see how many organs would be needed to satisfy all the candidates who might be considered suitable for grafts - comparing the model with and without regrafts - and to contrast the numbers on dialysis.

For an 80pmp total intake, 34 new organs would satisfy first grafts only for that mix. With a 16% regraft rate, 39 new organs would be required. The greater number of grafts successfully being carried is offset by the smaller number on long term dialysis.

The footnote to this page identifies the need to model intakes of 20 medium risk patients. Even if 5 of these are not grafted, Tableau 3 indicates a need for 43 new organs.

Unfortunately, there is a limited number of organs available in any year and the effect of this is demonstrated in Tableaux 4 and 5, both of which constrain to 30 organs pmp. Tableau 4 takes an input of 10pmp medium risk patients, three quarters of whom are grafted, and 35 high risk; tableau 5 accepts an input of 20 medium risk patients, of whom a little over one half receive grafts, and 25 high risk.

Footnote.

35 pmp of patients between the ages of 15 and under 55, with no complicating conditions, was used when running the model in the eighties. The summary of the questionnaire returns in appendix 1 indicate that, based on age mix, 36.8pmp of the 1992 intake were of that age. Some will be diabetics which will reduce this figure. However without more detailed information on the age structure and eligibility for transplant of the diabetics the figure of 35 pmp will be used as a benchmark intake figure for standard risk patients.

The unit questionnaires reveal that, of the new intake in 1992:
55% were 55 and over; of these 61% were 65 and over
Hence on an age mix basis only,
45% are 15<55, 21% are 55<65 and 34% are 65 and over

Hence the 1992 intake of approximately 80 pmp implies a mix of 35, 17 and 28pmp for the standard, medium and high risk streams - based on age only.

This becomes approximately 35, 25 and 20pmp if a constant 15% proportion of diabetes patients in the younger age group is introduced. However, not all these would be eligible for transplant so the mix chosen for two of the tableaux was

35pmp   standard risk
20pmp   medium risk
25pmp   high risk

The results of this input, together with the effect of a constraint on organs to approximately 30pmp, including 16% used for regrafts, is shown in Tableau 5.

8.3   Discussion on the output from the model

The simplest model, depicted in tableau 1, which excludes regrafts, produces an overall estimate of need for a little under 11,000 people - with the stock in the ratio 45% on transplant to 55% on dialysis.

Tableau 2 reveals that the effect of 16% regrafting is to increase the number on treatment by less than 4%, and to change the stock ratios to 49% on transplant to 51% on dialysis.   However, the significant change has been the increased need for donor organs from 34 to 39.

If the number in the medium risk category doubled, in tableau 3 - to reflect what appears to be happening, the number of organs rises by a further 4 to 43. The total number of people on treatment rises to slightly over 12000 and the stock mix becomes evenly split between those on transplant and those on dialysis.

When the number of organs is constrained to 30, as in the last two tableaux, the stock mix falls away to the more costly 60+% on dialysis with 40-% on transplant, with the total numbers on treatment falling back to 11,600 for the reasonable intake assumption of 35pmp standard risk, 20pmp medium risk and 25pmp high risk.

It must be said that the summary numbers from each tableau are not widely different. The most significant difference lies in the number of donor organs required.   That number is governed by only a small amount of data/assumption error. It is in the realm of hard fact, since the number is derived at an early stage in the treatment process. The overall numbers on treatment must be subject to greater error as a higher proportion of them arises from long term graft survival, or long term dialysis, in the middle and end periods of the process. These numbers will depend upon the validity of the estimated value for expected life and on its holding until steady state. From that point of view, the numbers in the model appear to be saying that 11,500 people will need treatment in steady-state, with a little more stock on dialysis than on transplant - the major variable lies in the number of organs available, and how these will be allocated between the risk groups. Within the dialysis stock, there is a planning decision to be reached regarding the balance achieved between haemodialysis and CAPD.

Appendix 1 reveals that, from the Thames region's questionnaires, the total stock on transplant is 232.6pmp - compared with a tableau 5 estimate of 270.8 with an established graft and 30 at the start of their first year with a transplant.   193.4 are currently on dialysis - compared with 528 at all stages of dialysis in tableau 5. Thus, the Thames regions are at approximately 77% of the transplant and 37% of the dialysis stock levels estimated by the intakes to the model in tableau 5, with its 30 organ constraint.

8.4   Checking the model

It is a relatively straightforward task to check tableau 1, the implementation of the model without regrafts, by calculator. The fact that when the writer did this, towards the end of the project, and found an error, albeit a small one, points to the usefulness of this characteristic of the model. The model had undergone many transformations and such errors are a natural manifestation of their human developers. The fact that it is possible

21

to pick them up at the end stage of the task gives confidence to the use of models allowing some form of simple check.

Each cell in the Source Array in Tableau 1 can be tested by chain multiplying the transfer probabilities out of each stage through the treatment process.

For example, referring to figure 6 and the summary of parameters in section 4.1, for each unit input to stream A, 0.5 enter the first year of grafting after a wait of less than one year in the pool, a further 0.96 x 0.44 will enter after a longer wait; the total entering the graft operation is thus 0.9224; ie for an intake of 28 transplantable patients to that stream 25.827 will receive grafts.

Of the proportion 0.9224 entering the post-operative graft stage, 0.1 will suffer early failure of the graft (0.092 are seen in tableau 1 to be in that stage), and 0.9 of these will require a long term return to dialysis; since the expected life on dialysis after early graft failure is estimated to be 12.5 years, 0.9224 x .1 x .9 x 12.5 = 1.038 are in this stage. In a similar way, all the cells in tableau 1 can be tested.

The addition of regrafts produces too complex an array to test in this manner but having obtained the results for the ungrafted tableau 1, a benchmark set of figures is obtained by which one can sense the validity, or otherwise, of the Source Array in the regraft tableau 2. The remaining tableaux all use the latter source array, only the Standard Intake numbers vary.

8.5   Five yearly projections - 'Winding up' the model

Computationally, there is little problem in projecting a succession of forecast projections for the number of people on treatment between the current year and the time when steady state arises. Equally, the mix of the current stock is available from either the questionnaire or the 1991 EDTA data. However, no entirely satisfactory answer has been found, in the time available, to matching the starting mix on treatment in each of the risk category bands - for the fundamental reason that the model identifies a patient in each risk band by the age at which that patient commenced ESRF treatment, whilst the stock figures from Thames data will relate to the current age of the patient.
It was noted in section 8.3 that the current Thames transplant stock was 77% of the steady state stock predicted in Tableau 5, and the current dialysis stock was 37% of its final number. On the assumption that these ratios are equally distributed across the risk groups, then starting numbers for each mode of therapy for each of the five streams, are inserted into the model which produce those overall proportions at zero time.

The 5, 7, 10 and 15 year projections for total transplant and dialysis numbers, presented as **a percentage of the steady-state total on that therapy** and based upon the standard intake mix of Tableau 5 are then;

Year	% on transplant	% on dialysis
5	84.3%	71.7%
7	86.5%	76.6%
10	89.2%	81.9%
15	92.5%	88.0%

Note:- The numbers entering dialysis receive a boost in the first year only as the new intake arrives.

8.6 Explanation of the abbreviations used in the following tableaux

Intake stream A - standard risk; transplantable
Intake stream B - standard risk; not suitable for transplantation
Intake stream C - medium risk; transplantable
Intake stream D - medium risk; not transplanted
Intake stream E - high risk; not transplanted

The fundamental Source Array - the numbers on treatment resulting from an input of 1 per year. All else is derived from this one array.

The Aggregated Source Array is simply a different summary of the above.
  The 'magnification' is the output/input ratio for each stream.

The Standardised Intake Array C applies the 80pmp in the mix shown at the left hand side to the last array

The Thames Estimate results from multiplying the previous array by the 14.03 million Thames population

The Percentage Distribution gives the mix of the Standardised Intake array in percentage terms

At the bottom is a textual summary in terms of 80pmp on the left and the Thames 14m on the right. It ends with a comment on backup places and assumes 2 weeks per year (ie n/26). These have not entered into any of the previous calculations.

Abbreviations
Dy1/WP1	First year on dialysis/First year in the waiting pool
WP2	Second year in the waiting pool
OpYr NEWtx	Number of people receiving a 1st graft and being in the post-op year
Succ Graft	Number of people carrying a successful graft
FlYr1 longt	Number of people in their first year of rejection after carrying a graft for a long time
LTDy longt	Number on long term dialysis following a late graft failure
FlYr1<1yr	Number of people in their first year of rejection after carrying a graft for less than one year
LTDy <1yr	Number on long term dialysis following an early graft failure
2ndGr	Number entering the second graft stage
LTDy nog	Number on long term dialysis for the not grafted groups

Tableau 1   80 pmp no regrafts   (See top line in each case)
Tableau 2   80 pmp 16% regraft
      these two done to test the number of organs needed
Tableau 3   as 2 but with twice as many medium risk intake
Tableau 4   as 2 but with organs constrained to 30pmp
Tableau 5   as 3 but constrained to 30pmp organ

Tableau 1 No regrafts 35+10+35pmp (0 in D stream)

Source Array

	Dy1/ WP1	WP2	OpYr NEWtx	Succ Graft	F1Yr1 longt	LTDy longt	F1Yr1 <1yr	LTDy <1yr	2ndGr	LTDy nog
A	1.000	0.440	0.922	9.173	0.471	3.177	0.092	1.038	0.000	
B	1.000									13.429
C	1.000	0.350	0.798	6.203	0.061	0.183	0.088	0.559	0.000	
D	1.000									7.155
E	1.000									2.692

Aggregated Source Array

	Dy1/2	OpYr	Carry	Fail1	LTD	Magnification
A	1.44	0.92	9.17	0.56	4.21	16.31
B	1.00				13.43	14.43
C	1.35	0.80	6.20	0.15	0.74	9.24
D	1.00				7.16	8.16
E	1.00				2.69	3.69

Standard Intake Array   35+10+35pmp (0 in D stream)

80pmp 0.8		Dy1	OpYr	Carry	Fail1	LTD
28	A	40.32	25.82	256.8	15.759	118.0
7	B	7				94
10	C	13.5	7.975	62.02	1.4913	7.420
0	D	0				0
35	E	35				94.23

Totals	95.82	33.80	318.8	17.250	313.6	8.134

Thames Estimate

14.03	Dy1	OpYr	Carry	Fail1	LTD		Grand Total
	1344	474	4474	242	4401		10935 people
		TX1	TXsucc			DysTot	
		474	4474			5987.	

Percentage Distribution Array

% distr	Dy1	OpYr	Carry	Fail1	LTD	
	5.2	3.3	33.0	2.0	15.1	
	0.9				12.1	
	1.7	1.0	8.0	0.2	1.0	
	0.0				0.0	total
	4.5				12.1	100
	12.29	4.336	40.91	2.2132	40.24	100
			45.24		54.75	
			TXP%		Dialysis%	

Summary per 80pmp   Thames 14.03

```
33.80 in post-operative year after grafting  (number at start of year)     474
318.8 are carrying a succesful graft                                      4474
17.25 in the first year of dialysis following graft rejection              242

95.82 in the first year of renal treatment on dialysis (at start of year) 1344
      either in the first year of waiting pool or first year of dialysis
313.6 are on long term renal dialysis                                     4401
```

Tableau 2 16% regrafts (in the A stream only)

Source Array

	Dy1/ WP1	WP2	OpYr NEWtx	Succ Graft	FlYr1 longt	LTDy longt	FlYr1 <1yr	LTDy <1yr	2ndGr	LTDy nog
A	1.000	0.440	0.922	10.566	0.542	2.815	0.153	0.764	0.189	
B	1.000									13.429
C	1.000	0.350	0.798	6.203	0.061	0.183	0.088	0.559	0.000	
D	1.000									7.155
E	1.000									2.692

Aggregated Source Array

	Dy1/2	OpYr	Carry	Fail1	LTD	Magnification
A	1.44	1.11	10.57	0.69	3.58	17.39
B	1.00				13.43	14.43
C	1.35	0.80	6.20	0.15	0.74	9.24
D	1.00				7.16	8.16
E	1.00				2.69	3.69

Standard Intake Array 35+10+35pmp (0 in D stream)

80pmp 0.8		Dy1	OpYr	Carry	Fail1	LTD
28	A	40.32	31.11	295.8	19.452	100.1
7	B	7				94
10	C	13.5	7.975	62.02	1.4913	7.420
0	D	0				0
35	E	35				94.23

Totals	Dy1	OpYr	Carry	Fail1	LTD	
	95.82	39.09	357.8	20.944	295.8	8.448

Thames Estimate

14.03	Dy1	OpYr	Carry	Fail1	LTD		Grand Total
	1344	548	5021	294	4151		11358 people
		TX1	TXsucc			DysTot	
		548	5021			5788.	

Percentage Distribution Array

% distr	Dy1	OpYr	Carry	Fail1	LTD		
	5.0	3.8	36.5	2.4	12.4		
	0.9				11.6		
	1.7	1.0	7.7	0.2	0.9		
	0.0				0.0	total	
	4.3				11.6	100	

	Dy1	OpYr	Carry	Fail1	LTD		
	11.83	4.828	44.20	2.5870	36.54	100	
			49.03		50.96		
			TXP%		Dialysis%		

Summary per 80pmp   Thames 14.03

39.09	in post-operative year after grafting (number at start of year)	548
357.8	are carrying a succesful graft	5021
20.94	in the first year of dialysis following graft rejection	294

95.82	in the first year of renal treatment on dialysis (at start of year)	1344
	either in the first year of waiting pool or first year of dialysis	
295.8	are on long term renal dialysis	4151

25

Tableau 3   16% regrafts (in the A stream only)

Source Array

	Dy1/WP1	WP2	OpYr NEWtx	Succ Graft	FlYr1 longt	LTDy longt	FlYr1 <1yr	LTDy <1yr	2ndGr	LTDy nog
A	1.000	0.440	0.922	10.566	0.542	2.815	0.153	0.764	0.189	
B	1.000									13.429
C	1.000	0.350	0.798	6.203	0.061	0.183	0.088	0.559	0.000	
D	1.000									7.155
E	1.000									2.692

Aggregated Source Array

	Dy1/2	OpYr	Carry	Fail1	LTD	Magnification
A	1.44	1.11	10.57	0.69	3.58	17.39
B	1.00				13.43	14.43
C	1.35	0.80	6.20	0.15	0.74	9.24
D	1.00				7.16	8.16
E	1.00				2.69	3.69

Standard Intake Array   35+20+25pmp (5 in D stream)

80pmp 0.8		Dy1	OpYr	Carry	Fail1	LTD
28	A	40.32	31.11	295.8	19.452	100.1
7	B	7				94
15	C	20.25	11.96	93.04	2.2369	11.13
5	D	5				35.77
25	E	25				67.30

Totals		Dy1	OpYr	Carry	Fail1	LTD	
		97.57	43.08	388.8	21.689	308.4	8.810

Thames Estimate

14.03	Dy1	OpYr	Carry	Fail1	LTD		Grand Total
	1369	604	5456	304	4327		12060 people
		TX1	TXsucc			DysTot	
		604	5456			6000.	

Percentage Distribution Array

% distr	Dy1	OpYr	Carry	Fail1	LTD		
	4.7	3.6	34.4	2.3	11.7		
	0.8				10.9		
	2.4	1.4	10.8	0.3	1.3		
	0.6				4.2	total	
	2.9				7.8	100	
	11.35	5.011	45.23	2.5231	35.87	100	
			50.25		49.74		
			TXP%		Dialysis%		

Summary per 80pmp   Thames 14.03

43.08 in post-operative year after grafting (number at start of year)	604
388.8 are carrying a succesful graft	5456
21.68 in the first year of dialysis following graft rejection	304

97.57 in the first year of renal treatment on dialysis (at start of year)	1369
either in the first year of waiting pool or first year of dialysis	
308.4 are on long term renal dialysis	4327

Tableau 4   16% regrafts (in the A stream only)

Source Array

	Dy1/ WP1	WP2	OpYr NEWtx	Succ Graft	FlYr1 longt	LTDy longt	FlYr1 <1yr	LTDy <1yr	2ndGr	LTDy nog
A	1.000	0.440	0.922	10.566	0.542	2.815	0.153	0.764	0.189	
B	1.000									13.429
C	1.000	0.350	0.798	6.203	0.061	0.183	0.088	0.559	0.000	
D	1.000									7.155
E	1.000									2.692

Aggregated Source Array

	Dy1/2	OpYr	Carry	Fail1	LTD	Amplification
A	1.44	1.11	10.57	0.69	3.58	17.39
B	1.00				13.43	14.43
C	1.35	0.80	6.20	0.15	0.74	9.24
D	1.00				7.16	8.16
E	1.00				2.69	3.69

Standard Intake Array   35+10+35pmp   (2.32 in D stream)   30 organs

		Dy1	OpYr	Carry	Fail1	LTD
0.8						
21.49	A	30.94	23.88	227.0	14.930	76.90
13.51	B	13.51				181.4
7.68	C	10.36	6.124	47.63	1.1453	5.699
2.32	D	2.32				16.6
35	E	35				94.23
Totals		92.14	30.00	274.7	16.075	374.8

8.549

Thames Estimate

	Dy1	OpYr	Carry	Fail1	LTD		Grand Total
14.03	1293	421	3854	226	5259		11052 people
	TX1	TXsucc			DysTot		
	421	3854			6777.		

Percentage Distribution Array

% distrbn.	Dy1	OpYr	Carry	Fail1	LTD	total
	3.9	3.0	28.8	1.9	9.8	
	1.7				23.0	
	1.3	0.8	6.0	0.1	0.7	
	0.3				2.1	total
	4.4				12.0	100
	11.69	3.809	34.87	2.0405	47.58	100
		38.67			61.32	
		TXP%			Dialysis%	

Summary per 80pmp (typical distribution)   Thames 14.03

30.00 in post-operative year after grafting (number at start of year)   421
274.7 are carrying a succesful graft   3854
16.07 in the first year of dialysis following graft rejection   226

92.14 in the first year of renal treatment on dialysis (at start of year) 1293
       either in the first year of waiting pool or first year of dialysis
374.8 are on long term renal dialysis   5259

Tableau 5   16% regrafts (in the A stream only)

Source Array

	Dy1/ WP1	WP2	OpYr NEWtx	Succ Graft	FlYr1 longt	LTDy longt	FlYr1 <1yr	LTDy <1yr	2ndGr	LTDy nog
A	1.000	0.440	0.922	10.566	0.542	2.815	0.153	0.764	0.189	
B	1.000									13.429
C	1.000	0.350	0.798	6.203	0.061	0.183	0.088	0.559	0.000	
D	1.000									7.155
E	1.000									2.692

Aggregated Source Array

	Dy1/2	OpYr	Carry	Fail1	LTD	Amplification
A	1.44	1.11	10.57	0.69	3.58	17.39
B	1.00				13.43	14.43
C	1.35	0.80	6.20	0.15	0.74	9.24
D	1.00				7.16	8.16
E	1.00				2.69	3.69

Standard Intake Array   35+20+25pmp (9.55 in D stream) 30 organs

		Dy1	OpYr	Carry	Fail1	LTD
0.8						
19.5	A	28.08	21.67	206.0	13.547	69.78
15.5	B	15.5				208.1
10.45	C	14.10	8.333	64.81	1.5584	7.754
9.55	D	9.55				68.33
25	E	25				67.30

Totals	Dy1	OpYr	Carry	Fail1	LTD	
	92.23	30.00	270.8	15.105	421.3	8.993

Thames Estimate

14.03	Dy1	OpYr	Carry	Fail1	LTD	Grand Total
	1294	421	3800	212	5911	11638 people
		TX1	TXsucc		DysTot	
		421	3800		7417.	

Percentage Distribution Array

% distrbn.	Dy1	OpYr	Carry	Fail1	LTD	
	3.4	2.6	24.8	1.6	8.4	
	1.9				25.1	
	1.7	1.0	7.8	0.2	0.9	
	1.2				8.2	total
	3.0				8.1	100
	11.11	3.617	32.65	1.8210	50.79	100
		36.26			63.73	
		TXP%			Dialysis%	

Summary per 80pmp (typical distribution)   Thames 14.03

30.00	in post-operative year after grafting (number at start of year)	421
270.8	are carrying a succesful graft	3800
15.10	in the first year of dialysis following graft rejection	212

92.23	in the first year of renal treatment on dialysis (at start of year)	1294
	either in the first year of waiting pool or first year of dialysis	
421.3	are on long term renal dialysis	5911

Appendix 1

Mean age of NEW patients and percentage aged 55 and over

| | 1991 | | | | | 1992 | | | | |
| | 15-55 | | >55 | | | 15-55 | | >55 | | |
	N	age	N	age	% >55	N	age	N	age	% >55
Guy's Adult	52	35.8	34	68.5	39.5	41	34.6	57	67.2	58.2
St Helier	45	39.3	36	66.4	44.4	50	40.8	60	71.3	54.5
Royal London	41	37.3	51	65.7	55.4	53	39.6	61	66.7	53.5
Charing Cross	30	38.7	29	68.3	49.2	25	35.2	45	73.8	67.1
K&C	17	40	22	67.7	56.4	24	40	29	65.9	54.7
Roy Free - incompatible age-bands										
Barts	29	39.7	39	66.9	57.4	32	40.9	40	64.8	55.6
Lister	17	41.2	24	70.8	58.5	24	42.1	20	63.5	45.5
Roy Sussex	22	36.8	38	67.1	63.3	32	37.5	31	68.1	49.2
St George's	12	42.5	14	65.7	53.8	15	40.7	23	67.8	60.5
St Thomas'	16	41.3	24	66.7	60.0	24	39.6	23	68.7	48.9
King's	22	40.5	26	68.8	54.2	36	41.1	37	71.6	50.7
Hammersmith	33	37.9	25	65.6	43.1	32	38.4	30	65.7	48.4
St Mary's	49	37.6	47	66.2	49.0	40	41.5	65	67.4	61.9
St Peter's	23	37.8	34	67.1	59.6	40	36.5	42	67.9	51.2
overall	N		N		%>55	N		N		%>55
	408		443		52.1	468		563		54.6
	av age 38.45		av age 67.13			av age= 39.12		av age 68.16		
	+68 RFree		Tot N= 919			+65 RFree+41Southend Tot N= 1137 **81.04pmp**				

Mean age of Stock and percentage aged 55 and over

| | Transplants | | | | | Dialysis | | | | |
| | 15-55 | | >55 | | | 15-55 | | >55 | | |
	N	age	N	age	% >55	N	age	N	age	% >55
Guy's Adult (91+92)	92	37.49	44	62.95	32.4					
St Helier all	168	39.5	80	63.3	32.3	52	40.94	114	67.9	68.7
Royal London	214	38.7	100	62.2	31.8	122	41	150	66.1	55.1
Charing Cross	123	41.8	45	62.2	26.8	97	40	133	68.5	57.8
K&C	72	38.5	18	65.6	20.0	53	41.1	77	66.8	59.2
Roy Free - incompatible age-bands										
Barts	167	41.2	102	62.5	37.9	119	40.6	120	65.3	50.2
Lister	10	39	11	61.8	52.4	62	40.6	81	68.5	56.6
Roy Sussex	96	37.5	49	61.8	33.8	49	41.6	90	69.1	64.7
St Georges	12	40.8	1	60	7.7	18	43.3	32	66.6	64.0
St Thomas'	110	41.5	64	63.8	36.8	71	41.84	92	66.85	56.4
King's	229	40.8	126	65.8	35.5	57	39.61	90	68.75	61.2
Hammersmith	164	40.5	66	62.7	28.7	66	42.1	57	66.1	46.3
St Mary's	195	40.4	61	62	23.8	85	39.91	141	67.7	62.4
St Peter's	139	40.9	60	64	30.2	107	39.3	100	67.9	48.3
overall	N		N		%>55	N		N		%>55
	1791		827		31.6	958		1277		57.1
	av age 40.06		av age 63.25			av age= 40.67		av age 67.41		
	+340 at RFree + 306 more at Guys					+192Guys+176RFree+58Southend				
	total N= 3264					total N= 2713				
or	**232.6pmp**					**or**	**193.4pmp**			

Diabetes intake as a %	1991 New	1992 New	Stock TXP	Dialysis Combined	or Split HD	HHD	CAPD
Guy's Adult	n/a	n/a	n/a	n/a			
St Helier	n/a	n/a	n/a		8%		25%
Royal London	19.6%	9.6%	6.7%	13.6%			
Charing Cross			22%	28%			
K&C			6%	15%			
Roy Free - incompatible age-bands			4.1%		4.2%		26%
Barts	17.7%	25%			8.3%		20.2%
Lister	7%	6%	14%	9%			
St George's	23%	13%	23.8% txp + dialysis				
St Thomas'	23%	17%					
King's			16%		15%		12%
Hammersmith (tx n/a)	23%	21%		19.5%			
St Mary's	11%	21%	4%		12%		25%
St Peter's	5.3%	11%	4.5%	8.2%			

29

EDTA analysis of stock in the Thames' regions 1991

NWT	HD	HHD	CAPD	IPD	TXP	TOTAL
children	0	1	0	0	9	10
15-55	117	48	142	0	496	803
55+	112	16	174	2	75	379
total	229	65	316	2	580	1192
diab15-54	11	1	30	0	32	74
diab>54.9	14	0	34	0	9	57
hence:-						
std-risk	106	47	112	0	464	729
hi-risk	123	17	204	2	107	453

NET						
children	4	0	3	0	51	58
15-55	76	59	92	3	457	687
55+	40	6	114	0	62	222
total	120	65	209	3	570	967
diab15-54	5	0	17	1	19	42
diab>54.9	3	0	13	0	4	20
hence:-						
std-risk	71	59	75	2	438	645
hi-risk	45	6	131	1	81	264

SET						
children	14	2	5	4	142	167
15-55	50	56	53	0	428	587
55+	62	10	73	2	72	219
total	126	68	131	6	642	973
diab15-54	6	1	15	0	21	43
diab>54.9	3	1	11	2	3	20
hence:-						
std-risk	44	55	38	0	407	544
hi-risk	68	11	88	2	93	262

SWT						
children	0	0	0	0	1	1
15-55	2	0	11	0	6	19
55+	1	0	17	0	0	18
total	3	0	28	0	7	38
diab15-54	0	0	3	0	0	3
diab>54.9	0	0	4	0	0	4
hence:-						
std-risk	2	0	8	0	6	16
hi-risk	1	0	20	0	0	21

All Thames	HD	HHD	CAPD	IPD	TXP	TOTAL
children	18	3	8	4	203	236
15-55	245	163	298	3	1387	2096
55+	215	32	378	4	209	838
total	478	198	684	11	1799	3170
tot adults	460	195	676	7	1596	2934
diab15-54	22	2	65	1	72	162
diab>54.9	20	1	62	2	16	101
hence:-						
std-risk	223	161	233	2	1315	1934
hi-risk	237	34	443	5	281	1000

30

CONFIDENTIAL

RENAL TRANSPLANTATION CENTRES IN THE THAMES REGIONS

Note for the London Renal Services Review Group.

SUMMARY

This paper summarises activity and outcome data for the 13 NHS centres carrying out adult cadaveric renal transplantation in the Thames regions. It also draws on national audit data to examine whether outcome is related to centre size : no such relationship was found.

The paper concludes that 4 to 5 centres would be sufficient, but the data does not in itself determine which these centres should be.

INTRODUCTION

At an earlier meeting, the London Renal Services review group discussed the arrangements for renal transplantaion in the four Thames regions, and decided tentatively that it would be advantageous to concentrate this work into a much smaller number of centres, so as to:-

a)   avoid single-handed working, and facilitate cross-cover,

b)   achieve substantial economies of scale,

c)   enhance the excellence of academic/research centres,

d)   perhaps improve outcome, if (as many believe) bigger centres are more likely to achieve better results,

e)   enable rational coordination and oversight of other renal services within defined catchment areas.

We were asked to examine available data bearing on these points.

There are two main sources of data, viz

a)   the replies to the questionnaire sent out by the group,
and
b)   routine returns to the United Kingdom Transplant Support Service Authority (UKTSSA). By good fortune, some of the UKTSSA data is currently being analysed in a national audit of renal transplantation in conjunction with the British Transplantation Society, (BTS) and on behalf of the Directors of Renal Transplant Units throughout the UK to whom we are grateful for permission to draw extensively on this as-yet unpublished material. (Note: The national audit data (eg relating to outcomes) are confidential and will be published only with the identities of the centres in coded form. The Thames region centres have all agreed that their data).

can be disclosed to the review group, so this paper includes a key to the audit codes and lists these centres by name rather than by code.

The data have been examined for the review group by Mark Belger and Rachel Bawden of UKTSSA, to whom we are grateful for Annexes 1 - 4, on which foundation these comments are based. There are a number of discrepancies between the questionnaire data and that from UKTSSA, mostly fairly minor for the present purpose. Moreover, the UKTSSA data for some London centres, notably Dulwich/Kings, is unsatisfactory because for historical reasons these centres have not participated fully in the national kidney sharing scheme nor in the collection of data. Annex 5, a draft of the BTS/UKTSSA national audit, includes at Tables 4.1 and 4.2 a summary of the proportion of grafts for which follow-up data is not available; the worst (highest) figures relate to 3 centres in the South Thames regions.

ADULT CADAVERIC TRANSPLANTS IN NHS CENTRES

There are at present 13 NHS centres engaged in adult renal cadaveric transplantation in the Thames regions, as follows -

Table 1

NHS CENTRES FOR ADULT RENAL TRANSPLANTATION IN THE THAMES REGIONS

Geographical region	Centre	Average Annual Transplants 1990 - 1992
NW Thames	St. Mary's	44
	Charing Cross	19
	Hammersmith	32
NE Thames	Royal Free	40
	St. Pauls/St Peter's (Middlesex)	26
	St. Bartholemew's	27
	Royal London	43
SE Thames	Brighton	30
	Canterbury	16
	St. Thomas'	20
	Dulwich / Kings	73
	Guys	66
SW Thames	Carshalton	49
TOTAL		485

(Source : Annex 1 Table 2.1)

Of these Brighton started in 1988 and Carshalton in 1986, Kings transferred to Dulwich in 198 while Canterbury started transplanting in 1988 but has now transferred this work to Guys.

OTHER RENAL TRANSPLANTS

Apart from the transplant activity summarised in Table 1, three other aspects of transplantation should be mentioned, viz children (Table 2), non-NHS hospitals (Table 3), and live related donor transplants (Table 4). These aspects are not considered further in this paper.

Table 2   CHILDREN

Centre	Total cadaveric renal transplants ages 0 -18, 1981 - 1991
St. Mary's	6
Charing Cross	1
Hammersmith	4
Royal Free	113
St. Pauls/St Peter's	2
St. Bartholemew's	5
Royal London	5
Brighton	1
Canterbury	0
St. Thomas'	2
Dulwich / Kings	13
Guys	240
Carshalton	2
Great Ormond Street	22
TOTAL	416

(Source Annex 2 Table 13.2(L)

Table 3   RENAL TRANSPLANTS IN NON-NHS CENTRES IN THAMES REGIONS

Centre	No of transplants
Cromwell	?
London Bridge	17
St. John & St. Elizabeth	5
Total	?

Note: The 22 transplants shown above were all carried out on overseas patients

Table 4   LIVE DONOR RENAL TRANSPLANTS IN NHS UNITS

Centre	Total live donors 1990 - 1992
St. Mary's	3
Charing Cross	7
Hammersmith	9
Royal Free	14
St. Pauls/St Peter's	16
St. Bartholemew's	6
Royal London	8
Brighton	14
Canterbury	2
St. Thomas'	11
Dulwich / Kings	1
Guys	17
Carshalton	2
TOTAL	110

(Source: Annex 1 Table 2.1)

ACTIVITY RELATED TO POPULATION

It is difficult to relate the figures for transplant activity to catchement populations in a meaningful way because of cross-flows within the Thames regions and more widely. South East and South West are in any case taken together, by agreement.

Table 5   RENAL TRANSPLANTATION RELATED TO POPULATION

Region	Population (millions)	Transplants (from table 1)	Transplants million
NW Th	3.47	95	27
NE Th	3.78	136	36
SE Th) SW Th)	6.61	254	38
TOTAL	13.86	485	35

If related to population over 16, rather than total population, the total figure becomes 44 transplants/million.

The national figure is approximately 29 transplants/million. To illustrate the extent of cross-boundary flows, Tables 4.3 and 4.4 of Annex 1 show different centres' stock of transplant recipients by region of residence.

CASE MIX

Age (leaving aside children):

Some centres appear to accept a higher proportion of older patients for transplantation. Table 13.2 of Annex 5 shows a range of <1% (Charing Cross) to 11% (Dulwich) in patients over 65 (the national average being 3%, see table 13.1 of Annex 5). Somewhat similar figures relating to patient stock are in Table 4.1 of Annex 1, and again Dulwich is shown as having proportionately more older patients.

Ethnicity

Table 4.2 of Annex 1 shows the ethnic mix of centres' patient stock. Three centres (Charing Cross, Dulwich, and St. Mary's,) report over 20% of non-white recipients; St. Mary's in particular reports 24% Asian, 4% Afro-Caribbean and 3% Other. The national figure, and the Thames region average, are not available.

Diabetes

Table 5.1 of Annex 1 shows the proportions of diabetic patients reported by centres; again Dulwich and Charing Cross stand out with 16% and 13% diabetics respectively. Diabetes is also listed in Table 12.2(L) of Annex 2 among the primary diseases of recipients; St. Thomas' (10%) and Hammersmith (9%) contrast most strongly with the national figure of 4%.

Other Factors

Other information reported re primary renal disease is not particularly helpful because such a high proportion of cases (circa 70%) is returned as unspecified/uncertain or other.

Kidney Retrieval

The numbers of kidneys retrieved over the years 1990 -1992 are shown in the questionnaires returned by centres, see Table 2.1 of Annex 1, and see also table A.2.1(L) of Annex 2. It is difficult to relate these figures to catchment populations because -

- catchment populations for calculating retrieval are not the same as those for transplantation
- the South Thames figures are pooled because kidney retrieval is organised on a regional rota system. Kidneys cannot be sensibly assigned to a given unit within SE or SW Thames.

Table 6   KIDNEY RETRIEVAL RELATED TO POPULATION (1989-1991)

Region	Population (millions)	Kidneys retrieved per annum	Retrievals/million
NW Th	3.16	98	31
NE Th	4.08	123	30
SE Th)			
SW TH)	6.27	190	30
TOTAL	13.51	411	30

(Source UKTSSA Annual Report 1991/92)

The national figure is approximately 31 retrievals/million.

WAITING LISTS AND PATIENT STOCK

Data on waiting lists is considered in section 7 of Annex 5, the national audit, and the relevant figures for London centres are extracted at Table 7.1(L) of Annex 2. As the discussion in Annex 5 shows, these figures are not always comparable because of the varying use of the 'suspended' category. Also, the figures do not indicate the proportion of dialysis patients on the transplant waiting list. There may be considerable variation between centres.

Additions to and removals from the waiting list are illustrated in Figures 7.4 and 7.2 of Annex 5, and numbers of those currently being followed up are in Table 2.1 of Annex 1.

These figures have not been analysed in detail nor related to catchment populations.

OUTCOME OF TRANSPLANTATION

For the first time, the national audit examines the outcomes of transplantation by centre over a ten-year period to 1991. Please see section 9 of Annex 5 for the full information in coded form. With the permission of the centres concerned, the Thames regions data is extracted (with a confidential key to the identity of the centres) as Annex 3 to this paper. Confidence limits are fairly wide, but it appears that there are some significant differences between centres. For example, in recent years (1987-1991) the one-year graft survival estimate at Charing Cross is 73%, and at the Royal London 94%. Similarly when one considers one year patient survival the figures range from 79% (Guys) and 96% (St Bartholomews) see Table 9.2(L) in annex 3. All these are of course crude figures, not corrected for age, ethnicity or other aspect of patient mix. We consider the figures are too small to allow for multifactorial analysis of the Thames data.

EFFECT OF CENTRE SIZE

In an attempt to see whether some of the diferences in outcome is related to the size of the centre (ie, the number of transplants carried out there), Mark Belger and Rachel Bawden have examined the national data taking into account other potentially significant factors such as donor age and closeness of match. Please see Annex 4 for their analysis, which concludes that from this data there is no evidence to suggest that the average number of transplants performed bears any relation to the oucome of the graft, nor to patient survival.

USE OF RESOURCES

We do not know the relative costs of transplantation at different centres, and have found it impracticable from the questionnaire returns to determine the numbers of nurses devoted to transplantation as contrasted with renal work generally. The questonnaires do however list (in Table 1.1 of Annex 1) the sessions spent by nephrologists, consultant surgeons, and other medical grades in the centres, and these can be crudely related to transplant activity as follows:

Table 7   MEDICAL STAFFING RELATED TO TRANSPLANT ACTIVITY

Centre	Transplants per session (nephrology)	Transplant persession (surgeon)
St. Mary's	1.3	2.6
Charing Cross	0.5	6.3
Hammersmith	0.9	3.2
Royal Free		3.5
St. Pauls/St Peter's	0.8	2.6
St. Bartholemew's	0.8	
Royal London	1.9	6.1
Brighton	1.4	15.
Canterbury	0.7	
St. Thomas'	0.7	
Dulwich / Kings	2.2	6.6
Guys	1.5	6.0
Carshalton		

(Source: Table 1; Annex 1 table 1.1)

Note: Staffing figures of this kind are notoriously unreliable as indicators of workload.

HOW MANY CENTRES ARE NEEDED ?

The Renal Association suggests one Renal Transplant Unit per 1 to 3 million population. Using the top end of this range, ie favouring bigger units, for a population of 13.86 million, would suggest five units are needed. (The bottom end of the range of course suggests 14 units.)

The present average annual transplant activity (from Table 1) of 485 transplants, if divided between five centres, would give around 100 transplants/centre/year --- which figure is regularly exceeded in Manchester and Dublin, and sometimes in Leeds and Newcastle too.

Although some have postulated that the overall level of transplants required maybe as high as 50 per million population (as compared to the London figure of 35 per million population) it is probably more realistic to expect the ceiling set by donor availability and other constraints to be nearer to 40 per million population. On this basis 5 centres would on average each need to undertake 110 transplant per year. Hence it seems to us reasonable to conclude that 4 to 5 centres could properly cope with the predictable London workload.

CONCLUSION

The available data on activity and outcomes do not point firmly towards any single solution, nor to the elimination of any particular centre(s). They are consistent with concentration of renal transplant work in the Thames regions into, say, 5 centres suitably disposed geographically. The resource savings would be considerable but there is nothing in these data to suggest that transplantation outcomes would be better or worse.

ACKNOWLEDGEMENTS

We are grateful to Mark Belger and Rachel Bawden at UKTSSA for annexes 1-4, on which these commets are based, and particularly for their analysis of patient and graft survival related to centre size, Annex 4.

[We also wish to thank Professor M McKeown, Mr D Briggs, and Professor P Morris for their helpful comments, and the British Transplantation Society and the Directors of Renal Transplant units in the UK for permission to draw extensively on their as yet unpublished audit material.

LIST OF ANNEXES

This annex comprises information extracted from the London renal services review questionnaire.

Table 1.1 gives information concerning medical staff levels at each centre.

Table 2.1 considers recent transplant activity and follow-up.

Tissue typing laboratories are named for each centre in Table 3.1, and Table 3.2 gives the location of the transplant co-ordinators associated with each unit.

Table 4.1 gives the age/sex breakdown of each centre's stock of transplant recipients, Table 4.2 gives their ethnicity and Tables 4.3 and 4.4 show the region of residence for transplant recipients in each centre.

Finally Table 5.1 shows the percentage of transplant patients at each centre who are diabetic.

It should be noted that a dash (-) represents information which is unclear or missing from the questionnaire.

NUMBER OF MEDICAL STAFF AT EACH RENAL TRANSPLANT CENTRE IN THE THAMES REGIONS AS REPORTED IN THE LONDON RENAL SERVICES REVIEW QUESTIONNAIRE

CENTRE	STAFF	NUMBER	NUMBER OF SESSIONS
St Mary's	Consultant Nephrologists	4	35
	Consultant Surgeon	3	17
	Other Grades	8	–
Charing Cross	Consultant Nephrologists	4	42
	Consultant Surgeon	3	3
	Other Grades	6	–
Hammersmith	Consultant Nephrologists	4	35
	Consultant Surgeon	3	10
	Other Grades	7	77
Royal Free	Consultant Nephrologists	3	–
	Consultant Surgeon	1	11/12
	Other Grades	7	–
St Paul's/St Peter's	Consultant Nephrologists	3	31
	Consultant Surgeon	1	10
	Other Grades	8	–
St Bartholomew's	Consultant Nephrologists	3	32
	Consultant Surgeon	1	–
	Other Grades	9	90
Royal London	Consultant Nephrologists	3	23
	Consultant Surgeon	1	7
	Other Grades	8	–
Brighton	Consultant Nephrologists	2	21
	Consultant Surgeon	1	2
	Other Grades	3	33

CENTRE	STAFF	NUMBER	NUMBER OF SESSIONS
Canterbury	Consultant Nephrologists	2	22
	Consultant Surgeon	0	–
	Other Grades	4+	–
St Thomas'	Consultant Nephrologists	3	30
	Consultant Surgeon	0	–
	Other Grades	6	–
Dulwich/King's	Consultant Nephrologists	3	33
	Consultant Surgeon	1	11
	Other Grades	7	–
Guy's (Adults)	Consultant Nephrologists	4	44
	Consultant Surgeon	1	11
	Other Grades	9	–
Guy's (Paeds)	Consultant Nephrologists	4	44
	Consultant Surgeon	1	3
	Other Grades	4	44
Carshalton	Consultant Nephrologists	2	–
	Consultant Surgeon	1	–
	Other Grades	8	–

TRANSPLANT ACTIVITY AT RENAL TRANSPLANT CENTRES IN THE THAMES REGIONS AS REPORTED IN THE LONDON RENAL SERVICES REVIEW QUESTIONNAIRE 1 JANUARY 1990 - 31 DECEMBER 1992

CENTRE		YEAR			TOTAL
		1990	1991	1992	
St Mary's	Patients transplanted	51	35	46	132
	Live Donors				3
	Cadaver Donors				99
	Kidneys retrieved		44	44	88
	Follow-up				
	- Total survivors				263
	- Currently followed				263
	- Followed at other centres				0
Charing Cross	Patients transplanted	21	20	16	57
	Live Donors				7
	Cadaver Donors				50
	Kidneys retrieved		10	10	20
	Follow-up				
	- Total survivors				-
	- Currently followed				168
	- Followed at other centres				0
Hammersmith	Patients transplanted	31	45	21	97
	Live Donors				9
	Cadaver Donors				88
	Kidneys retrieved		44	32	76
	Follow-up				
	- Total survivors				333
	- Currently followed				230
	- Followed at other centres				103
Royal Free	Patients transplanted	47	53	41	121
	Live Donors	7	1	6	14
	Cadaver Donors	40	32	35	107
	Kidneys retrieved		18	22	40
	Follow-up				
	- Total survivors				340
	- Currently followed				352
	- Followed at other centres				7
St Paul's/St Peter's	Patients transplanted	30	20	29	79
	Live Donors				16
	Cadaver Donors				63
	Kidneys retrieved		6	19	25
	Follow-up				
	- Total survivors				199
	- Currently followed				199
	- Followed at other centres				0
St Bartholomew's	Patients transplanted	28	34	19	81
	Live Donors				6
	Cadaver Donors		29	10	75
	Kidneys retrieved				39
	Follow-up				
	- Total survivors				269
	- Currently followed				269
	- Followed at other centres				2

CENTRE		YEAR			TOTAL
		1990	1991	1992	
Royal London	Patients transplanted	52	28	49	129
	Live Donors				8
	Cadaver Donors				121
	Kidneys retrieved	52	33	47	132
	Follow-up				
	- Total survivors				111
	- Currently followed				320
	- Followed at				
	other centres				10
					(approx)
Brighton	Patients transplanted	24	29	38	91
	Live Donors				14
	Cadaver Donors				78
	Kidneys retrieved				6
	Follow-up				
	- Total survivors				138
	- Currently followed				138
	- Followed at				
	other centres				0
Canterbury	Patients transplanted	17	20	10	47
	Live Donors				2
	Cadaver Donors				45
	Kidneys retrieved				-
	Follow-up				
	- Total survivors				122
	- Currently followed				90
	- Followed at				
	other centres				32
St Thomas'	Patients transplanted	25	19	17	61
	Live Donors				11
	Cadaver Donors				50
	Kidneys retrieved				-
	Follow-up				
	- Total survivors				168
	- Currently followed				168
	- Followed at				
	other centres				<5
Dulwich/King's	Patients transplanted	79	67	74	220
	Live Donors				1
	Cadaver Donors				219
	Kidneys retrieved				220 (+75)
	Follow-up				
	- Total survivors				379
	- Currently followed				355
	- Followed at				
	other centres				24
Guy's	Patients transplanted	62	87	50	199
	Live Donors				17
	Cadaver Donors				182
	Kidneys retrieved		210	200	410
	Follow-up				
	- Total survivors				-
	- Currently followed				442
	- Followed at				
	other centres				57

CENTRE		YEAR			TOTAL
		1990	1991	1992	
Guy's (Paeds)	Patients transplanted	12	21	13	46
	Live Donors				3
	Cadaver Donors				43
	Kidneys retrieved				–
	Follow-up				
	- Total survivors				–
	- Currently followed				83
	- Followed at				
	other centres				–
Carshalton	Patients transplanted	50	41	57	148
	Live Donors				2
	Cadaver Donors				148
	Kidneys retrieved				55
	Follow-up				
	- Total survivors				260
	- Currently followed				250
	- Followed at				
	other centres				10

TISSUE TYPING LABORATORIES FOR ALL THAMES RENAL TRANSPLANT CENTRES AS REPORED IN THE LONDON RENAL SERVICES REVIEW QUESTIONNAIRE

CENTRE	TISSUE TYPING LABORATORY
St Mary's	St Mary's
Charing Cross	Dept of Immunology of Rheumatic Diseases
Hammersmith	RPMS
Royal Free	Dedicated Renal Unit Lab
St Paul's/St Peter's	St Peter's
St Bartholomew's	Royal London
Royal London	London Hospital Medical College
Brighton	Guy's
Canterbury	Guy's
St Thomas'	Guy's
Dulwich/King's	Guy's
Guy's	Guy's
Guy's (Paed.s)	SE Thames Regional Unit
Carshalton	Guy's

TRANSPLANT CO-ORDINATOR CENTRE FOR ALL THAMES RENAL TRANSPLANT UNITS, AS REPORTED IN THE LONDON RENAL SERVICES REVIEW QUESTIONNAIRE

CENTRE	TRANSPLANT CO-ORDINATOR CENTRE
St Mary's	NW Thames RHA
Charing Cross	NW Thames RHA
Hammersmith	SHA
Royal Free	-
St Paul's/St Peter's	NE Thames RHA
St Bartholomew's	NE Thames RHA
Royal London	-
Brighton	-
Canterbury	-
St Thomas'	-
Dulwich/King's	S Thames RHA (King's)
Guy's	King's/Dulwich
Guy's (Paed.s)	SE Thames RHA
Carshalton	SE/SW Thames RHA

STOCK OF TRANSPLANT RECIPIENTS FOR EACH RENAL TRANSPLANT CENTRE IN THE THAMES REGIONS BY RECIPIENT AGE AND SEX, AS REPORTED IN THE LONDON RENAL SERVICES REVIEW QUESTIONNAIRE

CENTRE	SEX	AGE OF RECIPIENT								TOTAL
		15-24	25-34	35-44	45-54	55-64	65-74	75-84	85+	
St Mary's	Male	8	25	40	47	32	7	0	0	159
	Female	7	12	29	27	17	5	0	0	97
	TOTAL	15	37	69	74	49	12	0	0	256
	%	6	14	27	29	19	5	0	0	
Charing Cross	Male									88
	Female									80
	TOTAL	8	18	41	56	35	10	0	0	168
	%	5	11	24	33	21	6	0	0	
Hammermsith	Male	NOT AVAILABLE ON QUESTIONNAIRE								
	Female									
	TOTAL									
	%									
Royal Free	Male	NOT AVAILABLE ON QUESTIONNAIRE								
	Female									
	TOTAL									
	%									
St Paul's/ St Peter's	Male	4	21	22	34	24	15	1	0	121
	Female	2	10	25	21	13	7	0	0	78
	TOTAL	6	31	47	55	37	22	1	0	199
	%	3	16	24	28	19	11	0	0	
St Bartholomew's	Male									
	Female									
	TOTAL	4	40	55	68	77	25	0	0	269
	%									
Royal London	Male	14	35	46	42	44	13	0	0	194
	Female	2	28	22	25	34	9	0	0	120
	TOTAL	16	63	68	67	78	22	0	0	314
	%	5	20	22	21	25	7	0	0	
Brighton	Male	NOT AVAILABLE ON QUESTIONNAIRE								
	Female									
	TOTAL									
	%									

CENTRE	SEX	AGE OF RECIPIENT								TOTAL
		15-24	25-34	35-44	45-54	55-64	65-74	75-84	85+	
Canterbury	Male									60
	Female									30
	Total	2	26	25	19	9	8	1	0	90
	%	2	29	28	21	10	9	1	0	
St Thomas'	Male	0	14	21	29	23	12	2	0	101
	Female	1	13	15	17	19	8	0	0	73
	TOTAL	1	27	36	46	42	20	2	0	174
	%	<1	16	21	26	24	11	1	0	
Dulwich/King's	Male	6	33	56	44	39	40	9	0	227
	Female	3	17	28	42	24	13	1	0	128
	TOTAL	9	50	84	86	63	53	10	0	355
	%	3	14	24	24	18	15	3	0	
Guy's	Male	1	20	14	14	21	11	0	0	81
	Female	6	15	10	12	10	2	0	0	55
	TOTAL	7	35	24	26	31	13	0	0	136
	%	5	26	18	19	23	10	0	0	
Carshalton	Male	2	16	10	22	17	7	0	0	74
	Female	5	5	10	5	7	1	0	0	33
	TOTAL	7	21	20	27	24	8	0	0	107
	%	7	20	19	25	22	7	0	0	

CENTRE	SEX	AGE OF RECIPIENT			TOTAL
		0-4	5-14	15-24	
Guy's (Paed.s)	Male	1	31	27	59
	Female	1	11	15	27
	TOTAL	2	42	42	86
	%	2	49	49	

STOCK OF TRANSPLANT RECIPIENTS FOR ALL RENAL TRANSPLANT CENTRES IN THE THAMES REGIONS BY RECIPIENT ETHNICITY AS REPORTED IN THE LONDON RENAL SERVICES REVIEW QUESTIONNAIRE (% OF TOTAL)

| CENTRE | RECIPIENT ETHNICITY | | | | |
	WHITE	AFRO-CARIBBEAN	ASIAN	OTHER	TOTAL
St Mary's	-(69%)	-(4%)	-(24%)	-(3%)	-
Charing Cross	129(77%)	7(4%)	30(8%)	2(1%)	168
Hammersmith	NOT AVAILABLE ON QUESTIONNAIRE				
Royal Free	271(80%)	21(6%)	38(11%)	10(3%)	340
St Paul's/St Peter's	162(81%)	6(3%)	23(12%)	8(4%)	199
St Bartholomew's	211(89%)	15(6%)	27(11%)	16(7%)	238
Royal London	263(84%)	10(3%)	32(10%)	9(3%)	314
Brighton	NOT AVAILABLE ON QUESTIONNAIRE				
Canterbury	89(99%)	0	1(1%)	0	90
St Thomas'	NOT AVAILABLE ON QUESTIONNAIRE				
Dulwich/King's	275(78%)	38(11%)	28(8%)	14(4%)	355
Guy's	109(80%)	17(13%)	5(4%)	5(4%)	136
Guy's (Paed.s)	65(76%)	8(9%)	13(15%)	0	86
Carshalton	NOT AVAILABLE ON QUESTIONNAIRE				

STOCK OF TRANSPLANT RECIPIENTS FOR RENAL TRANSPLANT CENTRES IN THE THAMES
REGION BY REGION OF RESIDENCE. AS REPORTED IN THE LONDON RENAL SERVICES
REVIEW QUESTIONNAIRE (% OF TOTAL)

REGION/CENTRE	REGION OF RESIDENCE				
	NW THAMES	NE THAMES	SE THAMES	SW THAMES	OTHER*
St Mary's	196(80%)	13(5%)	3(1%)	10(4%)	23(9%)
Charing Cross	96(57%)	7(4%)	6(4%)	38(23%)	21(13%)
Hammersmith	167(73%)	8(3%)	3(1%)	24(10%)	28(12%)
Royal Free	126(38%)	160(48%)	–	–	48(14%)
St Paul's/St Peter's	88(44%)	61(31%)	19(10%)	17(9%)	14(7%)
St Bartholomew's	17(6%)	249(90%)	3(1%)	3(1%)	5(2%)
Royal London	9(3%)	294(92%)	13(4%)	0	2(1%)
Brighton	NOT AVAILABLE ON QUESTIONNAIRE				
Canterbury	–	–	90	–	–
St Thomas'	19(11%)	14(8%)	48(28%)	83(48%)	10(6%)
Dulwich/King's	12(3%)	34(10%)	249(70%)	52(15%)	8(2%)
Guy's	2(1%)	3(2%)	124(91%)	5(4%)	2(1%)
Guy's (Paed.s)	UNABLE TO SORT BY POSTCODE				
Carshalton	–	–	–	107	–

DISTRICT OF RESIDENCE FOR ALL RECIPIENTS IN 'OTHER' CATEGORY IN TABLE 4.3 FOR EACH RENAL TRANSPLANT CENTRE IN THE THAMES REGIONS

REGION/CENTRE	REGION OF RESIDENCE					
	WESSEX	OXFORD	E ANGLIA	S WESTERN	WALES	OTHER
St Mary's	–	14	–	–	–	–
Charing Cross	1	16	2	1	1	0
Hammersmith	0	28	0	0	0	0
Royal Free	NOT AVAILABLE ON QUESTIONNAIRE					
St Paul's/St Peter's	3	8	0	1	0	2
St Bartholomew's	0	3	1	0	1	0
Royal London	0	0	1	0	0	1
Brighton	NOT AVAILABLE ON QUESTIONNAIRE					
Canterbury	NOT AVAILABLE ON QUESTIONNAIRE					
St Thomas'	3	3	1	3	0	0
Dulwich/King's	5	1	0	0	0	2
Guy's	1	1	0	0	0	0
Guy's (Paed.s)	UNABLE TO SORT POSTCODES					
Carshalton	NOT AVAILABLE ON QUESTIONNAIRE					

PERCENTAGE OF DIABETIC TRANSPLANT PATIENTS AT EACH RENAL TRANSPLANT CENTRE IN THE THAMES REGION, AS REPORTED IN THE LONDON RENAL SERVICES REVIEW QUESTIONNAIRE

CENTRE	% DIABETICS
St Mary's	4
Charing Cross	13.1
Hammersmith	-
Royal Free	4.1
St Paul's/St Peter's	4.5
St Barthlomew's	6.3
Royal London	6.7
Brighton	-
Canterbury	6
St Thomas'	-
Dulwich/King's	16
Guy's	-
Guy's (Paed.s)	<1
Carshalton	-

ANNEX 2
TABLE 2.1 (L)

Cadaveric kidney transplants reported to UKTSSA 1 January 1981 – 31 December 1991 : London centres only
(Extracted from Table 2.1 of the full audit report)

Centre	1981	1982	1983	1984	Year of Graft 1985	1986	1987	1988	1989	1990	1991	TOTAL
St Mary's	12	8	10	25	19	26	32	79	60	58	56	678
Charing Cross	5	9	16	27	27	27	34	27	32	50	35	276
Hammersmith	18	21	16	35	30	29	31	29	25	19	16	234
The Royal Free	19	26	28	45	51	27	44	24	35	21	40	300
St Paul's	7	7	5	20	25	20	23	35	33	41	32	381
St Bartholomew's	11	12	18	24	20	33	25	23	23	21	15	189
Royal London	22	21	37	40	25	24	33	33	48	28	31	283
Great Ormond Street	0	0	0	0	0	0	0	49	54	51	28	384
Brighton	0	0	0	0	0	0	0	0	7	5	10	22
Canterbury	0	0	0	0	0	0	0	22	22	19	25	88
St Thomas	7	16	9	28	28	21	20	3	13	16	17	49
King's College	40	35	56	46	80	97	37	24	22	22	16	213
Dulwich	1	1	0	0	0	0	35	0	0	0	0	391
Guys	82	100	97	154	98	120	88	54	26	73	46	236
Carshalton	0	0	0	0	0	1	42	50	36	48	40	217
TOTAL	224	256	292	444	403	425	444	438	446	466	432	4270

Cadaveric kidney transplant activity reported to UKTSSA 1 January 1989 - 31 December 1991 : London Centres only
(Extracted from Table 6.1 of the full audit report)

| Centre | No Kidney Transplants | | | Kidneys Transplanted Locally | | | | | | Exported Kidneys Transplanted | | | | | | Imported Kidneys Transplanted | | | | | |
| | | | | Ben | | | Non-Ben. | | | Ben | | | Non-Ben | | | Ben | | | Non-Ben | | |
	89	90	91	89	90	91	89	90	91	89	90	91	89	90	91	89	90	91	89	90	91
St Mary's	32	50	35	0	1	0	17	20	24	1	5	1	27	16	18	3	1	0	12	28	11
Charing Cross	25	19	16	0	0	2	11	12	6	1	4	2	6	7	9	2	5	4	12	2	4
Hammersmith	35	21	40	0	0	1	22	20	22	2	1	5	8	3	6	1	0	3	12	1	14
Royal Free	33	41	32	3	1	0	16	24	15	5	8	6	11	7	7	0	7	5	14	9	12
St Pauls	23	21	15	0	0	0	5	7	3	1	1	3	4	2	0	7	1	5	11	13	7
St Bartholomews	48	28	31	2	1	0	19	16	18	7	9	6	14	4	7	7	5	5	20	6	8
Royal London	54	51	28	1	7	3	24	24	16	5	9	7	5	10	3	14	12	5	15	8	4
Great Ormond St	7	5	10	0	0	0	0	0	0	0	0	0	0	0	0	1	1	2	6	4	8
SE/SW Thames	189	230	225	5	1	6	135	188	172	3	2	1	12	10	7	4	5	5	45	36	42
Total	446	466	432	11	11	12	249	311	276	25	39	31	87	59	57	39	37	34	147	107	110

Ben   = Beneficially matched transplant (0 mis-matches at DR locus, at most 1 mis-match at the A & B loci combined)
Non-Ben = Other matches

UKTSSA kidney recipient waiting lists 31 December 1990 and 1991 :
London centres only (Extracted from Table 7.1 of the full audit
report)

Centre	31 December 1990			31 December 1991			% Difference
	Act	Sus	Total	Act	Sus	Total	
St Mary's	53	2	55	68	3	71	+29
Charing Cross	52	13	65	52	19	71	+ 9
Hammersmith	76	15	91	79	12	91	-
Royal Free	73	18	91	85	9	94	+ 3
St Paul's	108	11	119	126	8	134	+13
St Bartholomews	92	7	99	79	11	90	- 9
Royal London	95	13	108	127	21	148	+37
Great Ormond St	9	1	10	0	0	0	-
Brighton	59	14	73	63	10	73	-
Canterbury	35	2	37	28	2	30	-19
St Thomas	58	13	71	68	11	79	+11
Dulwich	40	12	52	57	7	64	+23
Guys	45	16	61	31	17	48	-21
Carshalton	37	43	80	37	43	80	-
Total	832	180	1012	900	173	1073	+6

Act = Active on the waiting list
Sus = Suspended from the waiting list

Primary renal disease of recipients receiving a cadaveric kidney transplantation 1 January 1989 - 31 December 1991 as reported to UKTSSA, by centre. Londons centres only
(Extracted from Table 12.2 of the full audit report)

| Centre | Primary renal disease (percent of total) | | | | | | | | | Total |
	1	2	3	4	5	6	7	8	9	
St Mary's	67 (57)	6 (5)	7 (6)	7 (6)	3 (3)	12 (10)	1 (1)	–	14 (12)	117
Charing Cross	30 (50)	6 (10)	4 (7)	6 (10)	3 (5)	4 (7)	3 (5)	2 (3)	2 (3)	60
Hammersmith	45 (47)	3 (3)	4 (4)	4 (4)	2 (2)	5 (5)	9 (9)	–	24 (25)	96
Royal Free	71 (67)	1 (1)	–	6 (6)	3 (3)	1 (1)	3 (3)	1 (1)	20 (19)	106
St Paul's	31 (53)	–	–	12 (20)	2 (3)	2 (3)	2 (3)	2 (3)	8 (14)	59
St Bartholomew's	74 (69)	6 (6)	1 (1)	8 (7)	5 (5)	2 (2)	4 (4)	–	7 (7)	107
Royal London	95 (71)	5 (4)	4 (3)	6 (5)	4 (3)	3 (2)	2 (2)	3 (2)	11 (8)	133
Great Ormond Street	18 (82)	–	–	2 (9)	–	–	–	–	2 (9)	22
Brighton	54 (82)	–	–	5 (8)	3 (5)	1 (2)	1 (2)	1 (2)	1 (2)	66
Canterbury	36 (78)	–	–	1 (2)	–	–	–	–	9 (20)	46
St Thomas'	22 (37)	1 (2)	5 (8)	3 (5)	4 (7)	10 (17)	5 (8)	1 (2)	9 (15)	60
Dulwich	119 (82)	–	1 (1)	16 (11)	–	–	2 (1)	–	7 (5)	145
Guy's	128 (63)	–	–	27 (13)	2 (1)	1 (1)	–	–	45 (22)	203
Carshalton	74 (60)	4 (3)	7 (6)	16 (13)	9 (7)	3 (2)	4 (3)	2 (2)	5 (4)	124
Total	864	32	33	119	40	44	36	12	164	1344

Live related kidney transplants reported to UKTSSA for 1 January 1989 - 31 December 1991 : London centres only
(Extracted from Table 14.1 of the full audit report)

Centre	1989	1990	1991	TOTAL
Charing Cross Hospital	1	2	4	7
Hammersmith Hospital	1	9	1	11
The Royal Free Hospital	6	7	0	13
St Paul's Hospital	10	9	3	22
St Bartholomew's Hospital	5	0	2	7
The Royal London Hospital (Whitechapel)	2	0	1	3
Great Ormond Street Hospital	0	0	1	1
Brighton	1	3	3	7
St Thomas' Hospital	14	2	0	16
Guy's Hospital	8	0	0	8
Dulwich Hospital (South Wing)	0	2	0	3
Carshalton	1	2	0	3
TOTAL	**49**	**36**	**15**	**101**

ANNEX 2
TABLE A.2.1. (L)

Cadaveric kidney donation reported to UKTSSA 1 January 1989 - 31 December 1991 : London centres only
(Extracted from Table A.2.1 of the full audit report)

Centre	No donors			Kidneys Retrieved			Kidneys Retained used			Kidneys Retained not used			Kidneys Exported used			Kidneys Exported not used		
	1989	1990	1991	1989	1990	1991	1989	1990	1991	1989	1990	1991	1989	1990	1991	1989	1990	1991
St Mary's	23	23	22	46	46	43	17	21	24	1	2	0	28	23	19	0	0	0
Charing Cross	9	13	10	18	24	20	11	12	8	0	1	2	7	11	10	0	0	0
Hammersmith	18	13	18	36	26	36	22	20	23	4	2	2	10	4	11	0	0	0
Royal Free	18	21	15	35	42	30	19	26	16	0	0	2	16	15	12	0	0	0
St Pauls	5	6	3	10	12	6	5	7	3	0	2	0	5	3	3	0	0	0
St Bartholomews	22	16	16	44	32	31	21	18	17	0	0	2	21	14	12	2	0	0
Royal London	20	28	16	40	55	31	25	31	19	3	5	1	10	19	10	2	0	1
SE/SW Thames	84	103	100	165	205	200	140	187	178	1	6	14	23	12	8	1	0	0
Total	199	223	200	394	442	397	260	322	288	9	18	23	120	101	85	5	0	1

Removals from the UKTSSA Active Transplant Waiting List during the calendar years 1989-1991 : London centres only   (Extracted from Table A.3.1 of the full audit)

Centre	1989						1990						1991					
	Sus-pend	Cad Tx	Live Tx	Removal	Death	No. Patients	Sus-pend	Cad Tx	Live Tx	Removal	Death	No. Patients	Sus-pend	Cad Tx	Live Tx	Removal	Death	No. Patients
St Mary's	1	27	0	2	2	31	1	26	0	1	2	30	1	29	0	0	0	31
Charing Cross	25	23	1	0	2	45	26	19	0	1	2	42	25	16	2	1	2	39
Hammersmith	2	29	1	3	1	36	1	9	0	0	0	10	8	38	0	8	6	59
Royal Free	4	31	3	6	1	45	17	40	3	0	4	64	4	31	0	1	5	41
St Pauls	8	22	3	1	11	44	7	19	4	2	5	37	10	14	3	5	0	31
St Bartholomews	23	44	3	3	3	72	10	23	0	0	3	34	13	31	2	1	6	52
Royal London	26	51	1	5	2	80	24	46	0	2	7	71	29	26	1	8	1	63
Great Ormond St	2	7	0	0	0	6	2	5	0	0	0	7	0	10	1	0	0	11
Brighton	1	14	0	1	2	18	1	14	2	8	0	25	1	22	2	6	0	30
Canterbury	7	11	0	1	1	19	2	14	0	0	1	17	0	6	0	0	0	6
St Thomas	10	15	0	0	4	27	12	23	0	0	1	35	3	16	0	1	2	21
Dulwich	4	15	0	2	0	20	1	45	0	29	0	74	0	29	2	14	0	45
Guys	26	50	2	5	5	82	8	24	0	0	3	35	7	31	0	1	1	38
Carshalton	83	36	0	0	4	75	67	45	0	2	2	84	76	38	0	0	2	77

Suspend = Patients whose status changed from active to suspended
Cad Tx = Patients registered on the Active waiting list who then receive a cadaveric transplant
Live Tx = Patients registered on the Active waiting list who then receive a live donor transplant
Removal = Patients permanently removed from the Active waiting list
Death   = Patients recorded as having died whilst on the Active waiting list
Note: Patients receiving a transplant, being removed or dying whilst on the suspended waiting list are not included

Additions to the UKTSSA Active Transplant Waiting List during calendar years 1989-1991 : London centres only (Extracted from Table A.3.2 of the full audit report)

Centre	1989				1990				1991			
	New Case	Renewal	Return from S	No Patients	New Case	Renewal	Return from S	No Patients	New Case	Renewal	Return from S	No Patients
St Mary's	18	7	3	28	36	20	1	56	33	12	0	44
Charing Cross	13	4	24	36	30	6	21	49	22	8	19	44
Hammersmith	27	5	1	32	30	10	2	42	43	18	5	65
Royal Free	38	11	2	48	49	19	3	69	36	12	10	56
St Pauls	43	6	5	53	33	6	9	48	39	7	6	50
St Bartholomews	50	10	8	66	31	3	13	43	25	5	9	34
Royal London	43	10	24	68	45	15	16	70	68	2	26	93
Great Ormond St	5	4	2	9	4	6	1	9	4	0	0	4
Brighton	17	5	0	22	41	8	0	49	25	6	1	32
Canterbury	14	1	6	21	19	1	3	23	0	1	0	1
St Thomas	27	10	9	45	30	3	6	39	17	12	3	31
Dulwich	23	13	2	37	54	21	1	75	44	19	2	65
Guys	34	30	15	74	12	1	3	16	22	14	3	37
Carshalton	31	5	79	73	45	7	56	74	44	6	67	78

New case   = new patients previously unknown to UKTSSA added to the Active waiting list
Return from S = patients whose status changed from Suspended to Active
Renewal   = patients who returned to the Active waiting list following a previous transplant or removal
No patients   = number of patients included in the analysis

Within the course of the year a patient may be counted several times, for example, a new patient registered as Active, who recieves a transplant which fails so the patient returns to the Active waiting list is counted twice, once as a new case and once as a renewal.

One year graft survival estimates after first cadaveric kidney transplant for grafts between 1 January 1981 and 31 December 1991 : London centres only
(extracted from Table 9.1 of the full audit report)

Centre	Transplant between 1981-1986			Transplant between 1987-1991		
	% Survival	95% Confidence Interval	No at risk at day 0	% Survival	95% Confidence Interval	No at risk at day 0
St Mary's	73	64-83	84	81	70-91	53
Charing Cross	73	64-82	89	73	63-82	97
Hammersmith	70	61-78	111	77	66-88	61
Royal Free	82	75-88	160	81	71-91	62
St Paul's	77	67-88	69	82	71-93	51
St Bartholomew's	85	78-92	103	93	87-99	73
Royal London	71	64-79	139	94	90-99	102
Great Ormond Street	-	-	-	-	-	9
Brighton	-	-	-	-	-	19
Canterbury	-	-	-	-	-	24
St Thomas'	79	70-87	94	81	73-90	82
King's	73	67-80	189	-	-	20
Dulwich	-	-	1	-	-	15
Guy's	81	77-85	434	-	-	47
Carshalton	-	-	1	-	-	47

Causes of graft failure reported to UKTSSA for grafts between 1 January 1981 - 31 December 1991 by centre
London centres only   (Extracted from Table 10.5 of full audit report)

Centre	Cause of Failure *												TOTAL
	1	2	3	4	5	6	7	8	9	10	11	12	
St Mary's	-	-	-	-	-	-	-	-	-	-	-	-	-
Charing Cross	-	8	-	-	-	2	-	-	-	-	-	6	16
Hammersmith	-	-	1	-	-	-	-	-	-	-	1	6	8
Royal Free	-	1	-	-	-	-	-	-	-	-	-	1	2
St Paul's	-	4	-	-	-	-	-	-	-	-	1	-	5
St Bartholomew's	-	-	-	-	-	-	-	-	-	-	-	-	-
Royal London	-	-	-	-	-	-	-	-	-	-	-	-	-
Great Ormond Street	-	4	-	1	-	2	-	-	-	-	-	-	7
Brighton	-	-	-	-	-	-	-	-	-	-	-	1	1
Canterbury	-	1	-	-	-	1	-	-	-	-	-	-	2
St Thomas'	1	8	-	-	1	-	-	-	-	4	1	2	17
King's	-	-	-	-	-	-	-	-	-	-	-	-	-
Dulwich	-	-	-	-	-	-	-	-	-	-	-	-	-
Guy's	-	-	-	-	-	-	-	-	-	-	-	1	1
Carshalton	-	-	-	-	1	-	-	-	-	-	-	-	1
TOTAL	7	27	1	1	2	5	-	-	-	4	3	17	58

* See Table 10.4

Cause of patient death after cadaveric kidney transplant reported to UKTSSA for grafts between 1 January 1981 and 31 December 1991 by centre : London centres only
(Extracted from Table 10.7 of the full audit report)

Centre	Cause of Death															TOTAL
	1	2	3	4	5	6	7	8	9	10	11	12	13	14	15	
St Mary's	3	–	–	–	–	–	–	–	–	–	–	–	–	–	–	3
Charing Cross	–	–	–	–	–	–	–	–	–	–	–	–	1	–	–	1
Hammersmith	1	–	–	–	–	–	–	–	–	–	–	–	1	–	–	2
Royal Free	–	–	–	–	–	–	–	–	–	–	–	–	–	–	–	–
St Paul's	–	–	1	–	–	1	–	–	–	–	–	–	–	–	–	2
St Bartholomew's	3	–	–	–	–	–	–	–	–	–	–	–	–	–	–	3
Royal London	1	–	–	–	–	–	–	–	–	–	–	–	1	–	–	2
Great Ormond Street	–	–	–	–	–	–	–	–	–	–	–	–	–	–	–	–
Brighton	1	–	–	–	2	–	–	–	–	–	–	–	–	–	–	3
Canterbury	–	–	–	–	1	–	–	–	–	–	–	–	–	–	–	1
St Thomas'	2	–	–	–	1	–	–	–	–	–	–	–	2	1	3	9
King's	–	–	–	–	–	–	–	–	–	–	–	–	–	–	–	–
Dulwich	1	–	–	–	–	–	–	–	–	–	–	–	–	–	–	1
Guy's	14	–	–	–	–	–	–	–	–	–	–	–	1	–	–	15
Carshalton	5	–	–	–	–	–	–	–	–	–	–	–	–	1	–	6
TOTAL	31	0	1	0	4	1	0	0	0	0	0	0	6	2	3	48

THE EFFECTS OF CENTRE SIZE ON ONE YEAR KIDNEY GRAFT SURVIVAL

The renal transplant centres were categorised into three size groups according to the average number of non-paediatric (>18 years) first cadaveric transplants carried out per year. The 1981-1991 time period was split into two groups which were considered separately: 1981-1986 and 1987-1991.

This gave the following distribution of centres:-

| | No of Centres | |
Centre Group	1981-1986	1987-1991
Small: 0-19 transplants per year on average	16	9
Medium: 20-39 transplants per year on average	12	16
Large: 40+ transplants per year on average	9	12
Total	**37**	**37**

One year graft survival plots were produced for recipients aged 19-55 years. In both cases (1981-1986 and 1987-1991) there was no difference in the survival distributions of the different centre size groups.

Multifactorial analyses were carried out for these two time periods, and these took other potentially significant factors into account. In addition to centre size group, donor age, shipping, year of graft and (for 1987-1991 data) beneficial matching were also considered. The model for 1981-1986 showed that graft year and donor age over 55 were significant (survival improves with time, but is worse for those whose kidney is from a donor aged over 55). For 1987-1991, donor age >55, matching and shipping were all significant (beneficially matched and local kidneys improve one year graft survival rates). In neither case was centre size group significant. Hence from this data there is no evidence to suggest that the average number of transplants performed bears any relation to the outcome of the graft.

This can be seen on the two accompanying graft survival plots.

One year patient survival was also investigated in the same way. This showed no real difference in survival for the 3 size groups for 1981-1986 or 1987-1991 (see accompanying patient survival plots), although the multifactorial analysis for 1981-1986 showed a marginally better survival rate for patients transplanted in large centres compared with those transplanted in small centres. No such differences were apparent for 1987-1991 and it is thus fair to say that centre size has not significantly affected patient survival in recent years.

One Year Graft Survival by Centre Size for All Centres, 1981–1986

(First Cadaveric Grafts for Recipients aged 19 to 55 Years Only)

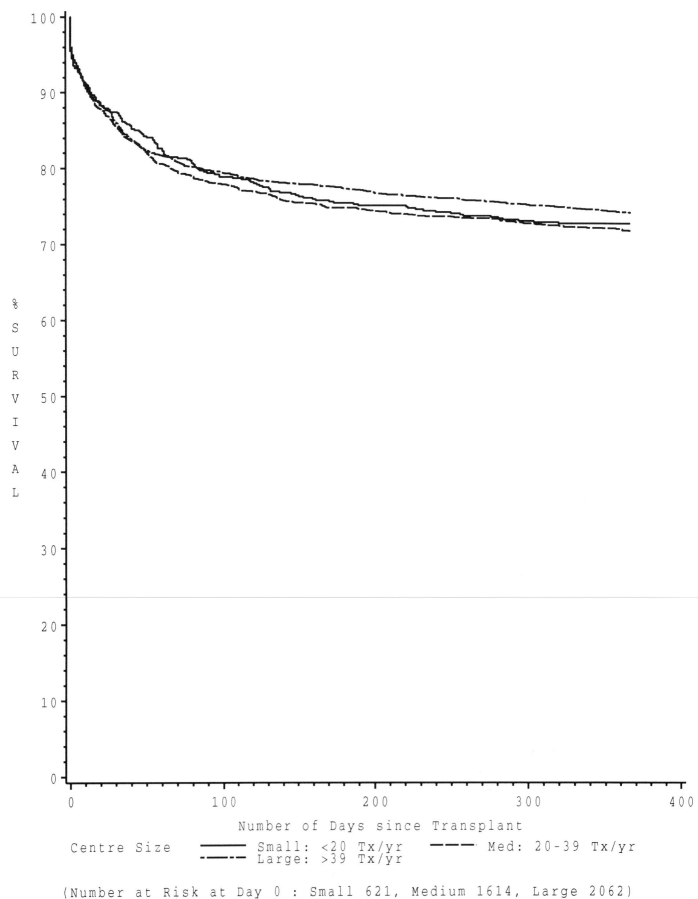

Number of Days since Transplant

Centre Size ——— Small: <20 Tx/yr ——— Med: 20-39 Tx/yr
–·–·– Large: >39 Tx/yr

(Number at Risk at Day 0 : Small 621, Medium 1614, Large 2062)

One Year Graft Survival by Centre Size for All Centres, 1987–1991

(First Cadaveric Grafts for Recipients aged 19 to 55 Years Only)

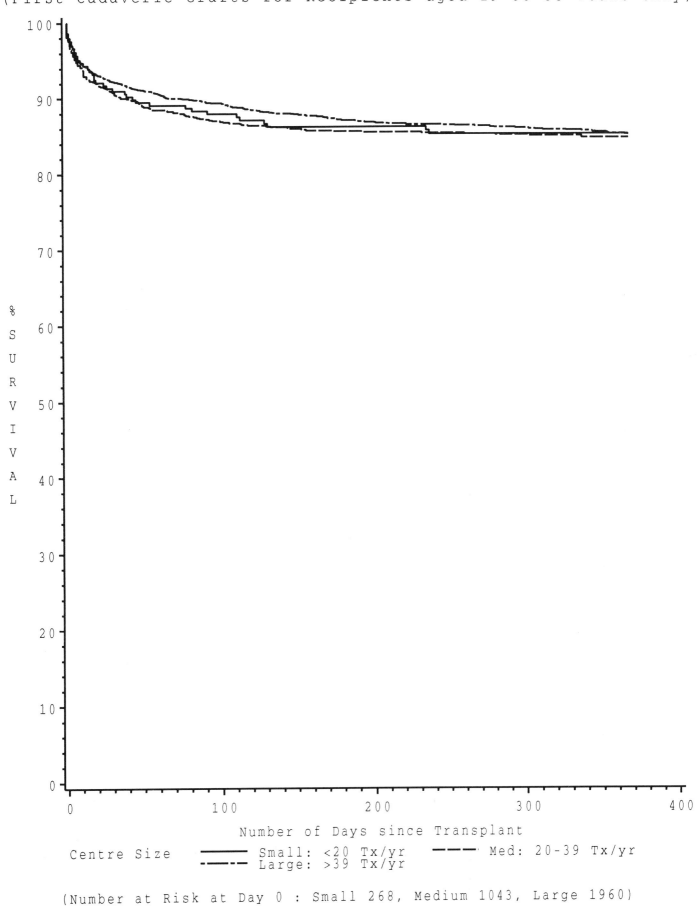

Number of Days since Transplant

Centre Size ———— Small: <20 Tx/yr – – – Med: 20-39 Tx/yr
–·–·– Large: >39 Tx/yr

(Number at Risk at Day 0 : Small 268, Medium 1043, Large 1960)

One Year Patient Survival by Centre Size for All Centres, 1981–1986

(First Cadaveric Grafts for Recipients aged 19 to 55 Years Only)

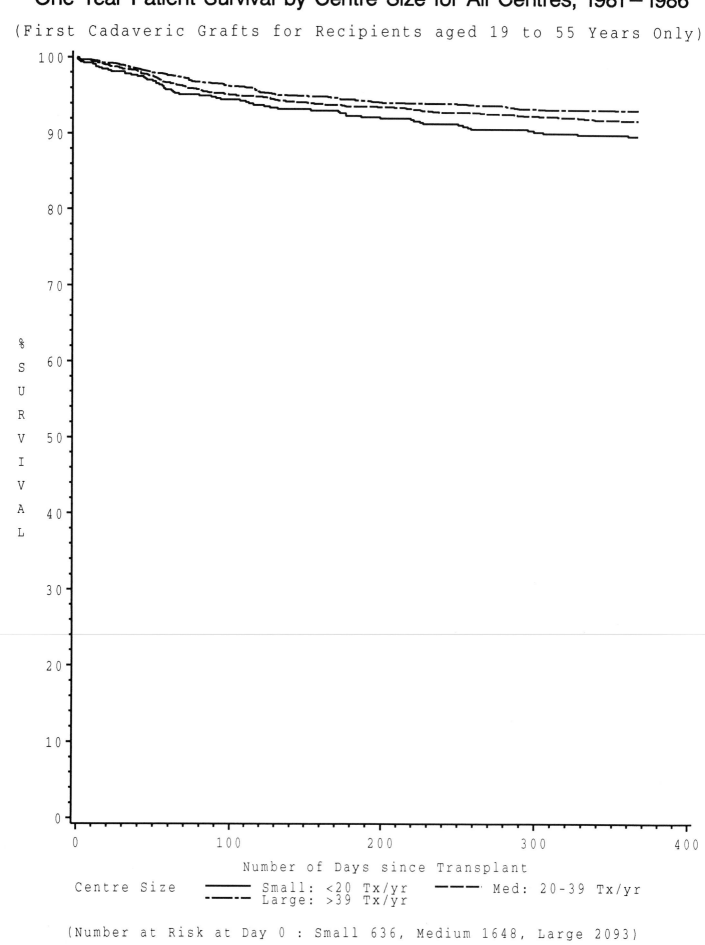

Number of Days since Transplant

Centre Size ——— Small: <20 Tx/yr —— Med: 20-39 Tx/yr
—·—·— Large: >39 Tx/yr

(Number at Risk at Day 0 : Small 636, Medium 1648, Large 2093)

One Year Patient Survival by Centre Size for All Centres, 1987−1991

(First Cadaveric Grafts for Recipients aged 19 to 55 Years Only)

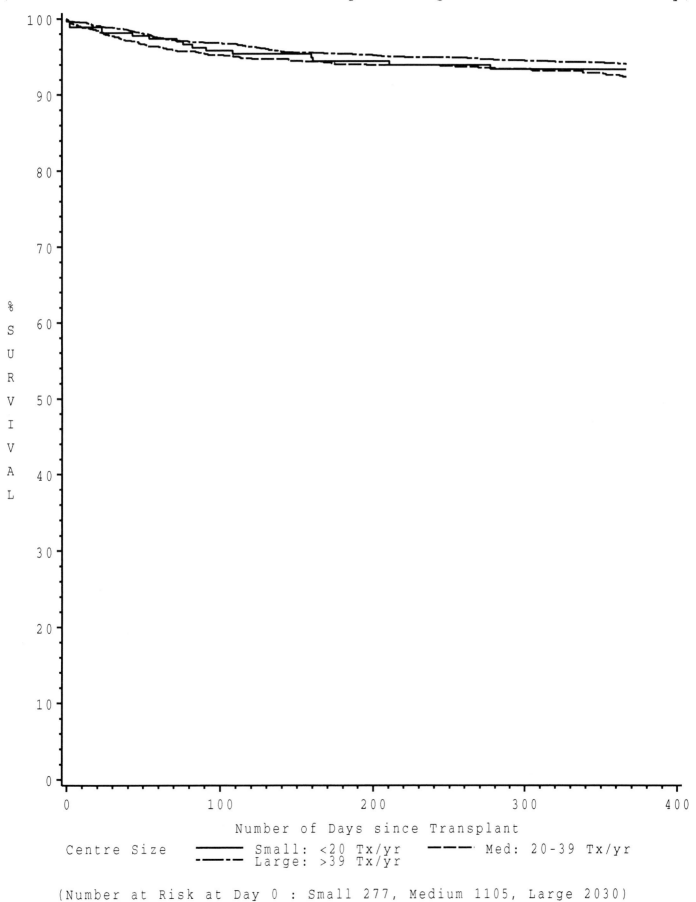

Number of Days since Transplant

Centre Size ———— Small: <20 Tx/yr ——–—— Med: 20-39 Tx/yr
—·—·— Large: >39 Tx/yr

(Number at Risk at Day 0 : Small 277, Medium 1105, Large 2030)

Review of London Renal Services

Technical Report

on

Financial Analysis

Review of London Renal Services

Technical Report on Financial Analysis

1. This report provides full details of the financial analysis work undertaken in support of the review of Renal Services for the London Implementation Group. It is structured to provide information on:

- the objectives set for the financial analysis work;
- the approach adopted to creating the financial analysis;
- a summary of running costs for the proposed renal facilities;
- a first assessment of potential investment requirements.

In addition it provides recommendations on the further financial analysis work required to produce a more robust assessment.

2. A further technical report is being prepared on patient life cycle costs for renal maintenance and transplant services. This separate report will be available to the London Implementation Group in early June 1993.

Objectives

3. The key objectives for the financial analysis work which were identified at the commencement of the review work can be summarised as:

- identify the actual full cost of the renal maintenance and transplant services currently provided in London;

- determine the running costs and potential additional capital costs of the services proposed for London by the review group;

- identify life cycle costs for patients in the maintenance and transplant programmes.

Approach Adopted

Determining the current cost of London Renal Services

4. The Renal Services questionnaire which was send to each of the renal centres in London requested each centre to supply Business Plans for 1992/93 and 1993/94 and to provide details of service costings. It was anticipated that the responses received would assist in building a picture of the full cost of running renal services in London and provide an indication of the relative cost efficiency of each centre. In addition some of the financial information would be used to construct cost profiles to provide an estimate of the cost of the services now being proposed for London by the Review Group.

5. In the event the response to this request has been extremely varied with only two centres providing detailed financial information, some providing

none and most providing only summary information and treatment tariffs by modality. It has therefore not proved possible at this stage to prepare baseline costs against which the cost and relative efficiency of the proposed services can be measured. We consider that it is likely that such information can be made available for most of the London renal centres and recommend that it should be collected on the basis of an agreed cost template to ensure like for like costing of services in the different centres.

6. An analysis of the response received from each centre is included in Schedule 1 (not included as part of this report) together with a table of those service costs and treatment tariffs which have been provided to the Review Group. This information is obviously incomplete and has not been used in any part of the further cost analysis work which we have undertaken.

Provincial Cost Profiles

7. In the absence of robust baseline information for the London centres it was decided that the most pragmatic solution to constructing the cost of the services proposed for London would be built cost profiles from other renal centres where information was readily available to the Review Group. For this reason we stress that our costing of the services proposed by the Review Group must be considered as very provisional until such time as it can be validated against the profiles of current service costs.

8. Reasonable full cost and budget information was available to the Group from two large provincial teaching hospitals, both providing fully integrated end stage maintenance and acute dialysis services and transplant services with patient throughputs at least equal to those in the London centres. In both of these provincial hospitals a full range of dialysis modalities are offered and full back up nephrology services are provided. Both hospitals have been subjected to detailed cost and budget analyses during the last two years.

9. The operational information for both hospitals is as follows:

> *Provincial 1*: provides both adult and paediatric dialysis and transplant services. During 1992/93 the hospital managed a total of 312 dialysis patients of which 24 were children. 63 out of the 288 adult patients were managed in four satellite units. The dialysis modalities were as follows:
>
> | | | |
> |---|---|---|
> | • | Hospital haemodialysis | 133 patients |
> | • | Satellite haemodialysis | 63 patients |
> | • | Home haemodialysis | 30 patients |
> | • | CAPD | 86 patients. |
>
> 102 patients were transplanted during 1992/93. The total cost of dialysis and transplant services is currently assessed at about £7.4 million.

Provincial 2: provides adult dialysis and transplant services. 226 dialysis patients are maintained with a modality split as follows:

- Hospital haemodialysis   49   patients
- MCU haemodialysis   13   patients
- Home haemodialysis   15   patients
- CAPD   149   patients.

About 22 (approximately 30%) of the patients receiving haemodialysis treatment are using bicarbonate fluids. A total of 132 patients were transplanted in 1992/93. The total cost of dialysis and transplant services is currently assessed at about £6.1 million.

10. The cost analyses for these two renal centres are included in Schedule 2 and Schedule 3 to this Report.

11. Even though a significant amount of cost analysis work has been undertaken on both of these sites, it should be noted that:

- the budgets held by the Clinical Directors are significantly less than the service costs shown above, and as part of this work it has been necessary to use apportionment and cost allocation routines to calculate true service costs - we expect that the same will be true for each of the London renal centres;

- on each site the cost knowledge - whilst being appropriate for most operational purposes - is still incomplete and further detailed research work has been required for some cost items, mainly based on patient profiles.

12. The main areas where detailed cost knowledge is still inadequate are in the allocation of costs for drugs, investigative services and theatre time for access surgery and organ transplants, all three of which are significant cost components of these high cost specialties. These are not specifically budgeted for on either of the provincial sites and in order to arrive at a full cost quantum all three cost items have been determined for the provincial 2 site on the basis of patient treatment profiles and validated at a later stage of our analysis as part of the life cycle costing exercise.

13. In addition the cost apportionment routines for general hospital overheads are likely to vary from site to site and can lead to significant distortions in any comparative analysis of unit costs. The allocation of capital charges will always give rise to variations across sites as a result of differences in the valuation of buildings and the fact that depreciation on premises is calculated on the written down life of the asset, which again will vary from site to site.

14. Each of the two cost schedules contains a unit cost calculation based on:

- the cost per patient year averaged over all modalities and including the costs of running Satellite or Minimum Care Units;

- the cost per transplant operation for transplant service costs.

15. The cost schedules show a reasonably consistent calculation of unit costs for dialysis and nephrology services across these two sites, Provincial 1 at £21,870 per dialysis patient and Provincial 2 at £20,470 per patient. Both of these costs include the apportionment of general hospital overheads and capital charges. There are however significant differences in staffing complements across these two sites.

16. We have not attempted as part of this exercise to compare individual cost items across these two sites since there will inevitably be differences in operational practices which will impact on manning levels, and similarly there will be differences on each site in allocation methodologies and the categorisation of costs.

17. A summary comparison of similar unit cost items shows a reasonably satisfactory level of consistency as shown in the table below.

Analysis of selected unit cost items

	£	£	+/-
Medical staff	1778	1648	-7%
Nursing staff	4796	4220	-12%
All other staff	1486	1511	+2%
Total staff costs	**8060**	**7379**	**-8%**
Drugs and medical and surgical items	6362	6744	+6%
Overheads & capital items	4954	4136	-16%

18. The significantly higher nursing costs shown in Provincial 1 tend to reflect the differences in staff complements noted in paragraph 14 above. Differences in overhead costs probably result from the use of different calculation methodologies.

19. Our overall assessment is that the individual cost calculations for dialysis and nephrology services are reasonably close enough to be used as a good practice template for estimating the costs of the services proposed for London centres.

20. The same is not true however for transplant services where the unit cost

per transplant operation is significantly different between the two sites:

- Provincial 1   £ 6,010
- Provincial 2   £ 11,718.

This difference is mainly accounted for by the under identification of cost items for Transplant Services in the Provincial 1 site.

21. Different parts of each of these two cost analyses have been used to create separate Provincial Cost Profiles for:

- a 200 place Renal Dialysis Unit with nephrology services;
- a 130 place Renal Transplant Unit.

22. A large part of each cost profile has been created from the Provincial 2 analysis with Provincial 1 costs being used where cost items are not otherwise available or where there are suspicions that cost items have been wrongly calculated or are incomplete. The cost calculations for Dialysis and Nephrology services are as follows:

Dialysis and Nephrology Services

	Total Cost £	Unit Cost £	% of budget
Medical staff	372,380	1,862	8%
Nursing staff	953,540	4,768	21%
Other staff	351,810	1,760	8%
less vacancy factor	-50,330	-252	-1%
Total staff	**1,627,400**	**8,137**	**35%**
Drugs	382,000	1,910	8%
Medical & surgical	1,063,400	5,318	23%
Investigative services	295,800	1,479	6%
Other non-pay	174,600	873	4%
Total non-pay	**1,915,800**	**9,580**	**42%**
Hospital overheads	583,480	2,917	13%
Capital charges	470,820	2,354	10%
Total service cost	**4,597,500**	**22,988**	**100%**

23. The cost calculations for Transplant Services are similarly set out overleaf. These tables demonstrate the importance of non-pay direct costs for both Dialysis and Nephrology and Transplant services - where they account for 42% and 40% respectively of total costs - and therefore the potentially high variable/marginal costs associated with changes in patient activity.

Transplant Services

	Total Cost £	Unit Cost £	% of budget
Medical staff	188,220	1,448	12%
Nursing staff	324,550	2,497	20%
Other staff	98,930	761	6%
less vacancy factor	18,350	-141	-1%
Total staff	**593,350**	**4,564**	**37%**
Drugs	275,600	2,120	17%
Medical & surgical	43,550	335	3%
Investigative services	11,310	87	1%
Theatre etc. costs	280,150	2,155	18%
Other non-pay	21,280	164	1%
Total non-pay	**631,890**	**4,861**	**40%**
Hospital overheads	201,480	1,550	13%
Capital charges	160,000	1,231	10%
Total service cost	**1,586,720**	**12,206**	**100%**

24. The detailed Provincial Cost Profiles are included as Schedule 4 and Schedule 5 to this Report. A three page cost summary is provided at the beginning of each of the schedules. Note that capital costs for land and buildings infrastructure have been recalculated on the basis of:

- an asset valued at £4 million for dialysis and nephrology services, with 25 years remaining life for the building;

- an asset valued at £1.5 million for transplant services, with 25 years remaining life for the building.

25. The cost profiles can be analysed to show the relative size of fixed, semi-variable and variable cost items so that the potential additional costs of managing additional patients can be estimated. For the purposes of this exercise we have assumed the following division of costs across these three categories:

- fixed costs [deemed unlikely to change for the hospital as a whole as a result of changes in renal patient numbers] are deemed to include nurse manager and business manager posts, utilities, hospital overheads and capital charges;

- semi-variable costs [which will not change in a direct relationship to patient numbers but which will be subject to change at the point at which a cost threshold is crossed, i.e. the need for additional or maybe less nursing staff] are deemed to include all other staffing costs and costs of administration;

- variable costs [which can be expected to move in direct relationship to the number of patients in a programme] are deemed to include all patient consumable items, i.e. dialysis fluids and drugs, as well as investigative services and theatre time.

26. The analysis of costs on the basis outlined above is as follows:

Dialysis and Nephrology Services

	Total cost £	Cost per patient £	%
Fixed items	1,127,150	5,635	25%
Semi-variable items	1,606,150	8,031	35%
Variable items	1,864,200	9,322	40%
Total	4,597,500	22,988	100%

This analysis shows that the variable or marginal cost of accommodating each additional patient within the existing pattern of services is calculated as being £9,322.

27. A similar cost structure is apparent for Transplant Services as shown in the table below:

Transplant Services

	Total cost £	Cost per patient £	%
Fixed items	381,515	2,935	24%
Semi-variable items	577,305	4,441	36%
Variable items	627,900	4,830	40%
Total	1,586,720	12,206	100%

This table shows that the variable/marginal cost of each additional transplant operation in a Tertiary Centre is calculated at £4,830.

28. The detailed cost profiles have been used as the basis for building the London renal facilities costs.

29. The Provincial Cost Profiles have been used to construct the London Facilities Profiles, suitably adjusted to build in a 10% London weighting allowance to all staff items and some internal recharge budgets where staffing would be a significant proportion of cost. Additional resources have been included to allow for the more extensive use of bicarbonate fluids for haemodialysis patients and the much greater use of CAPD disconnect systems.

30. Eight different Facilities Profiles have been constructed, to reflect the four different types of centre at which it is proposed renal services will be provided and the use of dialysis stations in each centre on either a two shift or three shift per day basis. These profiles can be more fully described as follows:

- two profiles covering both University and non-University Tertiary Units, both working on a two shift basis for dialysis services, with 15 haemodialysis stations managing 60 haemodialysis patients attending for three dialysis sessions per week, backup services for a further 140 dialysis patients (including those attending Satellite Units and those on home CAPD regimes), with 25 nephrology beds, and undertaking between 100 and 150 transplant operations per annum;

- as above, two profiles covering both University and non-University Tertiary Units, but both working on a three shift basis for dialysis services, with 15 haemodialysis stations now managing 90 patients attending for three dialysis sessions per week, backup services for a further 156 dialysis patients (including those attending Satellite Units and those on home CAPD regimes), with 25 nephrology beds, and undertaking between 100 and 150 transplant operations per annum;

- Sub Regional Units in District General Hospitals, working on a two shift basis for dialysis services, with 10 haemodialysis stations managing 40 patients attending for three dialysis sessions per week, backup services for a further 140 dialysis patients (including those attending Satellite Units and those on home CAPD regimes)), with 18 nephrology beds;

- as above, Sub Regional Units in District General Hospitals, but each working on a three shift basis for dialysis services, with 10 haemodialysis stations now managing 60 patients attending for three dialysis sessions per week, backup services for a further 156 dialysis patients (including those attending Satellite Units and those on home CAPD regimes)), with 18 nephrology beds;

- Satellite Units, working on a two shift basis, with 8 haemodialysis stations managing 32 patients per week attending for three dialysis sessions per week;

- as above Satellite Units, but each working on a three shift basis, with 8 haemodialysis stations now managing 48 patients per week attending for three dialysis sessions per week.

31. In summary the financial models assume that the number of dialysis patients that can be managed from each of the Tertiary and Sub-Regional DGH facilities is as follows:

	Tertiary 2 Shift	Tertiary 3 Shift	DGH 2 Shift	DGH 3 Shift
Hospital Haemodialysis	60	90	40	60
Satellite Haemodialysis	32	48	32	48
CAPD	108	108	108	108
Total	200	246	180	216

32. The cost profiles for these facilities have been constructed as shown below:

- medical and nurse staffing manpower and cost budgets have been separately determined for each type of facility according to the functions performed in that facility;

- some other costs - mainly the remaining manpower budgets - have been based on the total budget for that item contained in the Provincial Cost Profiles;

- most other costs are calculated from the unit cost calculations contained in the Provincial Cost Profiles, without any adjustments;

- fluid costs have been increased to allow all haemodialysis patients to use bicarbonate fluids (equivalent to an increase of £1,020 per annum for each additional patient in excess of the 22 patients already funded for bicarbonate dialysis in the Provincial Hospitals Cost Profile);

- medical equipment costs have been increased to allow for 80% of CAPD patients to use disconnect systems (equivalent to an increase of about £3,000 per annum for each of 56 patients in addition to the 20% (30 in number) of CAPD patients already resourced for disconnect systems in the Provincial Hospitals Cost Profile),

- a reasoned assumption that hospital general overhead costs would increase in total only marginally as a result of introducing a third shift per day for dialysis services (and have therefore included a unit cost per additional patient of only 10% of the standard unit cost).

It should be noted that estimated capital charges have been excluded from these Cost Profiles.

33. The importance of non-staff costs within the total cost structure for renal services means that any generalised cost structure will be susceptible to inaccuracy as a result of the impact of different clinical practices across sites. An example of this is in the assumption about clinical practice regarding the use of disconnect caps and shields in some CAPD disconnect systems. The Provincial Cost Profile (and therefore the eight London Service Profiles) assumes that shields are not used and only one disconnect cap is used per day across four dialysis sessions. We are aware that this may not be the case on all sites where standard practice might be the use of new caps and shields for each dialysis session.

34. We have calculated that this practice might add a further £1,450 per annum to the total maintenance cost for each CAPD patient on these disconnect systems, which might total about £125,000 per centre. This is equivalent to adding about £510 to our calculated unit cost for dialysis and nephrology services. Clearly access to more detailed cost information on the present provision of services in London would provide a higher level of assurance to the Review Group about the acceptability and therefore robustness of the cost structures shown in Schedule 6 and summarised in the table below.

35. The estimated cost for providing dialysis and nephrology services (excluding capital charges) at each of these facilities is calculated as follows:

	Total Cost £	Unit Cost £
Academic Tertiary - 2 shift	4,983,600	24,918
Academic Tertiary - 3 shift	5,489,840	22,316
Non-academic Tertiary - 2 shift	4,782,630	23,913
Non-academic Tertiary - 3 shift	5,288,870	21,499
DGH - 2 shift	4,070,290	22,613
DGH - 3 shift	4,428,390	20,502
Satellite Unit - 2 shift (marginal)	204,770	1,138
Satellite Unit - 3 shift (marginal)	243,530	1,127

36. Note that the costs shown for Satellite Units are manpower and estates costs only - all consumables costs are deemed to be included in the Tertiary or DGH running cost budgets. The additional unit costs shown are based on the identified cost of running the Unit divided by an average of 200 patients, since

patients attending Satellites are assumed to be included in the cohort of patients managed and funded from either a Tertiary or DGH centre.

37. The table above allows us to calculate the marginal cost movement of extending the use of existing haemodialysis facilities from two shifts to three shifts per day. In the 15 station Tertiary Centres an additional 30 patients can be managed at an additional cost of £506,000, equivalent to £16,860 per patient place. This is significantly higher than the marginal cost demonstrated in the Cost Profile since the operation of an additional dialysis shift results in a cost threshold being crossed, principally as a consequence of the requirement for an additional nursing shift and extra utilities costs. In the 10 station DGH model the marginal cost per additional patient, again after allowing for an additional nursing shift, is calculated at £17,900.

38. The total cost of the Transplant service provided in each of the University Tertiary Centres is estimated at £1,405,900 (excluding capital charges), equivalent to £11,250 per transplant operation These figures for Transplant Services include follow up patient management costs in the first and subsequent years following successful transplantation. Further work on patient life cycle costing will allow this composite unit cost figure to be disaggregated into separate patient cost profiles for:

- transplant operation
- first year post transplant
- subsequent annual costs.

Running Costs of the Proposed London Facilities

39. The recommendations contained in the main Report of the Review Group regarding the provision of Renal Facilities within London are for:

- a central core of five University Tertiary referral centres;
- between five and seven other autonomous Tertiary centres;
- for each 3 million population, one Unit in a DGH;
- a network of Satellite Units, provided at the level of two Units per million population.

40. The size of each of these Facilities is assumed to be as shown in the Cost Profiles included in this Report, with an assumption that each Centre will operate their haemodialysis stations for three shifts per day and that each patient will attend for dialysis three times per week.

41. The patient demand model (which assumes the availability of 30 organs per million population and a requirement for 16% regrafts) predicts that in steady state there will be a requirement to provide maintenance dialysis facilities, through both hospital haemodialysis and CAPD facilities for a total of 7,420 patients and a further provision of back up facilities for 280 patients carrying grafts or on long term dialysis.

42. Each dialysis station is therefore assumed to be available to service 6 different patients. The recommended facilities would therefore have the (maximum) physical capacity to provide the following haemodialysis facilities:

	No. of Centres	No. of Dialysis Stations	No. of Haemodialysis Patients Managed
University Tertiary	5	75	450
Tertiary	5 - 7	75 - 105	450 - 630
DGH	4 - 5	40 - 50	240 - 300
Satellite	28	224	1344
Total	**42 - 44**	**414 - 454**	**2484 - 2724**

43. The requirement for haemodialysis places phased over the next 15 years might therefore be presented as follows:

	0 years	by 5 years	by 10 years	by 15 years
University Tertiary	5	5	5	5
Tertiary	3	5	5-7	5-7
DGH	2	4	4-5	4-5
Satellite (equivalent)	3	12	20	28

The balance of requirement would be met by patients dialysing on Home CAPD.

44. The revenue cost implications of this phased programme of dialysis and nephrology provision (excluding capital charges) have been determined using the Cost Profiles as summarised in paragraph 32 above, and in total are estimated as follows:

	No. of Centres	Running cost per centre £	Total Cost of Facilities £million
University Tertiary	5	5,489,840	27.5
Tertiary	5 - 7	5,288,870	26.4 - 37.0
DGH	4 - 5	4,428,390	17.7 - 22.1
Satellite (marginal)	28	243,530	6.8
Total	**42 - 44**		**78.4 - 93.4**

45. The phased programme of provision as shown in paragraph 40 above would lead to a build up in running costs as follows:

	0 years £m	by 5 years £m	by 10 years £m	by 15 years £m
University Tertiary	27.5	27.5	27.5	27.5
Tertiary	15.9	26.4	26.4 - 37.0	26.4 - 37.0
DGH	8.9	17.7	17.7 - 22.1	17.7 - 22.1
Satellite (equivalent)	0.7	2.9	4.9	6.8
Total	53.0	74.5	76.5 - 91.5	78.4 - 93.4

46. In addition, the running costs associated with providing Transplant Centres as part of the integrated services provided at each of the five University Tertiary Centres (providing a total capability for between 500 - 625 transplant operations per annum) is estimated at **£7 million per annum.**

47. Our provisional estimate of the full cost of providing all of the renal facilities described by the Review Group is therefore considered to be between **£85 million and £100 million per annum.**

48. The provision of a large number of Satellite Units based in greater proximity to patients will allow for some offsetting savings as a result in the reduction in the length of patient journeys to dialysis centres. Providing a reasonable estimate of what these savings might be is difficult. However, using the information on average journey times and average distance provided within the questionnaire by each of the centres and assuming that:

- the objective is to ensure that patients are not required to undertake a journey of longer that 30 minutes;

- savings in time equate pro rata to savings in the average length of a journey;

- the potential savings in journey costs would equate to £0.30 per mile;

we have broadly estimated that savings of about £550,000 would arise for the present population of hospital dialysis patients, rising to between **£1.6 million and £1.8 million** for the full steady state haemodialysis population.

Requirement for Capital Investment

49. We have shown above that the requirement for facilities across London has been determined as follows:

- a central core of five University Tertiary referral centres;

- between five and seven other autonomous Tertiary centres;
- between four and five Units attached to District General Hospitals
- a network of about 24 Satellite Units.

50. At this stage of the Review insufficient site information exists to allow for a full analysis of the estimated capital costs of providing or reproviding dialysis, supporting nephrology and transplant facilities within the geographical area being considered. Some information has been collected from other Renal Centres which might be of use in the next stage of capital planning. This is presented in the remaining paragraphs of this section.

51. One of the centres - from which the Provincial 2 Cost Profile has been determined - has an Integrated Renal Dialysis and Transplant Unit housing:

- 10 haemodialysis maintenance stations;
- 1 emergency bed;
- 1 home training bed;
- 1 CAPD clinic room;
- 3 CAPD training beds;
- 12 transplant beds;
- minor operations room;
- perfusion room;
- a separate ward providing nephrology beds.

52. The space allocation has been identified as follows:

	square metres
Transplant	289
Haemodialysis	361
CAPD Training	219
Office Space	300
Storage	140
Centre Total	1209
Nephrology Ward	469
Total	1678

53. Some 21 dialysis machines are provided in the Centre with a further 11 machines maintained as stock to cover replacement to machines provided in the Hospital, in Minimum Care Units and those used by patients on Home Dialysis. The estimated cost of replacement per machine is about £15,000. It would be prudent to assume an average life expectancy per dialysis machine of between 5 and 7 years.

54. In addition the Centre maintains:

- CCPD machines
- CAPD bag warmers
- CAPD UVXD
- ECG recorders/monitors
- blood pressure monitors
- X ray viewer
- ultrasound scanner
- defibrillator
- water treatment equipment
- volumetric pumps
- computing equipment.

55. The replacement capital cost of these items is calculated at about £180,000.

56. Facilities in Provincial 1 will soon be reprovided in a purpose built integrated unit. The new specification provides for:

- 20 adult dialysis stations;
- 4 paediatric dialysis stations;
- 4 in-patient CAPD beds;
- 4 in-patient acute/high dependency beds;
- 10 Transplant Beds;
- 20 in-patient adult nephrology beds;
- out-patients suite;
- workshop, stores, laboratories and offices.

The total floor area for these facilities is determined at 300 square metres.

57. In addition separate provision will be made for isolation facilities, consultant and secretarial offices, administrative offices, a computer room, and a medical records facility, with an estimated additional space requirement of 960 square metres.

58. Provincial 1 Centre also has a responsibility for running four satellite units. The largest of these (which is likely to be the most representative of the London model) is housed in an existing building on a hospital site. The Provincial Centre is recharged for the cost of heating, lighting, cleaning, portering, waste disposal, buildings maintenance, pharmacy items, pathology services and catering and laundry facilities. A computer link is provided from the Satellite to the Main Centre.

59. Capital costs associated with this Satellite Unit (which was commissioned two years ago) are as follows:

- structural alterations & water treatment plant   £170,000
- equipment, furnishings and fittings   £160,000
- total assessed capital cost   £330,000.

60. Clearly further, more detailed research and review work will be required before a full summary of capital costs - and subsequent capital charges - can be provided.

Assessment of Further Work Required

61. Our assessment of the further work which will be required in order to arrive at a robust assessment of the resource implications of the service recommendations of the Review Group is as follows:

- a full detailed assessment of the full costs of providing the present range of renal services in London, based as far as possible on the cost template used for the construction of the service costs for the two Provincial Centres;

- assessment of the operational causes which give rise to cost differentials across the present London facilities and consideration of the impact these may have on the cost profiles included in this Report;

- a more detailed consideration of the capital implications of providing or reproviding the services required within the 15 year timeframe, and thereafter assessment of the potential net additional capital charges associated with the recommended pattern of service provision.

62. Completion of these further pieces of work will allow for the comparison of the costs of the present and proposed services to be undertaken and, importantly, will facilitate the construction of more robust estimates of the running costs and capital costs of the future provision of Renal Services as proposed by the Review Group.

28 May 1993

Schedule 1

**Summary of Identified Service Costs
for
Each Renal Centre in London**

[Not included in this Report]

Schedule 2

Provincial Site 1
Renal Services Budget
1993/94

Provincial Site 1 - Renal Services Budget for 1993/94

Version dated: 25 May 1993

Budget Heading	Total £	Unit Cost £	Manpower Total
SUMMARY STATEMENT			
Main Treatment Centre			
(as adjusted for items not charged)			
1.1 Medical Staff	553870	1778	11.00
1.2 Nurse Management	221400	711	13.00
1.3 Nurse Staff			
Haemodialysis Adults	671800	2156	46.13
1.4 Nurse Staff			
CAPD Adults	142400	457	8.00
1.5 Nurse Staff			
Haemodialysis/CAPD Children	136000	436	7.00
1.6 Nurse Staff			
Community	72500	233	3.00
1.7 Nurse Staff			
Outpatients	22400	72	1.50
1.8 Nurse Staff			
Nephrology	227680	731	15.30
1.9 Admin & Clerical Staff	190700	612	16.06
1.10 Paramedical Staff	82450	265	4.00
1.11 Technical Staff	179100	575	8.47
1.12 Other Staff Groups	10500	34	1.20
Total Staffing	**2510800**	**8058**	**134.66**
1.13 Drugs	507300	1628	0.00
1.14 Medical & Surgical Items	1475180	4734	0.00
1.15 Non-Clinical Service Recharges	25000	80	0.00
1.16 Estate Costs	20000	64	0.00
1.17 Equipment Maintenance	56500	181	0.00
1.18 Administration Costs	66700	214	0.00
Total Non-Staffing	**2150680**	**6902**	**0.00**
TOTAL MAIN TREATMENT CENTRE	**4661480**	**14961**	**134.66**

Provincial Site 1 - Renal Services Budget for 1993/94

Budget Heading	Total £	Unit Cost £	Manpower No.	Total
2. Satellite Units				
2a Y Satellite				
Staff	70600	227		3.91
Recharges	15000	48		0.00
Total Y Satellite	**85600**	**275**		**3.91**
2b B Satellite				
Staff	89200	286		4.77
Recharges	18400	59		0.00
Total B Satellite	**107600**	**345**		**4.77**
2c W Satellite				
Staff	112600	361		6.71
Recharges	26500	85		0.00
Total W Satellite	**139100**	**446**		**6.71**
2d H Satellite				
Staff	102000	327		6.50
Recharges	49700	160		0.00
Total H Satellite	**151700**	**487**		**6.50**
Total for 4 Satellite Units				
Staff	374400	1202		21.89
Recharges	109600	352		
TOTAL SATELLITES	**484000**	**1553**		**21.89**
TOTAL Dialysis and Nephrology	**5145480**	**16514**		**156.55**

Budget Heading	Total £	Unit Cost £	Manpower Total
3. Renal Transplant Unit			
Medical Staff	79430	779	1.70
Nursing Staff	248600	2437	13.00
Other Staff	5000	49	0.54
Other items	130000	1275	
TOTAL TRANSPLANT UNIT	**463030**	**4540**	**13.54**
Total of Dialysis & Nephrology	5145480	16514	156.55
Add overheads & missing items at 30%	1543644	4954	
Total inclusive cost	**6689124**	**21468**	**156.55**
Less cash abatement and CIP equal to 2.4% of direct budget	125414	403	
Total Dialysis & Nephrology	**6814538**	**21871**	**156.55**
Total of Transplant Services	463030	4540	13.54
Add overheads & missing items at 30%	138909	1362	
Total inclusive cost	**601939**	**5901**	**13.54**
Less cash abatement and CIP equal to 2.4% of direct budget	11286	111	
Total Transplant	**613225**	**6012**	**13.54**

Provincial Site 1 - Renal Services Budget for 1993/94

Total Service Cost	Budget £	Total £	Unit Cost £	Manpower No.	Total
1. Main Treatment Centre					
1.1 Medical Staff					
Consultants	130200		418	1.66	
Consultants - University Posts	44000		141	0.50	
Registrars	49070		157	2.00	
University Tutors (Registrars)	22400		72	1.00	
Senior House Officers	80700		259	4.00	
Medical Staff - Treatment of ESRF	94600		304	2.20	
Other Staff Expenses	1200		4		
Additional doctors hours	157600		506		
Fees - Domiciliary Visits	100		0		
University Staff o/head charge	3000		10		
Less recharges	-29000		-93	-0.36	
Sub Total		553870	1778		11.00
1.2 Nurse Management					
Senior Nurse Manager	29100		93	1.00	
Grade G	40300		129	2.00	
Grade F	24100		77	1.00	
Grade E	17900		57	1.00	
Grade D	84500		271	6.00	
Grade B	19600		63	2.00	
Associated staff overheads	5900		19		
Sub Total		221400	711		13.00

Provincial Site 1 - Renal Services Budget for 1993/94

Budget Heading	Budget £	Total £	Unit Cost £	Manpower No.	Total
1.3 Nurse Staff					
Haemodialysis Adults					
Grade H	23600		76	1.00	
Grade G	40600		130	2.00	
Grade F	97100		312	4.70	
Grade E	221200		710	13.55	
Grade D	100800		324	6.42	
Grade A	32000		103	3.00	
Health Care Assistant	36900		118	4.00	
Dialysis Assistant Grade A	119200		383	11.46	
Associated Staff overheads	400		1		
Sub Total		671800	2156		46.13
1.4 Nurse Staff					
CAPD Adults					
Grade G	22200		71	1.00	
Grade F	21600		69	1.00	
Grade E	65300		210	4.00	
Grade D	33300		107	2.00	
Sub Total		142400	457		8.00
1.5 Nurse Staff					
Haemodialysis/CAPD Children					
Grade H	22000		71	1.00	
Grade G	24100		77	1.00	
Grade F	20200		65	1.00	
Grade E	52600		169	3.00	
Grade D	15700		50	1.00	
Associated Staff overheads	1400		4		
Sub Total		136000	436		7.00

Provincial Site 1 - Renal Services Budget for 1993/94

Budget Heading	Budget £	Total £	Unit Cost £	Manpower No.	Total
1.6 Nurse Staff Community					
Grade H	46500		149	2.00	
Grade G	21000		67	1.00	
Associated staff overheads	5000				
Sub Total		72500	233		3.00
1.7 Nurse Staff Outpatients					
Grade E	14900		48	1.00	
Grade D	6300		20	0.50	
Associated Staff Overheads	1200		4		
Sub Total		22400	72		1.50
1.8 Nurse Staff Nephrology					
Apportionment of mixed ward	227680	227680	731	15.30	15.30
1.9 Admin & Clerical Staff					
Renal Services Administrator	18900		61	1.00	
Medical Secretaries	54400		175	4.82	
Computer staff	34600		111	2.00	
Other A&C Staff	46400		149	4.58	
Personal Secretary	16000		51	1.50	
Storekeeper Clerk	11000		35	1.16	
Ward clerks	9400		30	1.00	
Sub Total		190700	612		16.06
1.10 Paramedical Staff					
Medical Social Workers	21500		69	1.00	
Physiotherapy	19700		63	1.00	
Dietitian	41250		132	2.00	
Sub Total		82450	265		4.00

Provincial Site 1 - Renal Services Budget for 1993/94

Budget Heading	Budget £	Total £	Unit Cost £	Manpower No.	Total
1.11 Technical Staff					
Medical Physics Technician 05	26500		85	1.00	
Medical Physics Technician 03	128400		412	7.00	
Technician - ESRF	9700		31	0.47	
Associated Staff overheads	14500		47		
Sub Total		179100	575		8.47
1.12 Other Staff Groups					
General Porters	10500		34	1.20	
Sub Total		10500	34		1.20
1.13 Drugs					
Anticoagulants/ Antithrombics	21800		70		
Hormones - Trophic	40000		128		
Mineral, Nutritional & Vitamins	36600		117		
Plasma Expanders	30000		96		
EPO	237200		761		
All Other Drugs	61700		198		
Handling Charge	80000		257		
Sub Total		507300	1628		
1.14 Medical & Surgical Items					
Dressings	43300		139		
Needles & Syringes	35000		112		
Catheters & Cannulae	23800		76		
Giving Sets & Infusion Cassettes	200		1		
Gloves	10000		32		
Sutures	500		2		
Other Med & Surgical Items	725000		2327		
CAPD Fluids	461200		1480		
CAPD Supplies	157600		506		
Nephrology Ward	18580		60		
Sub Total		1475180	4734		

Provincial Site 1 - Renal Services Budget for 1993/94

Budget Heading	Budget £	Total £	Unit Cost £	Manpower No.	Total
1.15 Non-Clinical Service Recharges					
CSSD	25000		80		
Sub Total		25000	80		
1.16 Estate Costs					
Electricity	9000		29		
Sewage/Waste Removal	1000		3		
Maintenance of Cabins -					
Home Dialysis	6000		19		
Furniture & Furnishings	2000		6		
Minor Works	2000		6		
Sub Total		20000	64		
1.17 Equipment Maintenance					
Dialysis Equipment - Spares	29000		93		
M&S Repairs & Maintenance	25000		80		
M&S Maintenance Contracts	2500		8		
Sub Total		56500	181		
1.18 Administration Costs					
Telephone rentals	10900		35		
Photocopying	1700		5		
Computer costs	28400		91		
Quality Systems	1000		3		
Office Equipment	6500		21		
Printing & Stationery	5800		19		
Travel & Subsistence	8200		26		
Journals & Text Books	1200		4		
Study Leave	3000		10		
Sub Total		66700	214		
TOTAL MAIN TREATMENT CENTRE		4661480	14961		134.66

Provincial Site 1 - Renal Services Budget for 1993/94

Budget Heading	Budget £	Total £	Unit Cost £	Manpower No.	Total
2. Satellite Units					
2a Y SATELLITE					
Nurse Grade G	20800		67	1.00	
Nurse Grade E	41500		133	2.41	
Nurse Grade D	7100		23	0.50	
Associated Staff Overheads	1200		4		
Sub Total		70600	227		3.91
Recharges from Host Hospital	15000		48		
Sub Total		15000	48		
TOTAL Y SATELLITE		**85600**	**275**		**3.91**
2b B SATELLITE					
Nurse Grade G	22900		73	1.00	
Nurse Grade E	56300		181	3.13	
Nurse Grade D	9700		31	0.64	
Associated Staff Overheads	300		1		
Sub Total		89200	286		4.77
Recharges from Host Hospital	18400		59		
Sub Total		18400	59		
TOTAL B SATELLITE		**107600**	**345**		**4.77**

Provincial Site 1 - Renal Services Budget for 1993/94

Budget Heading	Budget £	Total £	Unit Cost £	Manpower No.	Total
2c W SATELLITE					
Nurse Grade G	21600		69	1.00	
Nurse Grade F	16000		51	0.80	
Nurse Grade E	48600		156	2.80	
Nurse Grade D	19400		62	1.31	
Dialysis Assistant Grade A	6500		21	0.80	
Associated Staff Overheads	500		2		
Sub Total		112600	361		6.71
Recharges from Host Hospital	26500		85		
Sub Total		26500	85		
TOTAL W SATELLITE		**139100**	**446**		**6.71**
2d H SATELLITE					
Nurse Grade G	21000		67	1.00	
Nurse Grade E	49700		160	3.00	
Nurse Grade D	22300		72	1.50	
Health Care Assistant	8600		28	1.00	
Associated Staff Overheads	400		1		
Sub Total		102000	327		6.50
Recharges from Host Hospital	49700		160		
Sub Total		49700	160		
TOTAL H SATELLITE		**151700**	**487**		**6.50**
TOTAL SATELLITES		**484000**	**1553**		**21.89**

Provincial Site 1 - Renal Services Budget for 1993/94

Budget Heading	Budget £	Total £	Unit Cost £	Manpower No.	Total
3. Renal Transplant Unit					
3.1 Medical Staff					
Consultant	54900		538	0.70	
Registrar	24530		240	1.00	
Sub Total		79430	779		1.70
3.2 Nursing Staff					
Nurse Grade I	25400		249	1.00	
Nurse Grade G	24300		238	1.00	
Nurse Grade F	19400		190	1.00	
Nurse Grade E	124500		1221	7.00	
Nurse Grade D	30400		298	2.00	
Health Care Assistant	11700		115	1.00	
Associated Staff Overheads	12900		126		
Sub Total		248600	2437		13.00
3.3 Other Staff					
Ward Clerks	5000		49	0.54	
Sub Total		5000	49		0.54
Other identified costs					
Cyclosporin	65000		637		
Diuretics/Antidiuretics	65000		637		
Sub Total		130000	1275		
TOTAL TRANSPLANT UNIT		383600	3761		13.54

Provincial Site 1 - Renal Services Budget for 1993/94

Activity Analysis

	Home Haemo	Hospital Haemo	CAPD	Satel	Total
	No.	No.	No.	No.	**No.**

End Stage Renal Failure

Adult

	Home Haemo	Hospital Haemo	CAPD	Satel	Total
Apr-92	32	119	73	53	**277**
May-92	34	121	73	54	**282**
Jun-92	33	130	74	52	**289**
Jul-92	32	124	77	54	**287**
Aug-92	30	126	77	56	**289**
Sep-92	30	120	78	67	**295**
Oct-92	30	119	72	69	**290**
Nov-92	30	119	72	69	**290**
Dec-92	27	125	71	67	**290**
Jan-93	28	119	72	72	**291**
Feb-93	28	118	69	72	**287**
Mar-93	27	117	70	73	**287**
Average number in programme	**30**	**121**	**73**	**63**	**288**

Paediatric

	Home Haemo	Hospital Haemo	CAPD	Satel	Total
Apr-92		10	11		**21**
May-92		10	11		**21**
Jun-92		12	12		**24**
Jul-92		11	12		**23**
Aug-92		11	11		**22**
Sep-92		11	12		**23**
Oct-92		12	13		**25**
Nov-92		12	13		**25**
Dec-92		13	13		**26**
Jan-93		11	14		**25**
Feb-93		11	15		**26**
Mar-93		10	14		**24**
Average number in programme	**0**	**11**	**13**	**0**	**24**
Total Adults & Paediatric	**30**	**133**	**86**	**63**	**312**

Provincial Site 1 - Renal Services Budget for 1993/94

No.

Transplant

Adults

Apr-92	1
May-92	5
Jun-92	1
Jul-92	3
Aug-92	4
Sep-92	3
Oct-92	4
Nov-92	6
Dec-92	9
Jan-93	4
Feb-93	3
Mar-93	3
Total for year	**46**

Paediatric

Apr-92	2
May-92	1
Jun-92	0
Jul-92	1
Aug-92	1
Sep-92	0
Oct-92	0
Nov-92	1
Dec-92	1
Jan-93	2
Feb-93	2
Mar-93	2
Total for year	**13**
Other Area patients	**43**
Adult & Paediatric total	**102**

Schedule 3

**Provincial Site 2
Adjusted Renal Services Budget
1993/94**

Provincial Site 2 - Adjusted Renal Services Budget for 1993/94

Version date: 19 May 1993

	Total £	Unit Cost £	Manpower Total
SUMMARY STATEMENT			
Main Treatment Centre			
1.1 Medical Staff	372380	1648	7.47
1.2 Nurse Management	42830	190	1.75
1.3 Nurse Staff			
Hospital Haemodialysis	333360	1475	19.53
1.4 Nurse Staff			
Hospital CAPD	144400	639	7.60
1.5 Nurse Staff			
Home dialysis	50000	221	2.10
1.6 Nurse Staff			
Out Patient Clinics	65500	290	4.64
1.7 Nurse Staff			
Nephrology Ward	317450	1405	20.48
1.8 Admin & Clerical Staff	121750	539	9.36
1.9 Support Services Staff	69950	310	3.60
1.10 Technical Staff	149610	662	6.90
1.11 Other Staff Groups	0		0.00
Total Staffing	**1667230**	**7377**	**83.43**

Provincial Site 2 - Adjusted Renal Services Budget for 1993/94

	Budget £	Total £	Unit Cost £	Manpower Total
1.12 Drugs		322000	1425	0.00
1.13 Medical & Surgical Items		1202000	5319	0.00
1.14 Other Service Recharges		80000	354	0.00
1.15 Estate Costs		0	0	0.00
1.16 Equipment Maintenance		0	0	0.00
1.17 Administration Costs		6000	27	0.00
1.18 Investigative Services		334191	1479	0.00
Total Non-Staffing		**1944191**	**8603**	**0.00**
TOTAL MAIN TREATMENT CENTRE		**3611421**	**15980**	**83.43**
Hospital Overheads		642340	2842	
Capital Charges		292442	1294	
TOTAL MAIN TREATMENT CENTRE		**4546203**	**20116**	**83.43**

2. Minimum Care Units

	Budget £	Total £	Unit Cost £	Manpower Total
Staff		67690	300	5.10
Recharges		12000	53	0.00
Total Minimum Care Units		**79690**	**353**	**5.10**
TOTAL MINIMUM CARE		**79690**	**353**	**5.10**
TOTAL Dialysis & Nephrology		**3691111**	**16332**	**88.53**
Hospital Overheads		642340	2842	0
Capital Charges		292442	1294	0
TOTAL Dialysis & Nephrology		**4625893**	**20469**	**88.53**

Provincial Site 2 - Adjusted Renal Services Budget for 1993/94

	Budget £	Total £	Unit Cost £	Manpower Total
3. Renal Transplant Unit				
Medical Staff		188220	1426	3
Nursing Staff		321930	2439	18.63
Technical Staff		35510	269	1.5
Admin & Clerical Staff		55120	418	4.05
Non Staff costs		345970	2621	
Theatre Costs		284460	2155	
Investigative Services		11540	87	
TOTAL TRANSPLANT UNIT		1242750	9415	27.18
Hospital Overheads		201480	1526	
Capital charges		102570	777	
TOTAL TRANSPLANT UNIT		1546800	11718	27.18
Total of all costs		6172693		115.71
Less vacancy factor (applied as 3.0% of pay budgets)		-64860		
Total Service Cost		6107833		115.71

Provincial Site 2 - Adjusted Renal Services Budget for 1993/94

Budget Heading	Budget £	Costing Adjustment £	Total £	Unit cost £	Manpower No.	Adj	Total
1. Main Treatment Centre							
1.1 Medical Staff							
Consultants	206450	-51800	154650	684	2.82	-0.70	2.12
Consultant Recharges	63830		63830	282			0.00
Registrars	31520		31520	139	1.00		1.00
Senior House Officers	62120	-10400	51720	229	2.00	-0.30	1.70
Clinical Assistants	46100	-9500	36600	162	1.35	-0.30	1.05
House Officers	40060	-8000	32060	142	2.00	-0.40	1.60
Management Fee	2000		2000	9			
Sub Total			372380	1648			7.47
1.2 Senior Nurse Management							
Grade I	19020		19020	84	0.75		0.75
Grade H	23810		23810	105	1.00		1.00
Sub Total			42830	190			1.75

Provincial Site 2 - Adjusted Renal Services Budget for 1993/94

Budget Heading	Budget Adjustment £	Costing Adjustment £	Total £	Unit cost £	Manpower No.	Adj	Total
1.3 Nurse Staff - Dialysis Hospital Haemo Dialysis							
Grade G	43800		43800	194	2.00	2.00	2.00
Grade F	51410		51410	227	2.53	2.53	2.53
Grade E	181570		181570	803	11.00	11.00	11.00
Grade D	46570		46570	206	3.00	3.00	3.00
Grade A	10010		10010	44	1.00	1.00	1.00
Sub Total			333360	1475			19.53
1.4 Nurse Staff Hospital CAPD							
Grade H	14280		14280	63	0.60	0.60	0.60
Grade G	43800		43800	194	2.00	2.00	2.00
Grade F	20320		20320	90	1.00	1.00	1.00
Grade E	66000		66000	292	4.00	4.00	4.00
Sub Total			144400	639			7.60

Provincial Site 2 - Adjusted Renal Services Budget for 1993/94

Budget Heading	Costing Budget Adjustment £	Total £	Unit cost £	Manpower No.	Adj	Total
1.5 Nurse Staff **Home Dialysis**						
Grade H	50000	50000	221	2.10	2.10	
Sub Total		50000	221			2.10
1.6 Nurse Staff **Out Patient Clinics**						
Grade F		20070	89	1.00	1.00	
Grade D		23620	105	1.64	1.64	
Grade B		21810	97	2.00	2.00	
Sub Total		65500	290			4.64
1.7 Nurse Staff **Nephrology Ward**						
Grade G	69560	69560	308	3.00	3.00	
Grade E	89630	89630	397	5.40	5.40	
Grade D	115150	115150	510	8.00	8.00	
Grade A	37760	37760	167	3.47	3.47	
Ward Clerk	5350	5350	24	0.61	0.61	
Sub Total		317450	1405			20.48

Provincial Site 2 - Adjusted Renal Services Budget for 1993/94

Budget Heading	Costing Budget Adjustment £	Total £	Unit cost £	Manpower No.	Adj	Total
1.8 Admin & Clerical Staff						
Senior Manager	21220	21220	94	1.00		1.00
Grade 5	13930	13930	62	1.00		1.00
Grade 4	48710	48710	216	3.82		3.82
Grade 3	33310	33310	147	3.00		3.00
Grade 2	4580	4580	20	0.54		0.54
Sub Total		121750	539			9.36
1.9 Support Services Staff						
Medical Social Workers	17250	17250	76		1.00	1.00
Physiotherapy	19700	19700	87		1.00	1.00
Dietetics	33000	33000	146		1.60	1.60
Sub Total		69950	310			3.60
1.10 Technical Staff						
Medical Physics Technician 04	34880	34880	154	0.90		0.90
Medical Physics Technician 03	30530	15260	68	0.50		0.50
SATO	75470	75470	334	5.50		5.50
Associated Overhead Costs	24000	24000	106			
Sub Total		149610	662			6.90

Provincial Site 2 - Adjusted Renal Services Budget for 1993/94

Budget Heading	Budget Adjustment £	Costing Adjustment £	Total £	Unit cost £	Manpower No.	Adj	Total
1.11 Other Staff Groups							
General Porters			0	0	0.00		
Sub Total			0	0		0.00	0.00
1.12 Drugs							
EPO			60000	265			
Misc (incl EPO)			0	0			
All Other Drugs	322000		262000	1159			
Handling Charge				0			
Sub Total			322000	1425			
1.13 Medical & Surgical Items							
Haemodialysis stations	128000		128000	566			
CAPD Teaching	20000		20000	88			
Nephrology Ward	22000		22000	97			
Home Dialysis	1032000		1032000	4566			
Sub Total			1202000	5319			

Provincial Site 2 - Adjusted Renal Services Budget for 1993/94

Budget Heading	Costing Budget Adjustment £	Total £	Unit cost £	Manpower No.	Adj	Total
1.14 Other Service Recharges						
CSSD		0	0			
Theatre - Access surgery	80000	80000	354			
Sub Total			354	80000		
1.15 Estate Costs						
Electricity		0	0			
Sewage/Waste Removal		0	0			
Maintenance of Cabins -						
Home Dialysis		0	0			
Furniture & Furnishings		0	0			
Minor Works		0	0			
Sub Total			0	0		
1.16 Equipment Maintenance						
Dialysis Equipment - Spares		0	0			
M&S Repairs & Maintenance		0	0			
M&S Maintenance Contracts		0	0			
Sub Total			0	0		

Provincial Site 2 - Adjusted Renal Services Budget for 1993/94

Budget Heading	Budget Adjustment £	Costing £	Total £	Unit cost £	Manpower No.	Adj	Total
1.17 Administration Costs							
Dialysis Unit Administration	6000		6000	27			
Sub Total		6000		27			
1.18 Investigative Services							
Programmed Investigation	26780	26780		118			
Nephrology Ward	161730	161730		716			
Outpatient Clinics	145681	145681		645			
Sub Total		334191		1479			
TOTAL MAIN TREATMENT CENTRE		3611421		15980			83.43
Hospital Overheads	642340	642340	642340	2842			
Capital Charges - Infrastructure	71624	71624	71624	317			
Capital Charges - Equipment	220818	220818	220818	977			
TOTAL MAIN TREATMENT CENTRE		4546203		20116			83.43

Provincial Site 2 - Adjusted Renal Services Budget for 1993/94

Budget Heading	Budget £	Costing Adjustment £	Total £	Unit cost £	Manpower No.	Adj	Total
2. Minimum Care Units							
Nurse Grade H	7140		7140	32	0.30		0.30
Nurse Grade B	45280		45280	200	4.30		4.30
Technician	15270		15270	68	0.50		0.50
Sub Total				67690	300		5.10
Recharges from Host Hospital		12000	12000	53			
Sub Total			12000	53			
TOTAL Minimum Care Units				79690	353		5.10

Provincial Site 2 - Adjusted Renal Services Budget for 1993/94

Budget Heading	Budget Adjustment £	Costing Adjustment £	Total £	Unit cost £	Manpower No.	Adj	Total
3. Renal Transplant Unit							
3.1 Medical Staff							
Consultant	75690		75690	573	1.00		1.00
Registrar	42100		42100	319	1.00		1.00
House Officer	21440		21440	162	1.00		1.00
Rech Tutor (Snr Reg)	48990		48990	371	1.00		1.00
Sub Total			188220	1426			3.00
3.4 Nursing Staff							
Nurse Manager	6340		6340	48	0.25		0.25
			6340	48			
Days							
Grade G	46860		46860	355	2.00		2.00
Grade F	48680	-20070	28610	217	2.49	-1.00	1.49
Grade E	84670		84670	641	5.00		5.00
Grade D	72990	-23620	49370	374	5.00	-1.64	3.36
Grade B	19190	-21810	-2620	-20	2.00	-2.00	0.00
Grade A	10370		10370	79	1.00		1.00
			217260	1646			12.85

Provincial Site 2 - Adjusted Renal Services Budget for 1993/94

Budget Heading	Costing Budget Adjustment £	Total £	Unit cost £	Manpower No.	Adj	Total
Nights						
Grade F	19030	19030	144	1.00		1.00
Grade E	59570	59570	451	2.93		2.93
Grade A	19730	19730	149	1.60		1.60
		98330	745			5.53
Sub Total		321930	2439			18.63
3.2 Technical Staff						
Scientist	20910	20910	158	1.00		1.00
Recharge Coordinator	14600	14600	111	0.50		0.50
Sub Total		35510	269			1.50
3.3 Admin & Clerical Staff						
Business Manager	13700	13700	104	0.50		0.50
Scale 5	16450	16450	125	1.00		1.00
Scale 3	11740	11740	89	1.00		1.00
Scale 2	8700	8700	66	1.00		1.00
Sub Total		50590	383			3.50
Ward clerk	4530	4530	34	0.55		0.55
3.4 Other Staff						
Dietetics	8300	8300		0.40	0.40	0.40
Total Staff Costs		609080	4614			27.58

Provincial Site 2 - Adjusted Renal Services Budget for 1993/94

Budget Heading	Budget Adjustment £	Costing Adjustment £	Total £	Unit cost £	Manpower No.	Adj	Total
Medical Staff non-pay	1000		1000	8			
Admin/Stationery costs	3000		3000	23			
Medical & Surgical Supplies	44200		44200	335			
Drugs	280200		280200	2123			
Tissue Collection	17570		17570	133			
Total Non-staff costs			345970	2621			
Theatre Costs	284460	284460	284460	2155			
Investigative Services	11540	11540	11540	87			
TOTAL TRANSPLANT UNIT			1251050	9478			27.58
Hospital Overheads	201480	201480	201480	1526			
Capital Charges	102570	102570	102570	777			
TOTAL TRANSPLANT UNIT			1555100	11781			27.58

Provincial Site 2 - Adjusted Renal Services Budget for 1993/94

Activity Analysis

	Home Haemo	Hospital Haemo	CAPD	Satel	Total
	No.	No.	No.	No.	No.
End Stage Renal Failure					
Adult					
Apr-92					0
May-92					0
Jun-92					0
Jul-92					0
Aug-92					0
Sep-92					0
Oct-92					0
Nov-92					0
Dec-92					0
Jan-93					0
Feb-93					0
Mar-93					0
Average number in programme	15	49	149	13	226
Total Adults	15	49	149	13	226

Provincial Site 2 - Adjusted Renal Services Budget for 1993/94

Transplant	No.
Adults	
Apr-92	
May-92	
Jun-92	
Jul-92	
Aug-92	
Sep-92	
Oct-92	
Nov-92	
Dec-92	
Jan-93	
Feb-93	
Mar-93	132
Total for year	132
Adult & Paediatric total	132

Schedule 4

**Provincial Cost Profile
for a
Renal Dialysis Unit Managing 200 Patients
with
Supporting Nephrology Services**

Provincial Cost Profile for a Renal Dialysis Unit Managing 200 patients with supporting Nephrology Services

Version date: 20 May 1993

	Predicted Cost £	Unit Cost £	Manpower wte	Notes
SUMMARY STATEMENT				
Main Treatment Centre				
1.1 Medical Staff	372380	1862	7.47	
1.2 Nurse Management	42830	214	1.75	
1.3 Nurse Staff				
Hospital Haemodialysis	333360	1667	19.53	
1.4 Nurse Staff				
Hospital CAPD	144400	722	7.60	
1.5 Nurse Staff				
Home dialysis	50000	250	2.10	
1.6 Nurse Staff				
Out Patient Clinics	65500	328	4.64	
1.7 Nurse Staff				
Nephrology Ward	317450	1587	20.47	
1.8 Admin & Clerical Staff	121750	609	9.36	
1.9 Support Services Staff	69950	350	3.60	
1.10 Technical Staff	149610	748	6.90	
1.11 Other Staff Groups	10500	53	1.00	
Total Staffing	**1677730**	**8389**	**84.42**	

Schedule 4

Page 1

Provincial Cost Profile for a Renal Dialysis Unit Managing 200 patients with supporting Nephrology Services

	Predicted Cost £	Unit Cost £	Manpower wte	Notes
1.12 Drugs	382000	1910		
1.13 Medical & Surgical Items	1063400	5317		
1.14 Other Service Recharges	86800	434		
1.15 Estate Costs	8800	44		
1.16 Equipment Maintenance	36200	181		
1.17 Administration Costs	42800	214		
1.18 Investigative Services	295800	1479		
Total Non-Staffing	**1915800**	**9579**		
TOTAL STAFF & NON-STAFF COSTS	**3593530**	**17968**		
Hospital Overheads	583480	2917		
Capital Charges	470820	2354		
TOTAL SERVICE COST	**4647830**	**23239**		
Less vacancy factor (applied as 3.0% of pay budgets)	-50330	-252		
TOTAL DIALYSIS & NEPHROLOGY	**4597500**	**22988**		

Schedule 4

Provincial Cost Profile for a Renal Dialysis Unit Managing 200 patients with supporting Nephrology Services

	Predicted Cost £	Unit Cost £	Manpower wte	Notes
1. Main Treatment Centre				
1.1 Medical Staff				
Senior Medical				
Consultants	154650	773	2.12	
Consultant Recharges	63830	319		
Junior Medical				
Registrars	31520	158	1.00	
Senior House Officers	51720	259	1.70	
Clinical Assistants	36600	183	1.05	
House Officers	32060	160	1.60	
Management Fee	2000	10		
Sub Total	372380	1862	7.47	
1.2 Senior Nurse Management				
Grade I	19020	95	0.75	Balance of 0.25 allocated to Transplant Services
Grade H	23810	119	1.00	
Sub Total	42830	214	1.75	

Page 3

Schedule 4

Provincial Cost Profile for a Renal Dialysis Unit Managing 200 patients with supporting Nephrology Services

	Predicted Cost £	Unit Cost £	Manpower wte	Notes
1.3 Nurse Staff - Dialysis				
Hospital Haemo Dialysis				
Grade G	43800	219	2.00	
Grade F	51410	257	2.53	
Grade E	181570	908	11.00	
Grade D	46570	233	3.00	
Grade A	10010	50	1.00	
Sub Total	333360	1667	19.53	
1.4 Nurse Staff				
Hospital CAPD				
Grade H	14280	71	0.60	
Grade G	43800	219	2.00	
Grade F	20320	102	1.00	
Grade E	66000	330	4.00	
Sub Total	144400	722	7.60	

Provincial Cost Profile for a Renal Dialysis Unit Managing 200 patients with supporting Nephrology Services

	Predicted Cost £	Unit Cost £	Manpower wte	Notes
1.5 Nurse Staff Home Dialysis				
Grade H	50000	250	2.10	
Sub Total	50000	250	2.10	
1.6 Nurse Staff Out Patient Clinics				
Grade F	20070	100	1.00	
Grade D	23620	118	1.64	
Grade B	21810	109	2.00	
Sub Total	65500	328	4.64	
1.7 Nurse Staff Nephrology Ward				
Grade G	69560	348	3.00	These costs are based on the provision of a 22 bed nephrology ward as per Provincial model 2. They are higher than those calculated for Provincial 1 [which equated to £731 per dialysis patient] which were derived for 18 renal beds within a 31 bed mixed general medicine ward, with a weighting of x1.2 for renal patients.
Grade E	89630	448	5.40	
Grade D	115150	576	8.00	
Grade A	37760	189	3.47	
Ward Clerk	5350	27	0.60	
Sub Total	317450	1587	20.47	

Page 5

Schedule 4

Provincial Cost Profile for a Renal Dialysis Unit Managing 200 patients with supporting Nephrology Services

	Predicted Cost £	Unit Cost £	Manpower wte	Notes
1.8 Admin & Clerical Staff				
Senior Manager / Administrator	21220	106	1.00	
Grade 5	13930	70	1.00	
Grade 4	48710	244	3.82	
Grade 3	33310	167	3.00	
Grade 2	4580	23	0.54	
Sub Total	**121750**	**609**	**9.36**	
1.9 Support Services Staff				
Medical Social Workers	17250	86	1.00	
Physiotherapy	19700	99	1.00	
Dietetics	33000	165	1.60	Balance of 0.4 wte allocated to Transplant services.
Sub Total	**69950**	**350**	**3.60**	
1.10 Technical Staff				
Medical Physics Technician 04	34880	174	0.90	
Medical Physics Technician 03	15260	76	0.50	
SATO	75470	377	5.50	
Associated Overhead Costs	24000	120		Represents travel and subsistence payments.
Sub Total	**149610**	**748**	**6.90**	

Schedule 4

Provincial Cost Profile for a Renal Dialysis Unit Managing 200 patients with supporting Nephrology Services

	Predicted Cost £	Unit Cost £	Manpower wte	Notes
1.11 Other Staff Groups				
General Porters	10500	53	1.00	
Sub Total	10500	53	1.00	
1.12 Drugs				
EPO	150000	750		Assumed at £2,500 per patient, 30% of patients [60 patients]
All Other Drugs	232000	1160		
Sub Total	382000	1910		
1.13 Medical & Surgical Items [including fluids]				
Haemodialysis stations	113200	566		Unit costs are calculated by averaging total costs over the quantum of all dialysis patients maintained by the hospital.
CAPD Teaching	17600	88		
Nephrology Ward	19400	97		
Home Dialysis	913200	4566		
Sub Total	1063400	5317		

Schedule 4

Provincial Cost Profile for a Renal Dialysis Unit Managing 200 patients with supporting Nephrology Services

	Predicted Cost £	Unit Cost £	Manpower wte	Notes
1.14 Other Service Recharges				
CSSD	16000	80		Unit cost from Provincial 1
Theatre - Access surgery	70800	354		Cost represents theatre time only. Other surgical costs are included in the Transplant budget and ward time in the nephrology budget.
Sub Total	86800	434		
1.15 Estate Costs				
Electricity	5800	29		Unit cost from Provincial 1
Sewage/Waste Removal	600	3		Unit cost from Provincial 1
Furniture & Furnishings	1200	6		Unit cost from Provincial 1
Minor Works	1200	6		Unit cost from Provincial 1
Sub Total	8800	44		
1.16 Equipment Maintenance				
Dialysis Equipment - Spares	18600	93		Unit cost from Provincial 1
M&S Repairs & Maintenance	16000	80		Unit cost from Provincial 1
M&S Maintenance Contracts	1600	8		Unit cost from Provincial 1
Sub Total	36200	181		

Provincial Cost Profile for a Renal Dialysis Unit Managing 200 patients with supporting Nephrology Services

	Predicted Cost £	Unit Cost £	Manpower wte	Notes
1.17 Administration Costs				
Telephone	7000	35		From Provincial 1 budget information
Photocopying	1000	5		From Provincial 1 budget information
Computer costs	18200	91		From Provincial 1 budget information
Quality Systems	600	3		From Provincial 1 budget information
Office Equipment	4200	21		From Provincial 1 budget information
Printing and Stationery	3800	19		From Provincial 1 budget information
Travel & Subsistence	5200	26		From Provincial 1 budget information
Journals/Books etc	800	4		From Provincial 1 budget information
Study Leave	2000	10		From Provincial 1 budget information
Sub Total	42800	214		
1.18 Investigative Services				
Programmed Investigation	23600	118		These costs will appear high because unit costs are calculated on the basis of the number of dialysis patients rather than finished consultant episodes or outpatient attendances.
Nephrology Ward	143200	716		
Outpatient Clinics	129000	645		
Sub Total	295800	1479		
TOTAL STAFF & NON-STAFF	3593530	17968	84.42	

Schedule 4

Provincial Cost Profile for a Renal Dialysis Unit Managing 200 patients with supporting Nephrology Services

	Predicted Cost £	Unit Cost £	Manpower wte	Notes
Hospital Overheads	583480	2917		Provincial 2 less Provincial 1 costs for estates and porters.
Capital Charges				
Infrastructure	250000	1250		Based on £4m asset, 25 years remaining life, av interest at 6%
Equipment	220820	1104		Provincial 2 information
Sub Total	470820	2354		
TOTAL DIALYSIS & NEPHROLOGY SERVICES	4647830	23239	84.42	

Schedule 5

**Provincial Cost Profile
for a
130 place Renal Transplant Unit**

Provincial Cost Profile for 130 place Renal Transplant Unit

	Predicted Cost £	Unit Cost £	Manpower wte	Notes
SUMMARY STATEMENT				
Renal Transplant Unit				
Medical Staff	188220	1448	3.00	
Nursing Staff	324550	2497	18.63	
Technical Staff	35510	273	1.50	
Admin & Clerical Staff	55120	424	4.05	
Other Staff	8300	64	0.40	
Less vacancy factor	-18350	-141		
Total Staff Costs	593350	4564	27.58	
Admin etc	3990	31		
Medical & Surgical Supplies	43550	335		
Drugs	275600	2120		
Tissue Collection	17290	133		
Theatre Costs	280150	2155		
Investigative Services	11310	87		
Total Non Staff Costs	631890	4861		
Staff and Non-Staff Costs	1225240	9425	27.58	
Hospital Overheads	201480	1550		
Capital charges	160000	1231		
TOTAL TRANSPLANT UNIT	1586720	12206	27.58	

Provincial Cost Profile for 130 place Renal Transplant Unit

	Predicted Cost £	Unit Cost £	Manpower wte	Notes
Medical Staff				
Consultant	75690	582	1.00	
Registrar	42100	324	1.00	
House Officer	21440	165	1.00	
Rech Tutor (Snr Reg)	48990	377		
Sub Total	188220	1448	3.00	
Nursing Staff				
Nurse Manager	6340	49	0.25	Shared post, 0.75 allocated to dialysis and nephrology services.
Days				
Grade G	46860	360	2.00	
Grade F	28610	220	1.49	
Grade E	84670	651	5.00	
Grade D	49370	380	3.36	
Grade A	10370	80	1.00	
Sub Total	219880	1691	12.85	

Provincial Cost Profile for 130 place Renal Transplant Unit

	Predicted Cost £	Unit Cost £	Manpower wte	Notes
Nights				
Grade F	19030	146	1.00	
Grade E	59570	458	2.93	
Grade A	19730	152	1.60	
Sub Total	98330	756	5.53	
Total Nursing [incl manager]	324550	2497	18.63	
Technical Staff				
Scientist	20910	161	1.00	
Recharge Coordinator	14600	112	0.50	What is this post holder responsible for?
Sub Total	35510	273	1.50	
Admin & Clerical Staff				
Business Manager	13700	105	0.50	
Scale 5	16450	127	1.00	
Scale 3	11740	90	1.00	
Scale 2	8700	67	1.00	
Sub Total	50590	389	3.50	

Schedule 5

Provincial Cost Profile for 130 place Renal Transplant Unit

	Predicted Cost £	Unit Cost £	Manpower wte	Notes
Ward clerk	4530	35	0.55	
Other Staff				
Dietetics	8300	64	0.40	
Less vacancy factor	-18350	-141		
Total Staff Costs	593350	4564	27.83	
Non Staff Costs				
Medical Staff non-pay	1000	8		
Admin/Stationery costs	2990	23		
Medical & Surgical Supplies	43550	335		
Drugs	275600	2120		Derived from Provincial 2, note that Prov 1 costs are lower at £1275 per patient episode. These costs need to be more fully verified by more detailed life cycle cost analysis.
Tissue Collection	17290	133		
Total Non-staff costs	340430	2619		
Theatre Costs	280150	2155		
Investigative Services	11310	87		
TOTAL TRANSPLANT UNIT	1225240	9425	27.83	

Schedule 5

Provincial Cost Profile for 130 place Renal Transplant Unit

	Predicted Cost £	Unit Cost £	Manpower wte	Notes
Hospital Overheads	201480	1550		From Provincial 2 calculations
Capital Charges - Infrastructure	93750	721		Based on £1.5m asset, 25 years remaining life, av interest at 6%
Capital Charges - Equipment	66250	510		Provincial 2 information
Sub total	160000	1231		
TOTAL TRANSPLANT UNIT	1586720	12206	27.83	

Schedule 6

New Cost Profiles

University Tertiary Centre - 2 Shift System for Dialysis

Dialysis/Nephrology Services

2 shift model for dialysis	£	Total £	Unit Cost £	Establishment wte no	Total wte no
Medical staff					
Consultant	401200		2006	5.00	
Senior Registrar/Registrar	121470		607	3.00	
Senior House Officer	66940		335	2.00	
House Officer	44080		220	2.00	
Total Medical		633690	3168		12.00
Nursing staff					
Nurse Management					
Grade I	27900		140	1.00	
Grade H	26190		131	1.00	
		54090	270		2.00
Haemodialysis					
Grade G	45170		226	2.00	
Grade F	19760		99	1.00	
Grade E	93350		467	5.40	
Grade D	30010		150	2.00	
Grade B	57360		287	5.00	
Grade A	20120		101	2.00	
		265770	1329		17.40
Acute Haemodialysis					
Grade G	45170		226	2.00	
Grade F	19760		99	1.00	
Grade E	86440		432	5.00	
Grade B	41300		207	3.60	
		192670	963		11.60
CAPD Training					
Grade G	22590		113	1.00	
Grade F	19760		99	1.00	
Grade E	51860		259	3.00	
Grade D	30010		150	2.00	
		124220	621		7.00

University Tertiary Centre - 2 Shift System for Dialysis

	£	Total £	Unit Cost £	Establishment wte no	Total wte no
Nephrology Ward					
Grade G	22590		113	1.00	
Grade F	19760		99	1.00	
Grade E	112370		562	6.50	
Grade D	172570		863	11.50	
Grade B	57350		287	5.00	
Ward clerk A&C2	10210		51	1.00	
		394850	1974		26.00
Community Staff/ Out Patient clinics					
Grade H	100300		502	4.00	
Grade B	34410		172	3.00	
		134710	674		7.00
Total Nursing		1166310	5832		71.00
Admin & Clerical Staff	133930	133930	670	9.36	9.36
Support Services Staff	76950	76950	385	3.60	3.60
Technical Staff	164570	164570	823	6.90	6.90
Other Staff Groups	11550	11550	58	1.00	1.00
Total Staffing		2187000	10935		103.86
Drugs	382000		1910		
Medical & Surgical Items	1302800		6514		
Other Service Recharges	86800		434		
Estate Costs	8800		44		
Equipment Maintenance	36200		181		
Administration	42800		214		
Investigative Services	325200		1626		
Total Non Staff		2184600	10923		
Total Staff & Non Staff		4371600	21858		103.86
All Other Overheads (excl capital charges)	612000	612000	3060		
Total Dialysis & Nephrology		4983600	24918		103.86

University Tertiary Centre - 2 Shift System for Dialysis

Transplant Services 150 patients per annum	£	Total £	Unit Cost £	Establishment wte no	Total wte no
Medical Staff					
Consultant	120360		963	1.50	
Senior Registrar/Registrar	40490		324	1.00	
House Officer	22040		176	1.00	
Total Medical		182890	1463		3.50
Nursing Staff					
Grade G	22590		181	1.00	
Grade F	35570		285	1.80	
Grade E	103720		830	6.00	
Grade D	105040		840	7.00	
Grade B	45880		367	4.00	
Total Nursing		312800	2502		19.80
Technical Staff	39060	39060	312	1.50	1.50
Admin & Clerical	60630	60630	485	4.05	4.05
Other Staff	9130	9130	73	0.40	0.40
Total Staffing		604510	4836		29.25
Administration etc	3875		31		
Medical & Surgical Supplies	41875		335		
Drugs	265000		2120		
Tissue Collection	16625		133		
Theatre Costs	269375		2155		
Investigative Services	10875		87		
Total Non Staff Costs		607625	4861		
Staff & Non Staff Costs		1212135	9697		29.25
All other overheads (excl capital charges)	193750	193750	1550		
Total Transplant Services		1405885	11247		29.25
Total All Services		6389485			133.11

London New Model 1

University Tertiary Centre - 3 Shift System for Dialysis

Dialysis/Nephrology Services

3 shift model for dialysis	£	Total £	Unit Cost £	Establishment wte no	Total wte no
Medical staff					
Consultant	401200		1631	5.00	
Senior Registrar/Registrar	121470		494	3.00	
Senior House Officer	66940		272	2.00	
House Officer	44080		179	2.00	
Total Medical		633690	2576		12.00
Nursing staff					
Nurse Management					
Grade I	27900		113	1.00	
Grade H	26190		106	1.00	
		54090	220		2.00
Haemodialysis					
Grade G	45170		184	2.00	
Grade F	39530		161	2.00	
Grade E	129650		527	7.50	
Grade D	45020		183	3.00	
Grade B	74560		303	6.50	
Grade A	30190		123	3.00	
		364120	1480		24.00
Acute Haemodialysis					
Grade G	45170		184	2.00	
Grade F	19760		80	1.00	
Grade E	86440		351	5.00	
Grade B	41300		168	3.60	
		192670	783		11.60
CAPD Training					
Grade G	22590		92	1.00	
Grade F	19760		80	1.00	
Grade E	51860		211	3.00	
Grade D	30010		122	2.00	
		124220	505		7.00

University Tertiary Centre - 3 Shift System for Dialysis

	£	Total £	Unit Cost £	Establishment wte no	Total wte no
Nephrology Ward					
Grade G	22590		92	1.00	
Grade F	19760		80	1.00	
Grade E	112370		457	6.50	
Grade D	172570		702	11.50	
Grade B	57350		233	5.00	
Ward clerk A&C2	10210		42	1.00	
		394850	1605		26.00
Community Staff/ Out Patient clinics					
Grade H	100300		408	4.00	
Grade B	34410		140	3.00	
		134710	548		7.00
Total Nursing		1264660	5141		77.60
Admin & Clerical Staff	133930	133930	544	9.36	9.36
Support Services Staff	76950	76950	313	3.60	3.60
Technical Staff	164570	164570	669	6.90	6.90
Other Staff Groups	11550	11550	47	1.00	1.00
Total Staffing		2285350	9290		110.46
Drugs	469860		1910		
Medical & Surgical Items	1509230		6135		
Other Service Recharges	106764		434		
Estate Costs	8800		36		
Equipment Maintenance	36200		147		
Administration	52644		214		
Investigative Services	399996		1626		
Total Non Staff		2583494	10502		
Total Staff & Non Staff		4868844	19792		110.46
All Other Overheads	621000	621000	2524		
Total Dialysis & Nephrology		5489844	22316		110.46

University Tertiary Centre - 3 Shift System for Dialysis

Transplant Services	£	Total £	Unit Cost £	Establishment wte no	Total wte no
150 patients per annum					
Medical Staff					
Consultant	120360		963	1.50	
Senior Registrar/Registrar	40490		324	1.00	
House Officer	22040		176	1.00	
Total Medical		182890	1463		3.50
Nursing Staff					
Grade G	22590		181	1.00	
Grade F	35570		285	1.80	
Grade E	103720		830	6.00	
Grade D	105040		840	7.00	
Grade B	45880		367	4.00	
Total Nursing		312800	2502		19.80
Technical Staff	39060	39060	312	1.50	1.50
Admin & Clerical	60630	60630	485	4.05	4.05
Other Staff	9130	9130	73	0.40	0.40
Total Staffing		604510	4836		29.25
Administration etc	3875		31		
Medical & Surgical Supplies	41875		335		
Drugs	265000		2120		
Tissue Collection	16625		133		
Theatre Costs	269375		2155		
Investigative Services	10875		87		
Total Non Staff Costs		607625	4861		
Staff & Non Staff Costs		1212135	9697		29.25
All other overheads (excl capital charges)	193750	193750	1550		
Total Transplant Services		1405885	11247		29.25
Total All Services		6895729			139.71

London New Model 2

Tertiary Centre - 2 Shift System for Dialysis

Dialysis/Nephrology Services

2 shift model for dialysis	£	Total £	Unit Cost £	Establishment wte no	Total wte no
Medical staff					
Consultant	240720		1204	3.00	
Senior Registrar/Registrar	80980		405	2.00	
Senior House Officer	66940		335	2.00	
House Officer	44080		220	2.00	
Total Medical		432720	2164		9.00
Nursing staff					
Nurse Management					
Grade I	27900		140	1.00	
Grade H	26190		131	1.00	
		54090	270		2.00
Haemodialysis					
Grade G	45170		226	2.00	
Grade F	19760		99	1.00	
Grade E	93350		467	5.40	
Grade D	30010		150	2.00	
Grade B	57360		287	5.00	
Grade A	20120		101	2.00	
		265770	1329		17.40
Acute Haemodialysis					
Grade G	45170		226	2.00	
Grade F	19760		99	1.00	
Grade E	86440		432	5.00	
Grade B	41300		207	3.60	
		192670	963		11.60
CAPD Training					
Grade G	22590		113	1.00	
Grade F	19760		99	1.00	
Grade E	51860		259	3.00	
Grade D	30010		150	2.00	
		124220	621		7.00

Tertiary Centre - 2 Shift System for Dialysis

	£	Total £	Unit Cost £	Establishment wte no	Total wte no
Nephrology Ward					
Grade G	22590		113	1.00	
Grade F	19760		99	1.00	
Grade E	112370		562	6.50	
Grade D	172570		863	11.50	
Grade B	57350		287	5.00	
Ward clerk A&C2	10210		51	1.00	
		394850	1974		26.00
Community Staff/ Out Patient clinics					
Grade H	100300		502	4.00	
Grade B	34410		172	3.00	
		134710	674		7.00
Total Nursing		1166310	5832		71.00
Admin & Clerical Staff	133930	133930	670	9.36	9.36
Support Services Staff	76950	76950	385	3.60	3.60
Technical Staff	164570	164570	823	6.90	6.90
Other Staff Groups	11550	11550	58	1.00	1.00
Total Staffing		1986030	9930		100.86
Drugs	382000		1910		
Medical & Surgical Items	1302800		6514		
Other Service Recharges	86800		434		
Estate Costs	8800		44		
Equipment Maintenance	36200		181		
Administration	42800		214		
Investigative Services	325200		1626		
Total Non Staff		2184600	10923		
Total Staff & Non Staff		4170630	20853		100.86
All Other Overheads	612000	612000	3060		
Total Dialysis & Nephrology		4782630	23913		100.86

London New Model 3

Tertiary Centre - 3 Shift System for Dialysis

Dialysis/Nephrology Services

3 shift model for dialysis	£	Total £	Unit Cost £	Establishment wte no	Total wte no
Medical staff					
Consultant	240720		979	3.00	
Senior Registrar/Registrar	80980		329	2.00	
Senior House Officer	66940		272	2.00	
House Officer	44080		179	2.00	
Total Medical		432720	1759		**9.00**
Nursing staff					
Nurse Management					
Grade I	27900		113	1.00	
Grade H	26190		106	1.00	
		54090	220		**2.00**
Haemodialysis					
Grade G	45170		184	2.00	
Grade F	39530		161	2.00	
Grade E	129650		527	7.50	
Grade D	45020		183	3.00	
Grade B	74560		303	6.50	
Grade A	30190		123	3.00	
		364120	1480		**24.00**
Acute Haemodialysis					
Grade G	45170		184	2.00	
Grade F	19760		80	1.00	
Grade E	86440		351	5.00	
Grade B	41300		168	3.60	
		192670	783		**11.60**
CAPD Training					
Grade G	22590		92	1.00	
Grade F	19760		80	1.00	
Grade E	51860		211	3.00	
Grade D	30010		122	2.00	
		124220	505		**7.00**

Tertiary Centre - 3 Shift System for Dialysis

	£	Total £	Unit Cost £	Establishment wte no	Total wte no
Nephrology Ward					
Grade G	22590		92	1.00	
Grade F	19760		80	1.00	
Grade E	112370		457	6.50	
Grade D	172570		702	11.50	
Grade B	57350		233	5.00	
Ward clerk A&C2	10210		42	1.00	
		394850	1605		26.00
Community Staff/ Out Patient clinics					
Grade H	100300		408	4.00	
Grade B	34410		140	3.00	
		134710	548		7.00
Total Nursing		1264660	5141		77.60
Admin & Clerical Staff	133930	133930	544	9.36	9.36
Support Services Staff	76950	76950	313	3.60	3.60
Technical Staff	164570	164570	669	6.90	6.90
Other Staff Groups	11550	11550	47	1.00	1.00
Total Staffing		2084380	8473		107.46
Drugs	469860		1910		
Medical & Surgical Items	1509230		6135		
Other Service Recharges	106764		434		
Estate Costs	8800		36		
Equipment Maintenance	36200		147		
Administration	52644		214		
Investigative Services	399996		1626		
Total Non Staff		2583494	10502		
Total Staff & Non Staff		4667874	18975		107.46
All Other Overheads	621000	621000	2524		
Total Dialysis & Nephrology		5288874	21499		107.46

London New Model 4

Sub Regional/District General Hospital - 2 Shift System for Dialysis

Dialysis/Nephrology Services

2 shift model for dialysis	£	Total £	Unit Cost £	Establishment wte no	Total wte no
Medical staff					
Consultant	120360		669	1.50	
Registrar	17335		96	0.50	
Senior House Officer	33470		186	1.00	
House Officer	22040		122	1.00	
Total Medical		193205	1073		4.00
Nursing staff					
Nurse Management					
Grade I	27900		155	1.00	
Grade H	26190		146	1.00	
		54090	301		2.00
Haemodialysis					
Grade G	22590		126	1.00	
Grade F	19760		110	1.00	
Grade E	51860		288	3.00	
Grade D	15010		83	1.00	
Grade B	41290		229	3.60	
Grade A	20120		112	2.00	
		170630	948		11.60
Acute Haemodialysis					
Grade G	45170		251	2.00	
Grade F	19760		110	1.00	
Grade E	86440		480	5.00	
Grade B	41300		229	3.60	
		192670	1070		11.60
CAPD Training					
[80 patients per year]					
Grade G	22590		126	1.00	
Grade F	19760		110	1.00	
Grade E	51860		288	3.00	
Grade D	30010		167	2.00	
		124220	690		7.00

Sub Regional/District General Hospital - 2 Shift System for Dialysis

	£	Total £	Unit Cost £	Establishment wte no	Total wte no
Nephrology Ward					
[18 beds]					
Grade G	22590		126	1.00	
Grade F	19760		110	1.00	
Grade E	77790		432	4.50	
Grade D	112540		625	7.50	
Grade B	45890		255	4.00	
Ward clerk A&C2	10210		57	1.00	
		288780	1604		19.00
Community Staff/					
Out Patient clinics					
Grade H	100300		557	4.00	
Grade B	34410		191	3.00	
		134710	748		7.00
Total Nursing		965100	5362		58.20
Admin & Clerical Staff	133930	133930	744	9.36	9.36
Support Services Staff	76950	76950	428	3.60	3.60
Technical Staff	164570	164570	914	6.90	6.90
Other Staff Groups	11550	11550	64	1.00	1.00
Total Staffing		1545305	8585		83.06
Drugs	343800		1910		
Medical & Surgical Items	1176060		6534		
Other Service Recharges	78120		434		
Estate Costs	8800		49		
Equipment Maintenance	36200		201		
Administration	38520		214		
Investigative Services	292680		1626		
Total Non Staff		1974180	10968		
Total Staff & Non Staff		3519485	19553		83.06
All Other Overheads	550800	550800	3060		
Total Dialysis & Nephrology		4070285	22613		83.06

London New Model 5

Sub Regional/District General Hospital - 3 Shift System for Dialysis

Dialysis/Nephrology Services

3 shift model for dialysis	£	Total £	Unit Cost £	Establishment wte no	Total wte no
Medical staff					
Consultant	120360		557	1.50	
Registrar	17335		80	0.50	
Senior House Officer	33470		155	1.00	
House Officer	22040		102	1.00	
Total Medical		**193205**	894		**4.00**
Nursing staff					
Nurse Management					
Grade I	27900		129	1.00	
Grade H	26190		121	1.00	
		54090	250		**2.00**
Haemodialysis					
Grade G	22590		105	1.00	
Grade F	19760		91	1.00	
Grade E	69150		320	4.00	
Grade D	30010		139	2.00	
Grade B	57360		266	5.00	
Grade A	30180		140	3.00	
		229050	1060		**16.00**
Acute Haemodialysis					
Grade G	45170		209	2.00	
Grade F	19760		91	1.00	
Grade E	86440		400	5.00	
Grade B	41300		191	3.60	
		192670	892		**11.60**
CAPD Training					
[80 patients per year]					
Grade G	22590		105	1.00	
Grade F	19760		91	1.00	
Grade E	51860		240	3.00	
Grade D	30010		139	2.00	
		124220	575		**7.00**

Sub Regional/District General Hospital - 3 Shift System for Dialysis

	£	Total £	Unit Cost £	Establishment wte no	Total wte no
Nephrology Ward					
[18 beds]					
Grade G	22590		105	1.00	
Grade F	19760		91	1.00	
Grade E	77790		360	4.50	
Grade D	112540		521	7.50	
Grade B	45890		212	4.00	
Ward clerk A&C2	10210		47	1.00	
		288780	1337		19.00
Community Staff/					
Out Patient clinics					
Grade H	100300		464	4.00	
Grade B	34410		159	3.00	
		134710	624		7.00
Total Nursing		1023520	4739		62.60
Admin & Clerical Staff	133930	133930	620	9.36	9.36
Support Services Staff	76950	76950	356	3.60	3.60
Technical Staff	164570	164570	762	6.90	6.90
Other Staff Groups	11550	11550	53	1.00	1.00
Total Staffing		1603725	7425		87.46
Drugs	412560		1910		
Medical & Surgical Items	1319120		6107		
Other Service Recharges	93744		434		
Estate Costs	8800		41		
Equipment Maintenance	36200		168		
Administration	46224		214		
Investigative Services	351216		1626		
Total Non Staff		2267864	10499		
Total Staff & Non Staff		3871589	17924		87.46
All Other Overheads	556800	556800	2578		
Total Dialysis & Nephrology		4428389	20502		87.46

London New Model 6

Satellite Unit - 2 Shift System for Dialysis

Satellite Unit

Dialysis Services 2 shift model for dialysis	£	Total £	Unit Cost £	Establishment wte no	Total wte no
1. Nursing staff					
Haemodialysis					
Grade F	19760		110	1.00	
Grade E	25930		144	1.50	
Grade B	28680		159	2.50	
Grade A	10060		56	1.00	
Total Nursing		84430	469		6.00
Recharges	70000	70000	389		
Capital charges [adaptations]	50340	50340	280		
Total Satellite Unit		204770	1138		6.00

Unit costs calculated on the basis of180 patients,
since Satellite patients are managed from
one of the 'parent' centres.

London New Model 7

Satellite Unit - 2 Shift System for Dialysis

Satellite Unit

Dialysis Services 2 shift model for dialysis	£	Total £	Unit Cost £	Establishment wte no	Total wte no
1. Nursing staff					
Haemodialysis					
Grade F	19760		91	1.00	
Grade E	43220		200	2.50	
Grade B	40150		186	3.50	
Grade A	10060		47	1.00	
Total Nursing		113190	524		8.00
Recharges	80000	**80000**	370		
Capital Charges	50340	**50340**	233		
Total Satellite Unit		**243530**	**1127**		**8.00**

Unit costs calculated on the basis of 216 patients,
since Satellite patients are managed from
one of the 'parent' centres.

London New Model 8

POPULATION WITHIN 30 MINUTES (NORMAL) DRIVE TIME OF THE FOLLOWING MEDICAL SITES

UNITS	PPOPULATION (000's)
Royal London	4033
UCH	4221
Middlesex	4145
Charing Cross	3740
St George's	2970
Guy's	3909
Chelmsford	592
Southend	349
North Middlesex	2831
Hillingdon	1253
Stevenage	849
Guildford	782
Brighton	597
Canterbury	508
Goodmays	2169
Colchester	602
Royal Free	3037
Barnet	1781
Watford	1009
RPMS	4078
St Mary's	4139
West Middlesex	2699
Northwick Park	2333
St Helier	1710
Cherlsey	1031
Kings	3465
Maidstone	673

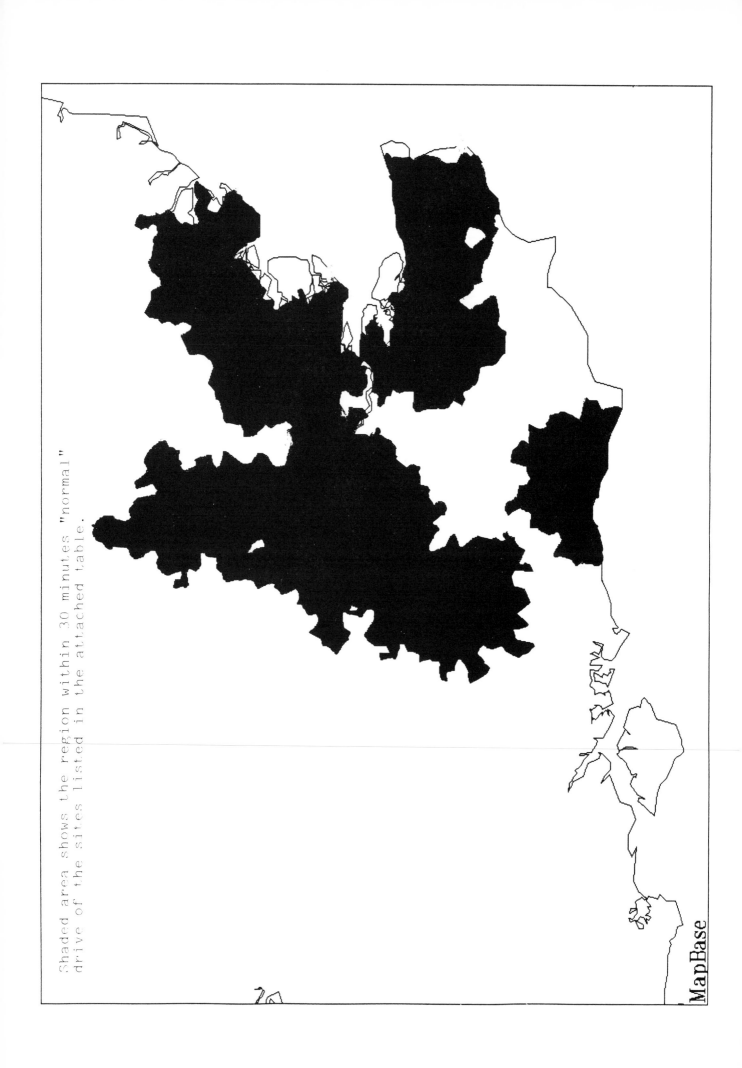

Shaded area shows the region within 30 minutes "normal" drive of the sites listed in the attached table.

MapBase

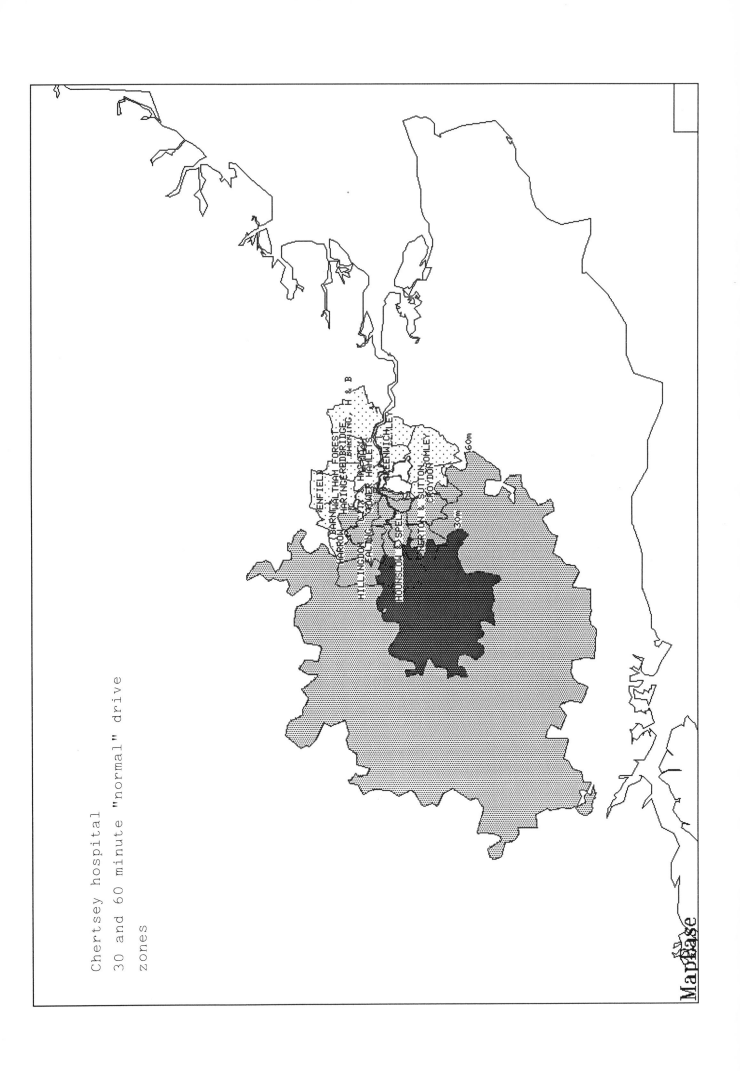

Chertsey hospital

30 and 60 minute "normal" drive

zones

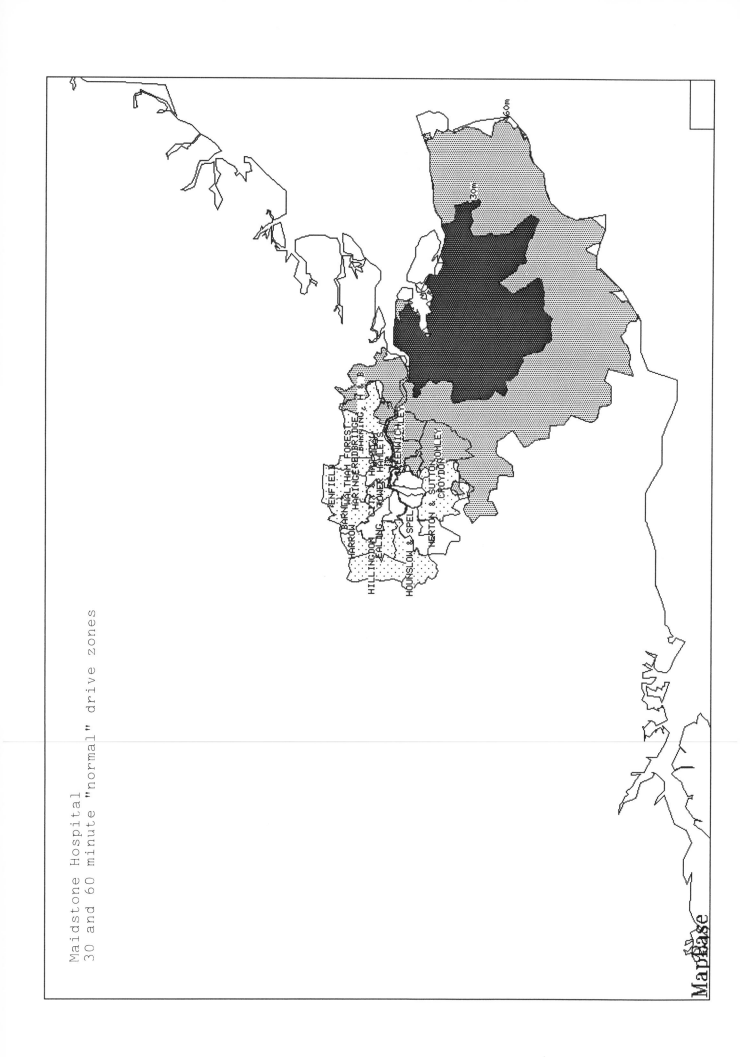

Maidstone Hospital
30 and 60 minute "normal" drive zones

MapBase

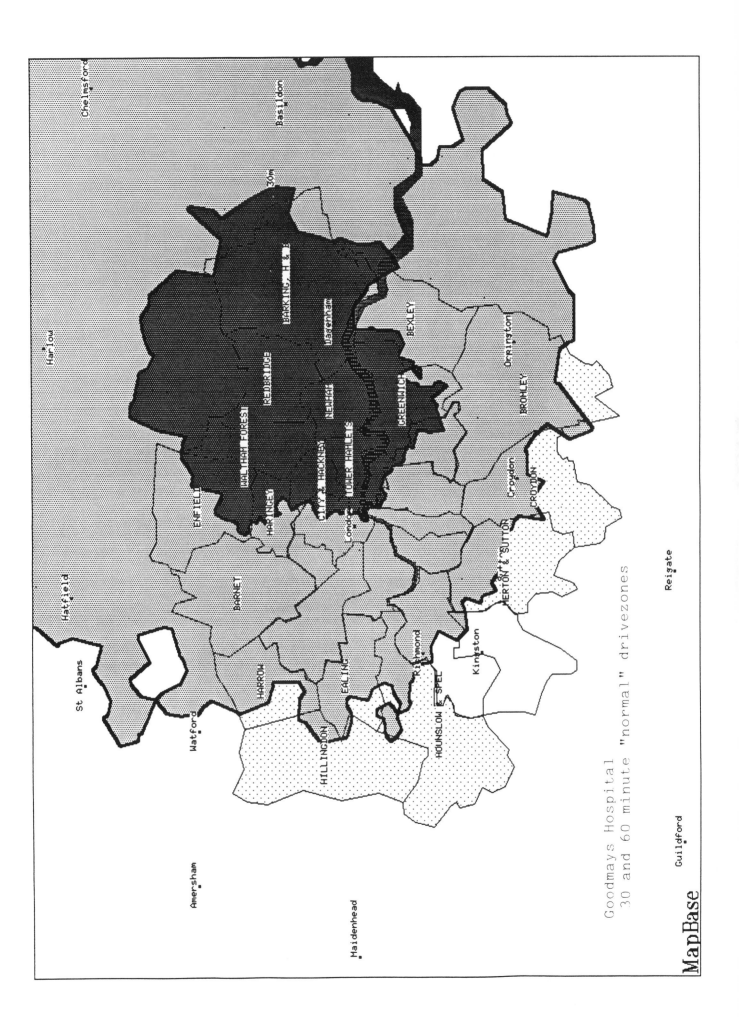

Goodmays Hospital
30 and 60 minute "normal" drivezones

MapBase

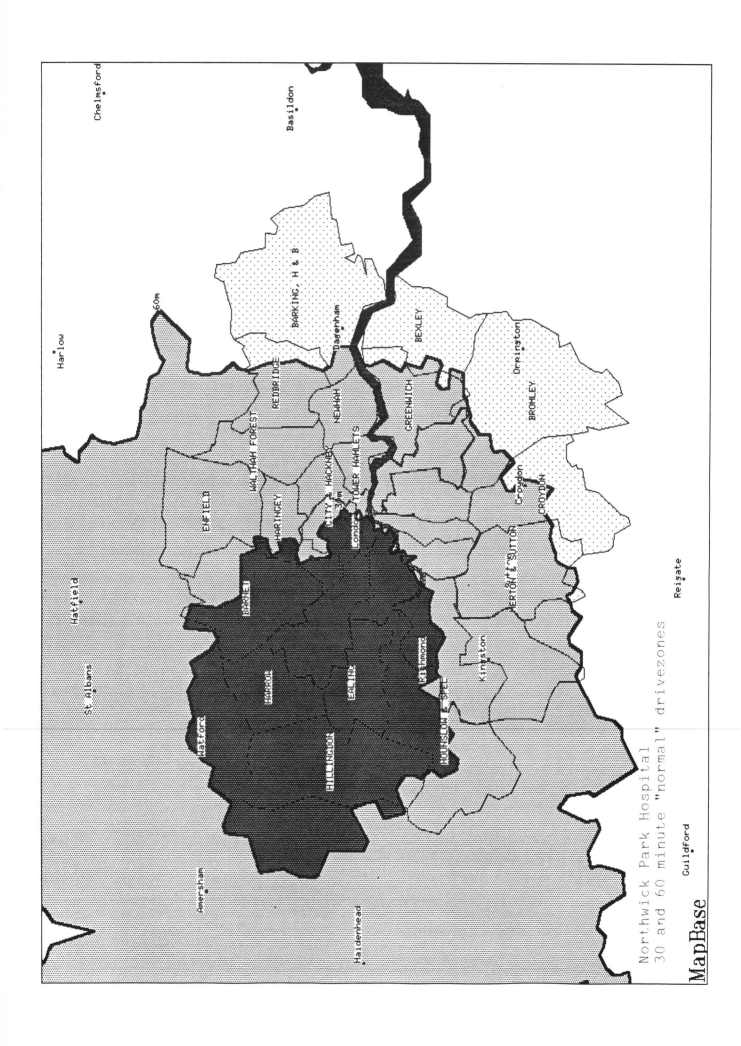

Northwick Park Hospital
30 and 60 minute "normal" drivezones

MapBase

RECOMMENDATIONS FOR FUTURE PROVISION OF SERVICES FOR RENAL REPLACEMENT THERAPY IN THE FOUR THAMES REGIONAL HEALTH AUTHORITIES

1. **University & Transplant Centres**

    -   these would be similar to the 'Autonomous Regional Units' as defined in the Renal Association report (Provision of Services for Adult Patients with renal disease in the United Kingdom, November 1991)

    -   they would be based at <u>five</u> of the twelve current central London Hospitals that have renal units

    -   there would be <u>one</u> of these units in <u>each</u> of the four Thames Regional Health Authorities; possibly with North East Thames having <u>two</u> centres

    -   such units should have adequate facilities for research into renal disease and the training of nephrologists

    -   such units would require approximately 50 beds in total for general nephrology, renal replacement therapy back up and transplantation.

2. **Peripheral Autonomous Renal Units**

    -   these would provide all services except renal transplantation (although they would provide follow-up facilities for transplanted patients)

    -   they would provide for patients from a wider area than the district itself.

    -   in some cases they would have associated 'satellite renal units'

    -   they would provide for a population of approximately 1,000,000 and would be staffed by three whole time equivalent physicians per million population (as recommended by the Renal Association document)

    -   they would require appropriate surgical back up support especially for access

    -   there would be <u>four or five</u> of these units in the four Thames Regional Health Authorities

    -   ultimately the location of autonomous renal units will presumably be determined by the 'purchasers'. However their decisions are likely to be heavily influenced by knowledge of the facilities already in existence.

North-East

There are two sites that are likely to be given consideration. Southend has had a 'satellite renal unit' (linked to the Royal London Hospital) for many years and has recently adopted a more autonomous role. They have 2 consultant physicians who have general medical as well as nephrological responsibilities. At present they look after 54 patients on unit haemodialysis and 4 on CAPD.

Chelmsford, which being more central is geographically rather better placed, is due to open a satellite renal unit later this year. There is a consultant physician on the staff who has had considerable previous experience of running a renal service.

North-West

There is a well developed renal service in the northern part of this sector but less development in the west.

Stevenage (Lister Hospital) has had a renal service since 1989 and has recently opened a Satellite unit at St Albans. There are 2 nephrologists and they look after over 140 patients treated with dialysis (Haemodialysis..75, CAPD..70). It is already undertaking the role of an autonomous renal unit and it would seem likely that this unit will continue to expand.

Watford has a satellite unit linked to St Marys where 25 patients are treated with haemodialysis. Their care is supervised by a general physician with interest in renal disease. However if there were to be a second autonomous unit developed in the west of this sector the purchasers would presumably determine the optimal site.

South-West

Brighton has had a renal unit for many years and currently 2 physicians, one of whom is a full time nephrologist, look after 140 dialysis patients. It seems likely that this unit will be developed further to serve as an autonomous renal unit for the southern half of South-West Thames although there is likely to be need for development of additional facilities with medical staff around the periphery of Greater London. Guildford would be geographically well situated to serve this role.

South-East

This sector already has one renal unit outside London at Canterbury. The Canterbury unit is run by two physicians, one of whom is a full time nephrologist. The programme includes hospital and home haemodialysis as well as CAPD. At one time transplantation was also performed in Canterbury although this has not been the case for a number of years. Geographically the unit is not ideally situated to provide an autonomous service to the outer half of the south-east sector and it may be that purchasers will favour further development at either Maidstone or Tunbridge Wells.

3.   Renal Unit in District General Hospital

As the stock of patients increases it is anticipated that there will be the need for the development of approximately 4 renal units staffed by general physicians with an interest in nephrology in the 'outer ring' of Greater London.

It is anticipated that there will be approximately 200 patients per million population needing unit based maintenance haemodialysis by the time the overall stock of dialysis patients reaches a plateau.

This implies that there will be approximately 2800 such patients in the 4 Thames RHA's. Assuming 3 treatment shifts per day (6 days per week) in each of the 13 units (15 stations in each) outlined above and thrice weekly dialysis for all patients 1170 ((15x3x2)x13) of these patients could be dialysed in these units. It is anticipated that the balance (1630 patients; needing 272 stations) will be treated either in 'satellite' facilities or by an increase in the number of stations in the 13 units.

4.   DHG sited satellite renal unit

-       situated so as to avoid the need for patients having to spend more than 1 hour travelling for unit based haemodialysis per day

-       they would be staffed adequately to cope with an elderly population of haemodialysis patients

-       a proportion of their patients would not have permanent vascular access

-       they would be linked clinically and professionally (but not necessarily managerially) to one of the University or DGH renal units which would provide backup facilities including emergency cover (eg. out of hours dialysis) and access surgery

-       the units should be of a size sufficient to cope with 150 patients needing unit haemodialysis per million population in the catchment area of the unit

-       there should be medical staff available to the unit on site within the hospital at all times when the unit is in operation

The Management of Satellite Renal Units

Three models have been used when establishing 'satellite' renal units in the UK during the past decade:

1. Minimal Care Facilities managed by the 'base' renal unit both medically and administratively. In many instances these have been 'free-standing' and have had no links with local hospitals.

Patients treated in these units have of necessity been stable chronic haemodialysis patients with permanent vascular access, often capable of undertaking dialysis without assistance.

Initially they were of particular value for patients needing haemodialysis who were only prevented from undertaking home haemodialysis because of inadequate social or domestic circumstances. Nowadays many of these patients are treated by CAPD.

2. Satellite renal units set up within district general hospitals and managed administratively as a part of that district general hospital.

Initially these often only treated 'stable' haemodialysis patients referred by the main renal unit, although in many cases they have gradually adopted a more independent role in keeping with the demands of an increasingly more elderly dialysis population.

When this has occurred a more comprehensive renal service has gradually developed with the provision of other modes of therapy for the management of chronic end stage renal failure (including CAPD) as well as treatment for acute renal failure.

3. Satellite renal units contracted out to the private sector.

The first such units in UK were set up in **Carmarthen and Bangor** in 1985. In these original sites the private contractor (Community dialysis Services in Carmarthen and Travenol/Baxter in Bangor) was to provide a dialysis service which included the building, equipment, consumables and all the staff with the exception of the medical staff. In return the NHS, via the DHA, was charged an agreed fee for each dialysis session. Since then additional units have been established at a number of sites including.

Ipswich	Baxter	1987
Carlisle	Baxter	1988
Merthyr Tydfil	Baxter	1990
Cardiff	Baxter	1990
Accrington	Fresenius	
Gloucester	Cobe	1990
Rotherham	CDS	1993

The services offered by these units varies from one to another although most have 'expanded' beyond the remit of the original 'contract'. Some of these units (eg. **Ipswich, Bangor and Carlisle**) effectively now function as independent renal units providing a comprehensive service with the exception of transplantation on site. Others (eg. **Carmarthen, University Hospital, Cardiff and Merthyr Tydfil**) have not developed a CAPD programme although in the case of Carmarthen and Merthyr they do provide haemodialysis facilities during the contracted working hours for patients with acute renal failure. With the exception of **Accrington and Rotherham** all of the units have had consultant cover based at the hospital.

There can be no doubt that the opening of these units allowed and encouraged the treatment of patients requiring renal replacement therapy who in previous years would not have been treated. However this is likely to have been due to the opening of a renal unit per se rather than of one that had been specifically contracted out to the private sector.

The role of the private sector in the provision of dialysis services in UK has been discussed in detail in two documents. In "Evaluation of renal services in Wales with particular reference to the role of subsidiary renal units. Report to the Welsh Office" Dr W G J Smith and his colleagues detailed the experience in Wales during the four years after the initial opening of the first two contracted-out dialysis facilities. More recently in a King's Fund project paper "Management and resource allocation in end-stage renal failure units: a review of current issues" published in 1990 N B Mays gave a more general overview but again largely based on the experience in Wales.

It is apparent from these documents that the use of the private sector for the provision of dialysis services allows rapid development in circumstances where problems with capital investment by the NHS would otherwise be a limiting factor. However, because of the lack of comparable NHS facilities in which similar capital investment has been committed to the creation of 'satellite units' that provide the same range of services as any of the 'contracted out units' it is not possible to directly compare the economics of the two.

Physicians who have been involved with the treatment of patients using contracted-out dialysis units have generally been satisfied with the service provided by the companies involved. 'Clinical' freedom has been maintained within the context of the original contract in all of the units and most of the physicians have found that the companies are prepared to be flexible when changes to the detail of the initial contract have been requested although this has sometimes involved more protracted negotiation than would have normally been necessary within the context of an NHS unit. It remains unclear whether a company that was running a dialysis facility and also involved with the production of dialysis consumables would be prepared to use products manufactured by a direct manufacturing competitor without levying a 'prohibitory' surcharge.

The majority of the physicians involved have found that the shift of responsibility to the contractors for the recruitment of nursing staff has in general been an advantage especially in some of the more remote districts where these units have been established. However it is widely recognised that this loss of involvement with the appointment of staff, especially those at the highest level could potentially present problems.

Another area in which problems can arise is due to the complex interface between the 'private sector' and NHS. All of the units currently in use are situated within the grounds of DGH's if not structurally attached to them. However in most cases they are understandably viewed as being 'separate' from the rest of the hospital and at times this opinion of the units can be extrapolated onto the patients who are treated by the units. In order to avoid this it is particularly important that all aspects of the service that the DGH will provide for the patients being dialysed in 'contracted-out' units are carefully and explicitly defined contractually beforehand. In this regard medical cover is of particular importance. When the initial negotiations took place, prior to the contracts for the earlier such units that were set up, it was assumed that virtually all of the patients dialysing in the units would be stable during dialysis and reasonably young and fit from other points of view. In reality experience has shown this to be far from correct and in several of the units more than half of the patients are aged over 70 years. Arrangements for adequate on-site medical cover are imperative.

The Choice between 'Contract' and NHS facilities for 'satellite' renal units in and around London should be primarily influenced by local circumstance. If capital is available for the development of such facilities or where conversion of pre-existing facilities is likely to be relatively inexpensive it would seem probable that local NHS providers would wish to explore with purchasers the feasibility of such developments... this avenue is now aided by the availability of dialysis 'hardware' on loan. Under circumstances where capital is a major limiting factor to the development of satellite services the use of 'contract dialysis' will be more attractive. Under both circumstances careful attention to the infrastructure required for the development of renal services will be needed and this will be particularly important if the option for the 'contracted services' is taken.

CONSULTATION WITH PATIENT GROUPS

1. Invitations to submit views and comments to the Review Steering Group were extended to the National Federation of Kidney Patients Associations (NFKPA), British Kidney Patients' Association (BKPA) and the twelve London-based Kidney Patients' Associations (KPAs) listed below. Ten submissions were received from KPAs, and the main points are summarised below.

Patient at home

2. Dialysis treatment in the patient's home appears to be highly favoured as being conducive to enhanced quality of life, and hopefully allowing patient to continue in employment. Home dialysis requires a support network operated by the renal unit that provides regular home visits by a specialist nurse and a welfare/social officer. Maintenance of equipment and the provision of supplies without worry and stress to the patient and carer is important. Regular and full review of the patients health, progress and family circumstances is vital.

Outpatients & day care facilities

3. Satellite units staffed by a specialist team linked to a central renal unit are preferable. Emphasis on appointments being kept promptly. Availability of refreshments for both patient and carer. Minimal care without full backup facilities in not an option.

Residential care

4. Residential accommodation for elderly or infirm patients is desirable. Also residential accommodation for patients requiring training.

Criteria for Tertiary Centres

*   A specialist team of staff

*   Patient and carers require full understanding of current medical condition and implications life style

*   Nursing care that is continually research based

*   Clinics - Nephrology, Low-Clearance, CAPD/Haemodialysis, and Transplant.

*   Acute Care.

*   Training facilities for patients, carers and staff.

*   Standards of care monitored in partnership with patients.

*   Counselling and support services, social services.

- A multi-disciplinary approach within the hospital.

- A transplant programme.

- Dietetic service of all renal patients, identifying and monitoring nutritional status.

- 24 hour direct contact support.

- Pathology services on site.

- Good public transport links.

- Ratio of patients to nurses of 2:1.

- Regular meeting between staff teams and patients.

- Full range of Dialysis treatments available.

- Well founded renal research facilities.

Accessibility, Timeliness and Communication

- Prompt and full resolution of telephoned problems to reduce stress in the patients home environment.

- Accessibility is considered to be of high importance, good transport links to the central renal unit are vital.

- Strong support for the development of satellite units. Emphasis placed on need to continually improve patient information and awareness regarding treatment. Contact and meetings involving medical staff, patients, carers, social services and counsellors to discuss and improve support services is highly desirable.

Collaboration With Social Services And Voluntary Agencies

5.   The renal social worker provides an essential service to patients particularly when first diagnosed. The Social Worker is an invaluable bridge between the patient and the social service and voluntary agencies. Contact should be developed with the Department of Employment to assess alternative employment opportunities.

KIDNEY PATIENT ASSOCIATIONS CONSULTED

Bart's

Charing Cross

King's

Guy's

Hammersmith

Harp (Royal London)

Royal Free

St Mary's

St Peter's (UCH/Middlesex)

St Thomas's

Tooting (St George's)

Shak (St Helier)

MEDICAL STAFFING PROFILE OF RENAL UNITS IN THE FOUR THAMES REGIONAL HEALTH AUTHORITIES

In the 16 hospitals with established adult renal units in the 4 Thames regional health authorities there are 46 consultant physicians who spend a substantial proportion of their time engaged in clinical nephrology. Twenty-one of these are aged between 35 and 45 years, 14 between 46 and 55 years and 11 are over 55 years. Additionally 4 units have associate specialists in nephrology. Twenty of the consultants have university appointments and 17 have general medical commitments (Fig.1). The sessional commitments of these consultants to general medicine varies considerably (Fig.2). In 7 units nephrologists do not have sessions in general medicine while in others as much as 40% of sessional time involves general medicine and in Southend the proportion is as high as 70%. In only 2 units (St Mary's & Stevenage) do the consultants have neither university appointments nor general medical commitments. In all units nephrologists are involved with the management of patients following renal transplantation.

There are 43 middle grade medical staff (Senior registrar, registrars & lectures) with clinical responsibilities distributed among the 16 renal units (Figs 1 & 3). In addition several units have research fellows with a clinical background. All of the central London units have a senior registrar and with the exception of St. George's all have at least 1 registrar. The units outside central London have 1 registrar. The number of middle grade staff with dual research/clinical appointments varies from 1 unit to another.

All 16 of the units have at least 1 senior house office (38 in total) although the majority do not use pre-registration house physicians. Three units employ clinical assistants on a sessional basis either for outpatient or haemodialysis unit duties (Fig.4).

WORKLOAD OF RENAL UNITS IN THE FOUR THAMES REGIONAL HEALTH AUTHORITIES

The workload can be broadly categorised as:

1. **General Nephrology**

    This involves the investigation and treatment of patients who have nephrological or metabolic disease, but who are not in renal failure. Most of this work is done on an outpatient basis, although some patients require admission to hospital for either special investigation (eg. renal biopsy) or treatment. Referrals will come both directly from general practitioners and from other hospital based clinicians. In general this work is of a high volume, low cost nature.

2. **Management of Chronic End Stage Renal Failure with renal replacement therapy.**

This involves three different categories of activity:

a. Investigation, treatment and long term follow up of patients with renal impairment who will ultimately require renal replacement therapy (ie. Dialysis or Transplantation). This component of a renal unit's workload requires a multi-disciplinary approach with involvement of nephrologist, dietician, surgeon, social worker, nurses, dialysis administrator and technicians in order to make the necessary preparations for dialysis treatment. Most of this work is carried out on an outpatient basis, but at some stage most of these patients need admission to hospital for vascular or peritoneal access surgery as well as in some cases for additional investigation.

b. Chronic Dialysis Programme. Most renal units will provide various different modes of dialysis treatment (eg. Hospital, satellite-unit and home haemodialysis, continuous ambulatory peritoneal dialysis, automated peritoneal dialysis, haemofiltration) along with the necessary support services for their patients. Most of the work is carried out on an outpatient basis although there is a significant inpatient component mainly due to complications of the treatment. Relatively low numbers of patients are involved but the cost per patient is considerable. Furthermore patients continue to generate costs for so long as they remain in the programme (ie. Until they either die, are transferred to another unit or are transplanted).

c. Transplantation. A successful renal transplant is the preferred treatment for a large proportion of patients requiring renal replacement therapy as it enables the patient to return to a virtually normal life style. During the first year following transplantation the costs are similar to those of dialysis but thereafter there is a considerable saving although patients require indefinite outpatient follow up. Despite its advantages the availability of transplantation is limited by the availability of cadaveric organs.

3. **Management of Acute Renal Failure**

The majority of patients with acute renal failure are extremely ill and often have disease involving more than one organ system. Because of this, as well as renal replacement therapy, they frequently require "intensive therapy" with medical input from several specialists in addition to nephrologists. In consequence their management is very expensive although in contrast to the patients with chronic renal failure the expenditure is for a limited period of time in relation to each patient.

4. Extra-corporeal therapy (eg. Dialysis, Haemofiltration, Haemoperfusion and Plasma Exchange) for conditions other than renal failure. For most renal units this aspect of their work is small by comparison with the workload generated by end stage of renal failure.

GENERAL NEPHROLOGY

BEDS

All renal units except Southend have designated nephrology beds. Bed numbers range from a nominal 3 beds at Southend to 34 beds at Kings, with an average of 20.5 per unit. Bed occupancy ranged from 83% at St Peter's to 140% at St Bartholomew's (with over spill into beds designated to other specialities). Some units include some general medical beds as part of their total complement (eg. Charing Cross & Hammersmith). Average bed occupancy in the 16 units was 101% (Figs.5&6).

The estimated requirement for beds for renal services is 27 pmp on reaching a stable "stock patient population" (1). The 1991 census figures for the population of the four Thames Regions of 14.026 million suggests a bed requirement of 379. The total of 323 beds for the area suggests a shortfall of 4 beds pmp(15%) on reaching a stable patient stock after a number of years of accepting 80 patients pmp. As stated in the report (1) this may be an underestimate, and the requirement for beds for managing patients other than ESRF, ARF or transplantation may be as many as 10 pmp increasing the total requirement to 34 pmp. Using this latter figure a total bed requirement would be 477 with a shortfall of 11 beds pmp (33%).

RENAL BIOPSIES

Approximately 1200 native renal biopsies were performed annually (Fig.7) and 125 patients treated with plasma exchange (Fig.8)

MANAGEMENT OF CHRONIC END STAGE RENAL FAILURE WITH RENAL REPLACEMENT THERAPY

Approximately 6,000 patients with chronic end stage renal failure are currently looked after by one of the 16 renal units in the Thames regional health authorities. 55% of these patients have functioning renal transplants (3226) while the remainder are treated with dialysis (Fig.9). In these units in 1992, 1091 patients started renal replacement therapy (Fig.10) and an average of 485 transplants have been performed annually during the past 3 years. Of the 2,660 patients being treated with chronic dialysis in March 1993 (Fig. 11), 33% were undergoing unit based haemodialysis, 10% were haemodialysing at home, 3% were haemodialysing inn satellite renal units, 53% were treated with continuous ambulatory peritoneal dialysis (CAPD) and 2% were receiving automated peritoneal dialysis (CPD).

The size of the renal units in terms of end stage renal failure patient load varies from at the one extreme Southend and St George's who look after 58 and 66 patients respectively to at the other Guy's with 637 (195 dialysis & 442 transplanted) and the Royal London with 584 adult patients . With the exception of Southend and St. George's all of the units look after more than 100 patients treated with dialysis and five units have more than 200 such patients (Royal London, St Bartholomew's, St Mary's, Charing Cross and St Peter's).

The recently published document "Provision of Services For Adult Patients with Renal Disease in the United Kingdom" recommends 3 whole time equivalent physicians per million population on achieving a stable stock of patients needing renal replacement therapy with a take on rate of 80 patients per million population per year. With this treatment rate each such renal physician would look after about 25 new patients per year. Physicians with academic appointments might be expected to spend less time than their 'NHS' colleagues undertaking clinical commitments and as such will equally take on fewer new patients per year". Assuming that on this basis academic appointments will have half the workload of "clinical" appointments Table 1 shows the annual new end stage renal failure patient workload for consultant nephrologists in and around London for 1992. Thus defined, the consultant staff in all 16 units in the 4 Thames Regional Health Authorities are responsible for the care of as many or more patients than would be recommended on achieving a stable patient stock. Serving a population of approximately 14,000,000 the 46 consultant nephrologists undertake 300 NHS sessions in nephrology with 100 academic sessions. This can be considered to equate with 350 clinical nephrology sessions or 32 whole time equivalent (WTE) consultants which based on the Renal Association guidelines will represent a deficit of 10 consultants once a stable stock is achieved; although this is unlikely to occur for a number of years. In these calculations responsibility for partaking in an active transplant programme has not been considered and in at least one of the units (St Mary's) a consultant post was vacant. In 3 units (St Helier, St George's and Southend) the workload as measured in this way is far greater than is recommended although the latter 2 being relatively new units have a small pool of patients by comparison with the others. Even when allowing for the presence of an associate specialist at St Helier more than 60 new patients per Whole Time Equivalent of consultant time were taken onto the renal replacement programme during 1992.

PROPOSALS FOR MEDICAL STAFFING PROFILE IN THE FUTURE

In each of the four sectors serving a population of 3.5 million it is suggested that there will be:

A <u>University/Transplant Centre</u> in Central London with 15 Haemodialysis stations. These would be staffed medically with:

-	Transplant Surgeons	x3
	Academic Nephrologists	x2
	Clinical Nephrologists	x4
-	Senior Registrars (nephrology)	x2
	Senior Registrars (transplants)	x1
-	Registrar (nephrology)	x1
-	SHO/HP	x5

A <u>Main District General Hospital Renal Unit</u> outside London with 15 Haemodialysis stations which would be staffed medically with:

-	Nephrologists	x3
-	Surgeons (access)	x1
-	Senior Registrar (nephrology)	x1
-	Registrar (nephrology)	x1
-	SHO/HP	x4

In the outer ring of greater London it is anticipated that there will be the need for an <u>additional DGH renal unit</u> with 15 haemodialysis stations staffed with 2 consultant physicians with an interest in Nephrology.

Thus in total in the four sectors (assuming 2 <u>Transplant/University Centres</u> in one of them) there would be the need for:

15 Transplant Surgeons
10 Academic Nephrologists
32 Consultant Nephrologists
 8 Consultant Physicians with interest in Nephrology
14 Senior Registrars in Nephrology
 9 Registrars in Nephrology
41 SHO/HP's

NB :   This does not take into account the junior staffing requirements of the 4 DGH's that are likely to develop renal units in the outer ring of greater London nor the support staff needed to provide medical cover for the 'satellite' units that are proposed in and around London on DGH sites.

LONDON RENAL UNITS
Medical Staffing Profile
March 1993

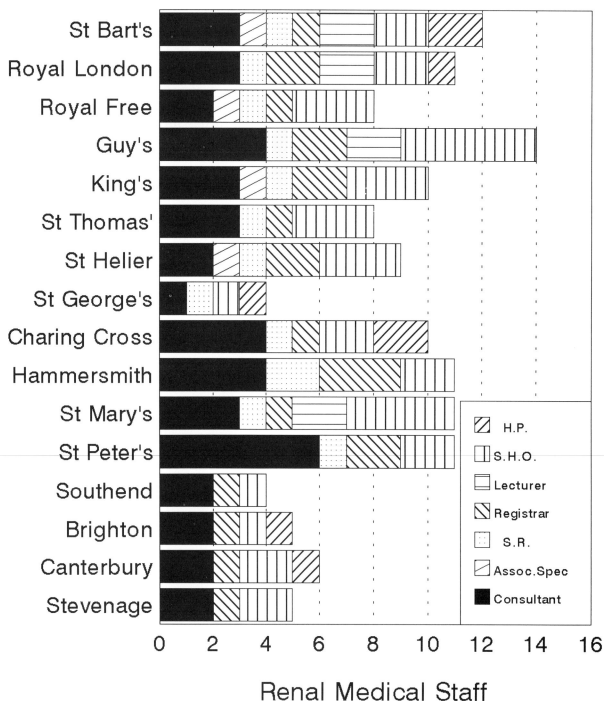

Hospital

Renal Medical Staff

Legend:
- H.P.
- S.H.O.
- Lecturer
- Registrar
- S.R.
- Assoc.Spec
- Consultant

Figure 1

LONDON RENAL UNITS
Consultant Nephrologist Sessional Commitments.
March 1993

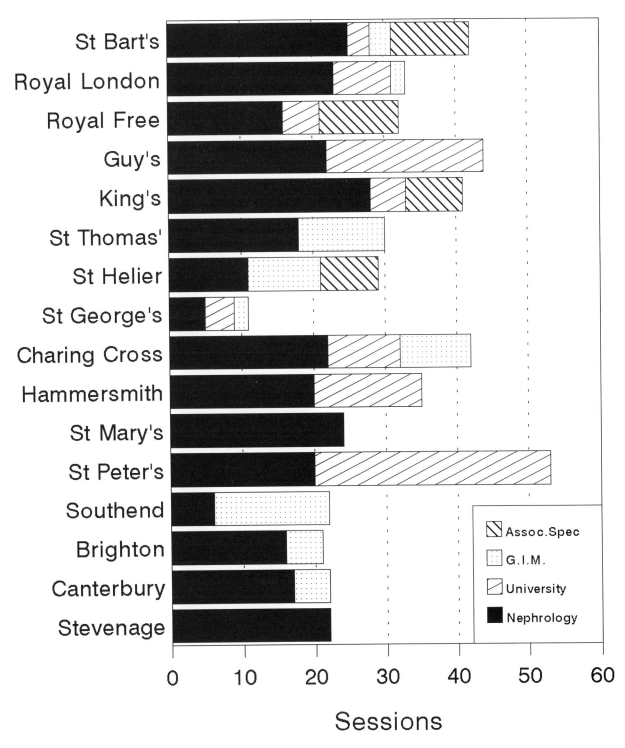

Hospital

Figure 2

LONDON RENAL UNITS
Middle Grade Sessional Commitments.
S.R.'s, Registrars & Lecturers

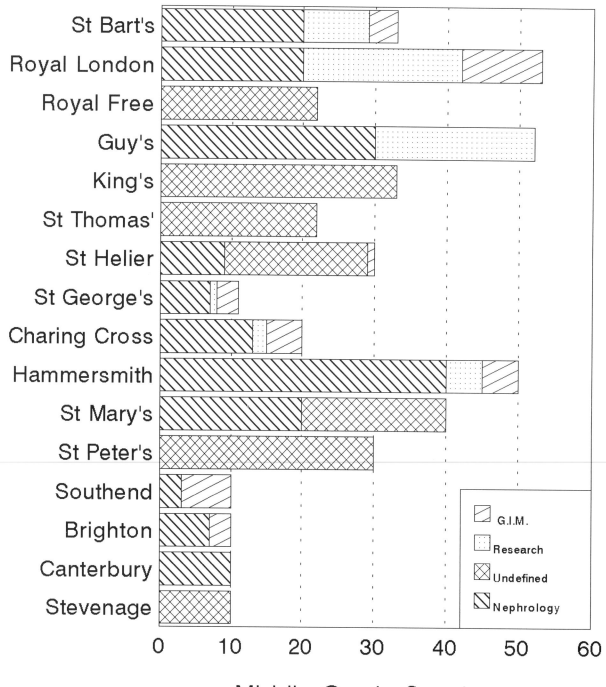

Figure 3

LONDON RENAL UNITS
Junior Grade Sessions in Nephrology
S.H.O.'s, H.P.'s & Clinical Assistants

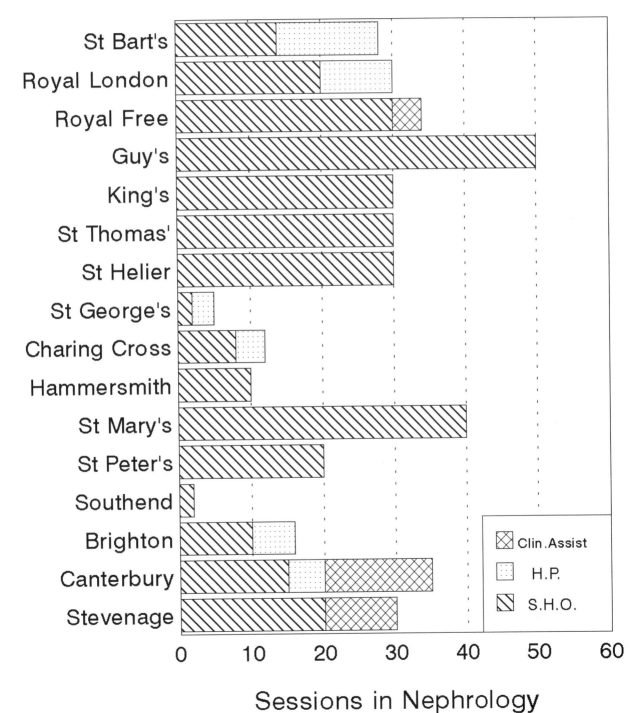

Figure 4

LONDON RENAL UNITS
Inpatient Bed Complement
March 1993

Hospital

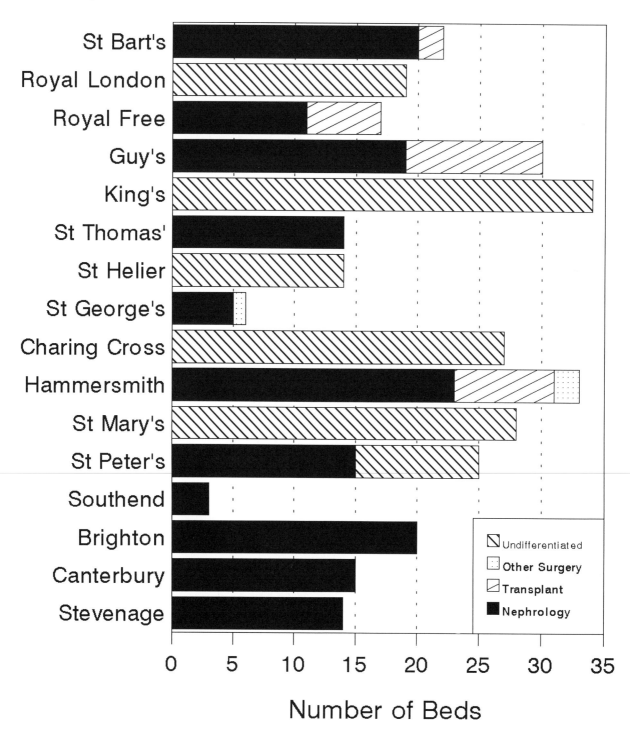

Figure 5

LONDON RENAL UNITS
Average Number of Inpatients
1992

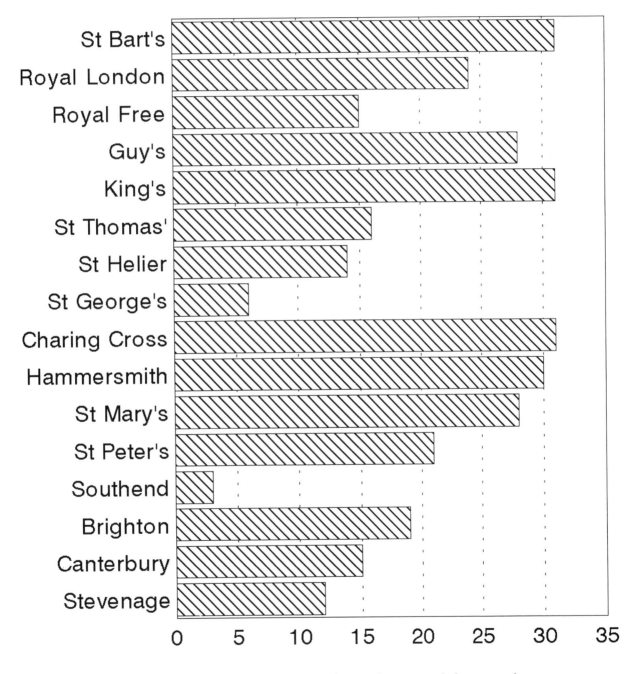

Hospital

Average Number of Inpatients

Includes Nephrology & Transplant Patients

Figure 6

LONDON RENAL UNITS
Renal Biopsies in Adults
1991-1992

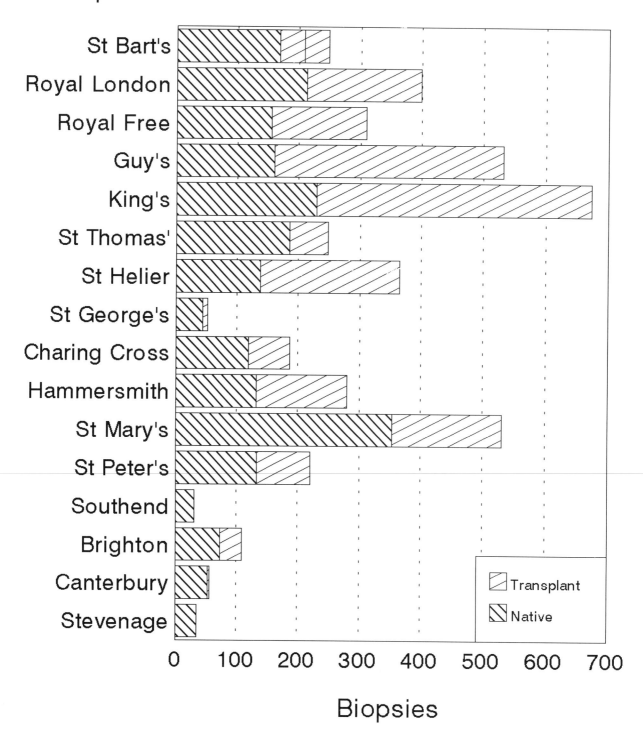

Figure 7

LONDON RENAL UNITS
Patients Treated with Plasma Exchange
1991-1992

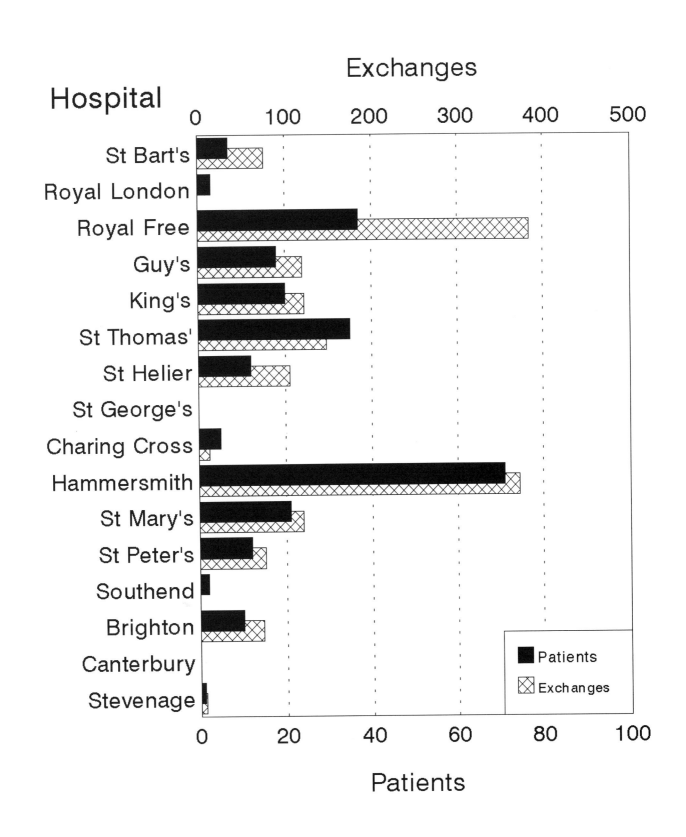

Figure 8

LONDON RENAL UNITS
Chronic Renal Replacement Therapy
March 1993

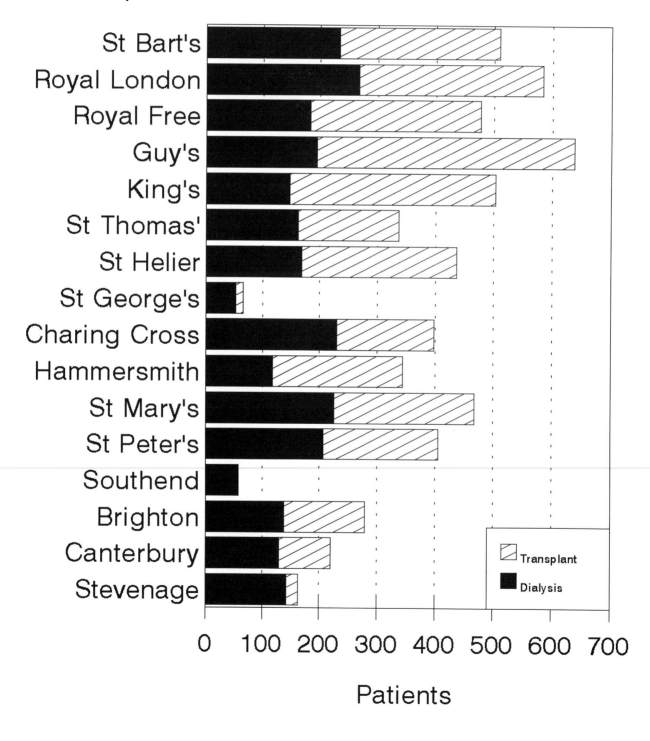

Figure 9

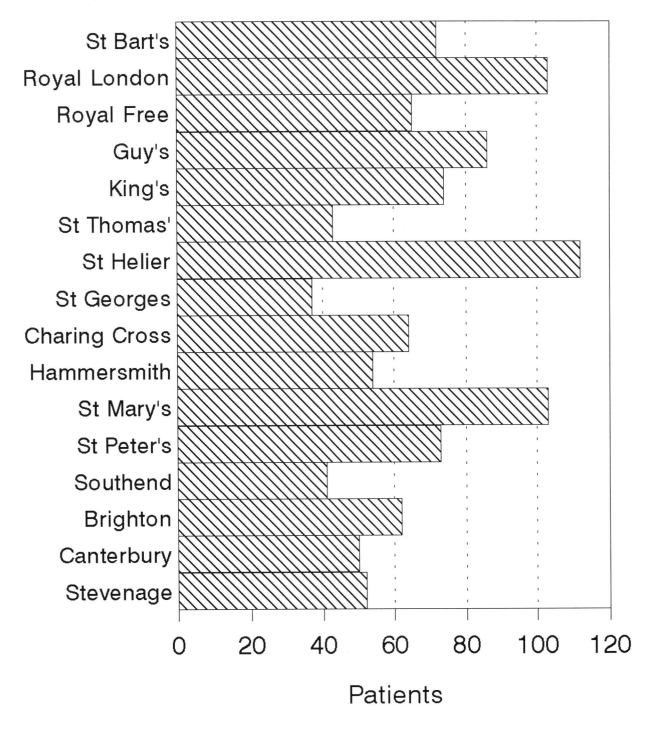

LONDON RENAL UNITS
Chronic Renal Replacement Therapy
New Patients 1992

Hospital

Figure 10

LONDON RENAL UNITS
CHRONIC DIALYSIS PATIENT POPULATION
March 1993

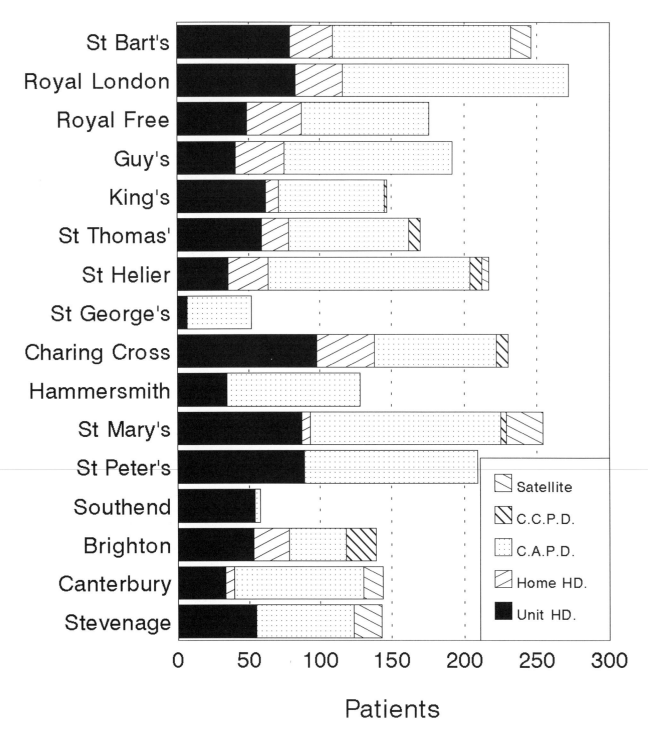

Figure 11

LONDON RENAL UNITS
Patients Treated for Acute Renal Failure
Annual Average (from 1991 & 1992)

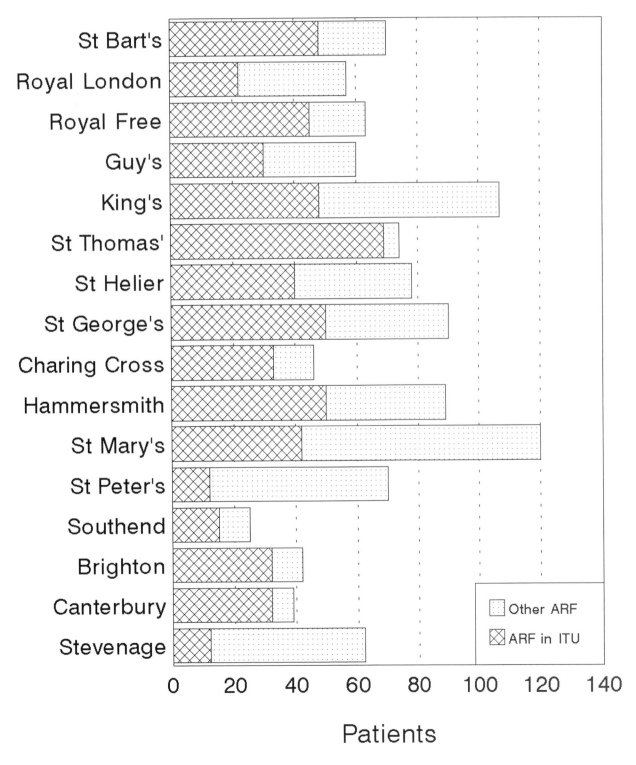

Hospital

Figure 12

REPORT OF THE REVIEW OF LONDON RENAL SERVICES

NURSING REPORT

This report is based on the information contained in the Nursing questionnaire returns and the interviews with representatives from individual units and represents an analysis of the current provision of renal nursing services in London. Statements are supported through reference to the appropriate sections of the questionnaire.

Nursing Establishment (Sections 1.1 to 1.6 and 7.6 to 7.7)

Only six units had a senior nurse with specific responsibility for clinical areas (1.1). Units where this was not provided were thought to be lacking a high quality service to patients, including those to satellite units. All units should have this support. We have allowed for this in the staffing profiles of the various levels of unit which have been costed in Appendix D.

4 units had clinical nurse specialists or equivalent. These are important posts providing education, training, support etc. to nursing staff. Again, all units should provide this support, and these too have been allowed for in our structures.

Inspection of sections 1.2 to 1.6 and 7.6 to 7.7 shows that the grade mix was high over all. There are very few support workers, HCAs (lower grades, but trained to specific competencies), resulting in an expensive grade-mix. we emphasise that well-trained HCAs can look after routine hospital dialysis - including venepuncture - and so free renal trained nursing staff to concentrate on acutely ill patients.

In general, there is inflexibility in staffing provision, so that high staff levels with a high grade mix are available, despite there being an uneven (and sometimes minimal) workload.

In the staffing structures we have recommended, grade mix has been adjusted and shift patterns brought into an economical framework.

Non-Nursing establishment (section 1.8)

All units had the support of dieticians and social workers, though in many cases they were not NHS funded. One source of funding was greater than others - the BKPA. BKPA funding was provided on a 1 or 2 year basis. Short-term funding of this nature is not conducive to the implementation of teamwork and the implementation of medium- to long-term policy.

Concerns were also expressed about the provision of Renal Social Worker support as a result of the changes effected with the implementation of Community Care legislation.

These have been accounted for in our costed NHS establishment profiles in Appendix D.

The provision of technical staff requires adjustment. Staffing structures do not reflect workload and call out rates of up to 20 times per month were reported. This expert, but costly service requires rationalisation. In many instances, patients requiring help out of hours can obtain this over the telephone and it is only in rare instances that the immediate attendance of a technician is required. In any case, this is most important for home haemodialysis patients, and with appropriate shift patterns and skill-mix, there should be little need for call out of technicians to a dialysis unit. Again, we have allowed for these factors in our cost profiles.

This working pattern is effective in terms of cost and quality:

a) It reduces the number of technicians required.
b) It reduces 'on-call' costs.
c) It reduces travelling costs and time.
d) It allows technicians to spend more time on the unit to service machines, teach staff and patients and to innovate.

This type of service can only function if the nursing staff are trained to be fully conversant with dialysis machinery. It therefore requires both the rotation and training of nursing staff.

Counsellors, computer staff, home dialysis administrators/ coordinators and secretarial staff comprise the bulk of other non-nursing establishment. The provision of these staff appears to be haphazard and uncoordinated, bearing little relation to the activity of the units concerned.

Provision of secretarial support appeared limited and good support in this area should facilitate greater high-level clinical and managerial provision by senior medical and nursing staff.

There is good liaison between all units and their patient associations. The associations can provide support, information, advice, education and counselling services for patients and staff. They have fund-raising potential.

Shift patterns (section 2)

In all areas of Renal Replacement Therapy, there was a large shift overlap of nurses (up to 3 hours in some areas, and 2.5 hours in many others) which is both expensive and inefficient.

Rotation of Staff (Section 4)

Rotation of staff around all areas of renal replacement therapy and between day and night duty varied from unit to unit and no single unit was able to rotate all staff to all areas of therapy, though most areas rotated junior staff to some areas. Some units saw staff rotation as a drawback as expensive agency nurses had to be brought in during periods of staff sickness etc..

Rotation of staff is recommended because it is a means of ensuring quality of care for patients as the individual nurse gains experience in all areas of RRT. This experience is essential in counselling and nursing patients and is also a means of promoting job satisfaction for the nurse. Inadequate rotation is a waste of skill. Nor is it cost-effective as nurses cannot cover for each other.

Senior staff should rotate for periods of time to maintain/update their skills in all areas of RRT and rotation of RDU and ITU staff may be desirable

ACTIVITY

In the staffing structures we have recommended - for all treatment modalities - grade mix and shift pattern adjustments to provide a more economical framework.

Maintenance/Hospital Dialysis (sections 2.1, 3.1, 7.1)

Most units operate 3 or 4 patient shifts: morning; afternoon; evening and/or night (section 3)

This area of RRT was working under capacity. For example, 1 unit reported (section 3.1):

    19 stations providing dialysis
    10 patients per day shift (52%)
     8 patients per night shift (42%)

All nursing shifts were fully staffed, with large overlaps between individual shifts (2.1), although the need for some overlap is recognised.

All haemodialysis patients in all units were on bicarbonate dialysis fluid, which more expensive than acetate fluid, but essential for the provision of quality care.

31 May 1993

Home haemodialysis should be provided for a small group of patients for whom transplantation is either not desirable or unsuccessful and for whom CAPD is not possible. Home haemodialysis for any other group of patients is an expensive form of treatment as the training of these patients ties up hospital dialysis stations and uses highly skilled nurses for long periods of training. It also needs the back up of technical staff to monitor and repair machinery.

Satellite Units were used minimally. Those that exist are not used to full capacity (medical questionnaire section 3.5).

There is great potential for satellite dialysis. The staff in these units should be trained by the tertiary centre and should be included in the rotation of staff. A good mix of trained and HCSW staff is desirable/achievable in these units. Patient relocation to satellite units also contributes to the quality of care as less travelling time is required and is also more cost-effective as transport costs are reduced.

CAPD (7.3)

This appeared to be a busy area of work, though operating under capacity. The number of stations provided are under-used, indicating over-provision of services for the number of patients being trained for CAPD.

Patient attendance tends to be '9 to 5, Monday to Friday' with or, in some cases, without overnight stay. Some training is done in the home, although this tends to be a 'polishing-off' technique. The grade-mix in this area is top-heavy; HCAs staff do not come into this scenario and the 'on-call' system operated by the nursing staff and technical staff tends to be heavily used.

We must question why this is:

a) Is the training given adequate for home care?
b) Is the training long enough?
c) Do patients get enough practice before going home?
d) Are the patients confident enough to home care?

The heavy call-out rate is not cost effective. It also takes nurses out of the teaching environment and into the community to deal with patient emergencies.

More long-standing patients are changing to hospital dialysis. Some centres are becoming increasingly selective about the type of patient they take on to the CAPD programme, i.e., only those who they know will succeed are taken on.

Having said that, the trend has been and remains that there is freedom of choice of treatment for patients: all patients can choose to be on a disconnect system.

Community Care

Hospital-based nurses should not be providing community care

There are only a few community-based staff - too few to have an impact on overall patient care (1.4).

Highly skilled nurses, preferably nurse practitioners, would be an efficient and cost-effective use of staff. These nurses could be trained to detect and treat peritonitis, educate families, allay fears, provide support for families and, above all, keep the patients in the home, resulting in:

- a) Home care - which is much cheaper than hospital care.
- b) Hospital-based staff being kept in the training area.
- c) Reduced need for medical staff time.
- d) Ongoing patient education, resulting in, for example, fewer episodes of peritonitis.
- e) The development of nurse practitioner clinics.
- f) Reduced drugs costs.
- g) Fewer costly in-patient episodes.
- h) Support for those patients who choose to die at home - patients would have the choice not to die in hospital (this is a quality, rather than cost issue).
- i) Reduced transport costs as fewer patients need to visit the hospital.
- j) The bulk of Renal work is in community/out-patient care.

Additional activity (section 7.2)

Immunoadsorption is performed in most units and patients are nursed by renal-trained staff.

Haemofiltration, CVVH tends to be performed on ICU. Some units have renal-trained nurses working on ICU.

Acute Dialysis (7.1, 7.2, 7.8, 7.9)

All units take acute haemodialysis patients and all staff are 'on-call' for acute work (7.1.3). Acute dialysis is an area of work which needs (and which London has got) a highly skilled work force.

Isolation facilities (7.8)

All units have access to isolation facilities and in some units, patients with Hepatitis B, C and HIV are receiving dialysis.

All units have a training/counselling programme for their nursing staff with regard to viral infections and all staff observe universal precautions when dealing with all patients.

All patients are tested for Hepatitis B and C. The testing of patients for HIV is inconsistent between units: some units test all patients; some units test patients for HIV only if joining the transplant programme.

We have found no data to support the claim that taking universal precautions is an adequate safeguard when dealing with HIV. The routine testing for all patients is recommended.

Ward activity (section 7.6)

The provision of nephrology beds varied tremendously between units. Nephrology wards on all sites accommodate nephrology patients, together with a combination of other specialty patients, for example, urology, general medicine and renal transplant.

There is scope on all wards to develop a better grade/skill mix.

Transplantation (Sections 1.5, 2.3, 7.7)

There is greater variety of provision in this area than any other. Where and how patients are nursed differs widely and all units appear to be working under capacity.

In some areas, it has the largest number of nurses for a small number of beds: a 7 bedded unit, fully staffed, has performed 2 transplants in 1993 to date. One unit has the same number of staff-to-bed ratio and performs 20 transplants per year as a provincial unit has performing 140 transplants per year. Another unit nurses all post-transplant cases on an intensive care unit (ICU).

Transplantation is an area which has the least rotation of staff.

A pooling of transplant services in 4 or 5 units would be desirable, resulting in great savings on costs associated with nursing, beds, medical and surgical services etc.

In this area of work, transport costs would not be seen as a necessary cost saving.

Clinics (sections 1.6, 7.5, 7.5a)

Renal services are becoming out-patient led - 90% of renal work is done on an out-patient basis and patient numbers attending clinics are growing. There is great divergence of nursing activity in this area: some clinics are staffed entirely by medical staff, with no nurse input. Others offer minimal nursing input, a few provide high grade nurse input. Only a few clinics are nurse led.

The nurse practitioner clinics that exist are functioning at minimal level; there is great scope for development in this area in relation to, for example, nurse diagnosis, nurse prescribing, nurses performing invasive procedures etc..

The clinical use of nurse practitioners is cost effective and contributes to the overall quality of care. It frees the time of medical staff, allowing them to spend longer with new or acutely ill patients and facilitates the implementation of Patient's Charter standards by, for example, reducing waiting time in clinics.

The nurse practitioner would work closely with the dietician and social worker, providing expert care along with information and patient education, s/he would be a highly trained and skilled renal/transplant nurse of high grade.

Community staff are the obvious personnel to develop in this field.

Student Nurse training

The Royal College of Nursing has stated that amalgamation of colleges of nursing has, or is in the process of taking place. For training purposes, student nurses are travelling up to 60 miles to gain the necessary clinical experience. The colleges have a full uptake of all places provided. The provision of newly qualified nursing staff for tertiary or secondary sites, therefore, is not seen as problematic.

Renal Nurse training (section 6)

Post-registration renal training is an essential element of a career structure. Not all hospitals providing renal services run a renal training course. The provision of this facility, together with a diabetes module are key factors in the development of skilled nephrology/transplant nurses. Provision of the renal course also aids recruitment and retention of nursing staff as job satisfaction is likely to be increased by the teaching opportunities offered. It will help to assure quality of care to all renal patients. It would be unsatisfactory, therefore, for a chosen tertiary site not to provide the ENB 136 Renal Nursing Course.

Training in computer skills is desirable, particulary for clinic and community staff. Nurses need the ability to access the large renal/transplant patient database.

Where HCAs are employed, 'in-house' training in renal patient care and renal technology is provided. Some HCAs are trained to NVQ II or III. This is seen as part of a career ladder for support workers. HCA training could be developed as a positive recruitment factor for high-quality applicants, although some units state that high quality support workers are difficult to find.

Travelling times (section 9)

There is a wide variation in respect of patient travelling times and distances. For example, 1 patient travelled 4 miles in one hour; another patient travelled 85 miles in $2^1/_2$ hours. These variations highlight the hidden costs of travel: the ambulance and hospital car service and the reimbursement of private and public travel.

Based on average distances travelled and the average numbers of patients using the hospital car service, an estimated cost of £613,043 can be calculated as the hidden cost of the hospital car service.

Furthermore, patients on low income, family support and family credit etc., are also entitled to claim for travelling expenses. Actual numbers of these patients has been impossible to define, but it is likely to be significant and would represent a substantial overlay on the costs highlighted above.

Also, when patients travel long distances, over many months, to hospital and back home, 2 or 3 times a week, with 4 to 6 hours of dialysis treatment between trips; it can be very tiring and detracts from the quality of the service provided.

Tertiary centres, therefore, appear to be an expensive and unattractive option for hospital haemodialysis for large numbers of patients.

The need for provision of transport is likely to increase. Satellite dialysis and satellite clinic provision, therefore, are issues with both cost and quality dimensions: a cheaper, higher quality service is likely to result following the provision of satellite units.

Modes of transport (9.3)

The largest proportion of patients do not travel to hospital by public or private transport. An aging and increasingly sick population of patients on dialysis require transport provided by the hospital. The three most commonly used are: hospital car service; ambulance and taxi. All three are expensive to provide (see above).

Nurse travel

Staff in all units stated that travel to and from the hospital to home was not a problem.

Nurses are already in the process of amalgamation in some areas. All units state that when rationalisation takes place, nursing staff should not find travelling to new venues a problem - should that be necessary.

31 May 1993

8

Nursing Research (section 1.7)

Within the M25, in renal services, there is a paucity of research nurses. There appears to be little research being done. The academic resource surrounding the capital and the specialty does not appear to be being tapped. The potential of nurses is not being exploited.

Initiatives

There appeared to be little in the way of Nursing-related initiatives. Areas suggested include:

- nurse practitioners
- CAPD staff to diagnose peritonitis
- insertion of central line by nurses

most of these initiatives coming from within 1 unit.

Miscellaneous points

a) Patient loyalty appears to be at a very high level.

b) The service provided to patients should be 'user-friendly'.

c) Business and Nursing management should be separated.

d) Good Grade/Skill-mix essential to make the best use of the staff.

e) Teamwork - all grades/disciplines/professions must work together.

f) The 'open door' policy that exists throughout the capital to patients over 80 with regard to dialysis should be reviewed:

> One hospital site has an elderly lady living in the ward. She has been abandoned by her family and is too old and frail to cope alone. Residential accommodation is not easily available and the limited supply is likely to be reduced in the future.

> Some sites have expressed a need for this review.

> An honest and forthright description of the treatment method (i.e., haemodialysis or CAPD) should be given so that the patient is aware of the commitment needed. If the patient decides not to accept treatment, that decision should be respected.

g) When implementation takes place, time and thought must be

X1

given to the staff of all professions who need to be relocated/replaced/retrained:

Vacancies occurring should provide opportunities for the assimilation of these staff members. Particularly with regard to highly skilled staff in whom large amounts of resources have been invested with regard to training.

Opportunities for retraining should be made available to those who cannot, for whatever reason, move to the newly rationalised sites.

h) It is essential that the people of London have access to renal care provided by highly skilled, caring personnel, nursing, medical and paramedical/support staff.

i) Standards of care must be maintained and improved in satellite units as they must in tertiary centres and DGHs.

j) Professions must establish and maintain good channels of communication between:

- individual units
- professions
- patients and clinicians.

Summary of Key Points - Nursing Report

	POINTS	EFFECT
1	Senior Nurse lead	Coordinated quality of care.
2	Senior Clinical Specialist support	Good staff training/patient care. Good morale.
3	Good grade/skill mix	Cost effective use of highly paid/skilled staff. Rationalises use of staff. Fully utilises nursing resource.
4	Minimal shift overlap	Cost effective. Releases staff.
5	Work to full capacity	Best use of facilities. Reduces costs.
6	Rotation of staff	Good use of skills. Promotes quality of care to patients. Is cost effective and increases job satisfaction.
7	Satellite dialysis	takes the treatment to the patient. Reduces travelling costs.
8	Provision of community staff nurse practitioner	Removes 'on-call' costs. Promotes quality of care and family support. Reduces use of medical staff time. Reduces in-patient stay.
9	Isolation facilities	Protects other patients/staff
10	Transplant patients	All to come under care of renal/nephrology nurses. Promotes quality of care. Develops nursing expertise.
11	Nurse practitioners	Promotes quality of care. Patients's Charter facilitated. Quality time at clinics. Saves medical and surgical time for service provision to new/acutely ill patients.
12	Secretarial support	Frees clinical staff for clinical practice. Promotes service provision.

13	Technicians	Rationalisation: lower costs; lower numbers; no 'on-call'; promotes quality.
14	Dieticians/Social workers	Part of the team. Fully funded. Longer term planning
15	Training	Provides for: well motivated staff; job satisfaction; staff recruitment/retention; career structure; promotes quality; cost effective.
16	Travelling distance	Long times are tiring. Long distances are expensive.
17	Nursing Research	Essential. Validates good quality care. Improves the service. Facilitates innovative practice.
18	Teamwork	All grades of professions working together. Good communication. Promotes quality of care. Increased patient survival rate.
19	Business Manager	Large budget better managed by a person with no added responsibilities.
20	Patient education	Prevents/delays onset of complications (e.g., diabetes).

Good practice helps maintain good quality of life (e.g., prevents peritonitis; maintains integrity of peritoneum)

Careful diet delays need for RRT

Dietary discipline prevents/ delays complications of RRT

Prepares families for coping with chronic sickness

Enhances the quality of life

Prolongs life expectancy

Reduces costs |

Nurse Staffing Profiles and Costs

This report sets out the staffing profiles and associated costs for the different levels of future renal nursing service provision.

Costs in this report are based on the average staff cost (minimum point + maximum point divided by 2). For the provinces, 17.5% has been added to cover on-costs and enhancements. This figure (average + 17.5%) has been increased by 10% to illustrate London-weighted costs. No distinction has been made between inner-and outer-London.

The proportion of trained staff to HCA reflects the current situation in respect of trained:untrained ratios. It is anticipated that as HCA training evolves, the proportion of HCAs will increase.

Where 2 and 3 shift staffing profiles have been developed, the following shift patterns have been assumed:

```
Morning shift        07.30 - 15.00 (7.0 hours - breaks deducted)
Afternoon Shift      11.00 - 19.00 (7.5 hours - breaks deducted)
Evening Shift        17.00 - 23.00 (5.5 hours - breaks deducted)
```

A more detailed cost profile is presented as Appendix D.

TERTIARY CENTRE   HAEMODIALYSIS

2 nurses need to be available to manage 5 stations at any one time; at full occupancy, 6 nurses need to be available.

(a)   15 stations operating 2 shifts per week, opening 6 days per week between 7.30am and 7pm. (equivalent to 60 patients per week).

Nurse Staffing Establishment:

Grade	WTE	Cost (provincial)	Cost (London)
G	2.0	41066	45173
F	1.0	17966	19762
E	5.4	84864	93351
D	2.0	27283	30012
C			
B	5.0	52141	57355
A	2.0	18295	20124
TOTAL	**17.4**	**241615**	**265777**

Establishment spilt = 60% trained to 40% untrained

Workload: maintenance haemodialysis
          home haemodialysis training (minimal)
          emergency haemodialysis (e.g. peritonitis - CAPD)

Nursing practice: 'on-call' 8pm. to 8am.
                     teaching input to ENB 136
                     teaching input to HCSW training programme
                     individual patient care

(b)   15 stations operating 3 shifts per week, opening 6 days per week between 7.30am. and 11pm. (equivalent to 90 patients per week).

Nurse Staffing Establishment:

Grade	WTE	Cost (provincial)	Cost (London)
G	2.0	41066	45173
F	2.0	35931	39525
E	7.5	117867	129654
D	3.0	40925	45018
C			
B	6.5	67783	74561
A	3.0	27442	30186
TOTAL	**24.0**	**331015**	**364117**

TERTIARY CENTRE   **ACUTE HAEMODIALYSIS**

2 Stations   Acute dialysis facility, including plasma exchange

Assuming full occupancy:

Nurse Staffing Establishment:

Grade	WTE	Cost (provincial)	Cost (London)
G	2.0	41066	45173
F	1.0	17966	19762
E	5.0	78578	86436
D			
C			
B	3.6	37541	41295
A			
TOTAL	**11.6**	**175151**	**192667**

Establishment spilt = 70% trained to 30% untrained

NB. In each Tertiary centre there will be 1 WTE I Grade Nurse Manager and 1 WTE H Grade Clinical Nurse Specialist. The 'London' Cost of the I Grade would be approximately £27627, the corresponding cost for the H Grade would be £25074 - giving a total nursing cost of £245368.

DGH HAEMODIALYSIS

2 nurses need to be available to manage 5 stations at any one time; at full occupancy, 4 nurses need to be available.

(a) 10 stations operating 2 shifts per week, opening 6 days per week between 7.30am and 7pm. (equivalent to 40 patients per week).

Nurse Staffing Establishment:

Grade	WTE	Cost (provincial)	Cost (London)
G	1.0	20533	22586
F	1.0	17966	19762
E	3.0	47147	51862
D	1.0	13642	15006
C			
B	3.6	37541	41295
A	2.0	18295	20124
TOTAL	**11.6**	**155123**	**170636**

Establishment spilt = 50% trained to 50% untrained

Workload: maintenance haemodialysis
                emergency haemodialysis
                acute haemodialysis (already costed)

Nursing practice: 'on-call' 8pm. to 8am.
                            for acute dialysis
                            teaching input to HSCW training programme
                            individual patient care

(b) 10 stations operating 3 shifts per week, opening 6 days per week between 7.30am. and 11pm. (equivalent to 60 patients per week).

Nurse Staffing Establishment:

Grade	WTE	Cost (provincial)	Cost (London)
G	1.0	20533	22586
F	1.0	17966	19762
E	4.0	62862	69149
D	2.0	27283	30012
C			
B	5.0	52141	57355
A	3.0	27442	30186
TOTAL	**16.0**	**208228**	**229050**

DGH Haemodialysis (continued from over page)

NB. In each DGH there will be 1 WTE I Grade Nurse Manager and 1 WTE H Grade Clinical Nurse Specialist. The 'London' Cost of the I Grade would be approximately £27627, the corresponding cost for the H Grade would be £25074 - giving a total nursing cost of for (a) £223337 and for (b) £281751

If a 20-station haemodialysis unit was being operated, staff numbers and costs would double accordingly - with the exception of the I and H Grade staff.

SATELLITE UNIT HAEMODIALYSIS

2 nurses need to be available to manage 8 stations at any one time; at full occupancy, 2 nurses need to be available.

(a) 8 stations operating 2 shifts per week, opening 6 days per week between 7.30am and 7pm. (equivalent to 32 patients per week).

Nurse Staffing Establishment:

Grade	WTE	Cost (provincial)	Cost (London)
G			
F	1.0	17966	19762
E	1.5	23573	25931
D			
C			
B	2.5	26070	28677
A	1.0	9147	10062
TOTAL	**6.0**	**76757**	**84433**

Establishment spilt = 40% trained to 60% untrained

Workload: maintenance haemodialysis

Verification: via maintenance dialysis formula
well patients
calculated on 6 stations (= 7.2 WTE)

(b) 8 stations operating 3 shifts per week, opening 6 days per week between 7.30am and 11pm. (equivalent to 48 patients per week).

Nurse Staffing Establishment:

Grade	WTE	Cost (provincial)	Cost (London)
G			
F	1.0	17966	19762
E	2.5	39289	43218
D			
C			
B	3.5	36498	40148
A	1.0	9147	10062
TOTAL	**8.0**	**102901**	**113191**

COMMUNITY STAFF/CLINICS

Assuming   1.0 WTE per 40 patients.
           160 home patients (= 4.0 WTE)
           8 practitioner clinics per week (= 2 clinics per practitioner)
           10 patients (max) per practitioner clinic
           20 patients seen at home/20 in clinic by each practitioner

H grade nurse practitioner with responsibility for:

        patient case load
        satellite - DGH cover
        nurse practitioner clinics

Each H grade supported in each half-day clinic by a B grade HCSW - i.e., 1 WTE at B grade to support 4 community H grade practitioners.

Clinics

Assuming all sites operate on a 2-clinic per session (morning/afternoon), 10 sessions per week (Monday-Friday), 20 clinics would need to be covered. 2 Grade B clinic staff would be required to meet this workload.

Nurse Staffing Establishment (community/clinics):

Grade	WTE	Cost (provincial)	Cost (London)
H	4.0	91180	100298
G			
F			
E			
D			
C			
B	3.0	31248	34413
A			
TOTAL	**7.0**	**122428**	**134711**

TERTIARY CENTRE   **CAPD TRAINING**

3 beds, operating 7 days per week.

Average time to train - 12 days (equivalent to 80 patients per year)

Nurse Staffing Establishment:

Grade	WTE	Cost (provincial)	Cost (London)
G	1.0	20533	22586
F	1.0	17966	19762
E	3.0	47147	51862
D	2.0	27283	30012
C			
B			
A			
TOTAL	**7.0**	**112929**	**124222**

no HCSW input at present

DGH   CAPD TRAINING

Training 8am.-4pm., Monday-Friday, with in-patient stay.

Staffing profile based on CAPD training profile (above)

80 patients per year	7.0 WTE	@ 112929 (provinces)	124222 (London)
70 patients per year	6.0 WTE	@ 98813 (provinces)	108694 (London)
60 patients per year	5.2 WTE	@ 84697 (provinces)	93167 (London)
50 patients per year	4.3 WTE	@ 70581 (provinces)	77639 (London)
40 patients per year	3.5 WTE	@ 56465 (provinces)	62111 (London)
30 patients per year	2.6 WTE	@ 42348 (provinces)	46583 (London)
20 patients per year	1.7 WTE	@ 28232 (provinces)	31056 (London)

NEPHROLOGY WARD

25 beds

1 WTE per bed.

a)   Nurse Staffing Establishment:

Grade	WTE	Cost (provincial)	Cost (London)
G	1.0	20533	22586
F	1.0	17966	19762
E	6.5	102152	112367
D	11.5	156880	172568
C			
B	5.0	52141	57355
A			
(A&C 2	1.0	9283	10211)
TOTAL	**25.0**	**349671**	**384638**
	(26.0)	(358954)	(394849)

Establishment spilt = 80% trained to 20% untrained

B grades would cover clinics if more than 2 clinics per session were being run (e.g., St. Mary's Hospital report occasionally running 3 or 4 clinics per am. or pm. session)

b)   At a DGH, an 18-bedded nephrology ward, with a nurse to bed ratio of 1:1 would have the following establishment:

Grade	WTE	Cost (provincial)	Cost (London)
G	1.0	20533	22586
F	1.0	17966	19762
E	4.5	70720	77792
D	7.5	102313	112544
C			
B	4.0	41712	45884
A			
(A&C 2	1.0	9283	10211)
TOTAL	**18.0**	**253245**	**278569**
	(19.0)	(262528)	(288780)

Establishment spilt = 80% trained to 20% untrained

Again, B grades would cover clinics if more than 2 clinics per session were being run.

31 May 1993

TRANSPLANT BEDS

15 beds

Assuming   5.8 WTE per bed for first 48 hours post-transplant
           1.0 WTE per bed thereafter i.e. 14 WTE plus 5.8 WTE
           3 transplants per week (c. 150 per year)

Nurse Staffing Establishment:

Grade	WTE	Cost (provincial)	Cost (London)
G	1.0	20533	22586
F	1.8	32338	35572
E	6.0	94294	103723
D	7.0	95492	105041
C			
B	4.0	41712	45884
A			
TOTAL	**19.8**	**284370**	**312807**

Establishment spilt = 80% trained to 20% untrained

Nursing Support Staff - Tertiary centre

Staff Group/Grade	WTE	Cost (provincial)	Cost (London)
Secretary (A&C3) (to Nurse Manager)	0.5	5369	5906
Home Dialysis Administrator (A&C5)	1.0	15586	17145
Computer Staff (A&C5)	1.0	15586	17145
Social Worker (senior)	1.0	21164	23281
Social Worker	1.0	17801	19581
Dietician (Senior I)	1.0	19916	21908
Dietician (Senior II)	1.0	17096	18806
Ward Clerk (A&C2) (.7 to Tx, .7 to Dx, .7 to ward)	2.1	19494	21443
Business Manager (SNM 19)	1.0	27025	29228
Technician (MTO5)	1.0	27608	30369
Technician (MTO4)	1.0	22692	24961
TOTAL	**11.6**	**209337**	**229773**

Re. Technician support: Minimum of 2 per unit:

       1 per 30 machines on site
       1 per 30 machines off site

       on-call for emergency telephone advice only

Nursing Support Staff - DGH

Staff Group/Grade	WTE	Cost (provincial)	Cost (London)
Secretary (A&C3) (to Nurse Manager)	0.25	2685	2953
Home Dialysis Administrator (A&C5)	1.0	15586	17145
Computer Staff (A&C5)	1.0	15586	17145
Social Worker (senior)	1.0	21164	23281
Social Worker	0.5	8901	9791
Dietician (Senior I)	1.0	19916	21908
Dietician (Senior II)	1.0	17096	18806
Ward Clerk (A&C2) (.7 to Dx, .7 to Ward)	1.4	12996	14295
Business Manager (SNM 19)	0.5	13513	14616
Technician (MTO5)	1.0	27608	30369
Technician (MTO4)	1.0	22692	24961
TOTAL	**9.65**	**177743**	**195270**

Re. Technician support: Minimum of 2 per unit:

    1 per 30 machines on site
    1 per 30 machines off site

    on-call for emergency telephone advice only

Printed in the United Kingdom for HMSO.
Dd.296539, 6/93, C35, 3396/4, 5673, 249611.